CITY OF OTHERS™

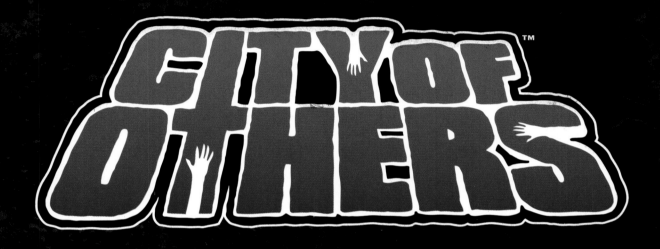

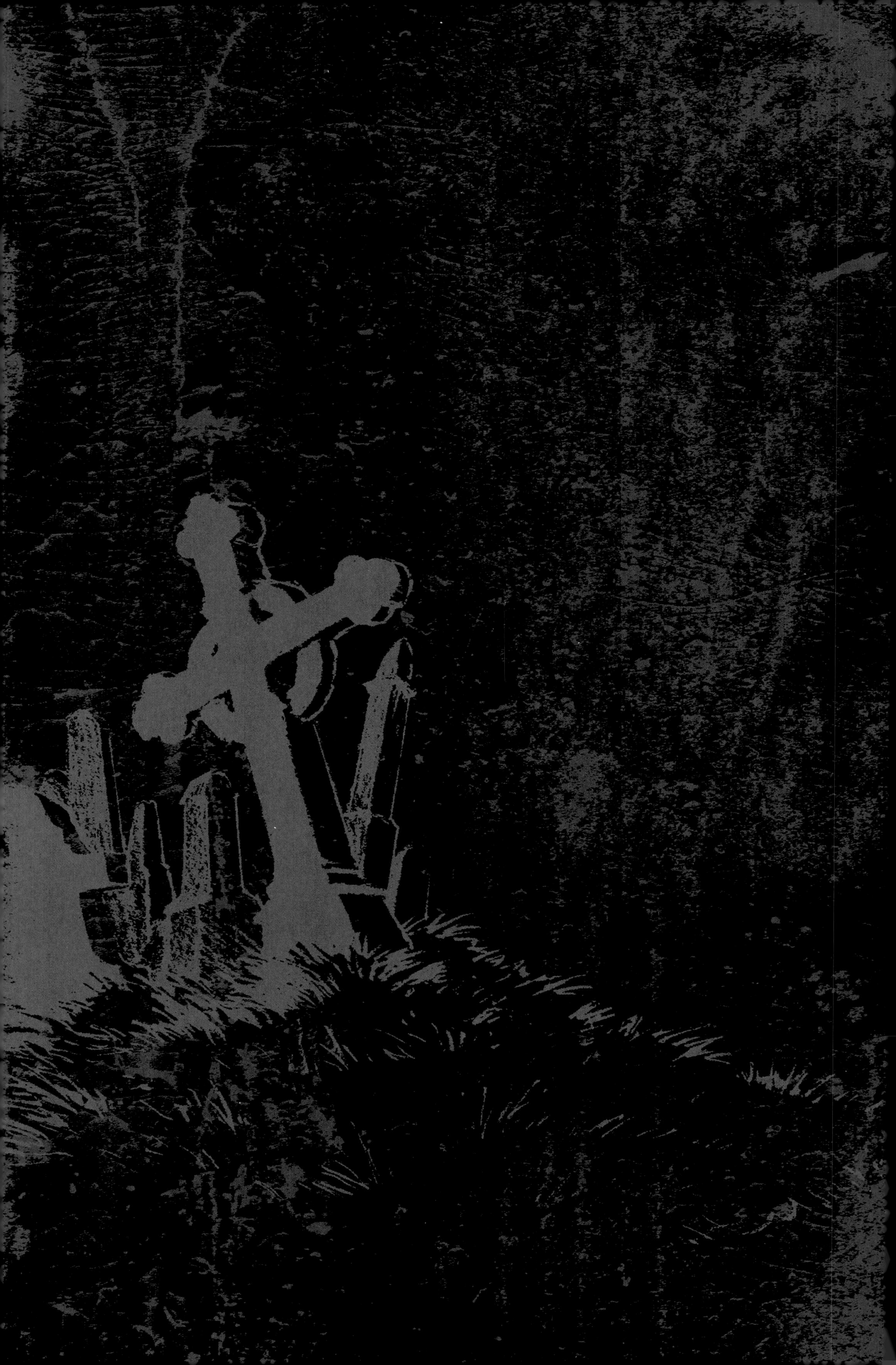

CITY OF OTHERS™

STORY BY
STEVE NILES AND
BERNIE WRIGHTSON

COVER AND INTERIOR ART BY
BERNIE WRIGHTSON

COLORS BY
JOSÉ VILLARRUBIA

LETTERED BY
MICHAEL DAVID THOMAS

PRESIDENT AND PUBLISHER

MIKE RICHARDSON

EDITOR

SHAWNA GORE

ASSISTANT EDITOR

JEMIAH JEFFERSON

DESIGNERS

DAVID NESTELLE
PATRICK SATTERFIELD

Published by Dark Horse Books
A division of Dark Horse Comics LLC.
10956 SE Main Street
Milwaukie, OR 97222

DarkHorse.com

CITY OF OTHERS: TENTH ANNIVERSARY EDITION

This volumes collects issues #1 through #4 of the Dark Horse comic-book series *City of Others*.

Tenth Anniversary Edition: June 2019 | ISBN 978-1-50671-202-4

1 3 5 7 9 10 8 6 4 2
Printed in China

Library of Congress Cataloging-in-Publication Data

Names: Niles, Steve, author. | Wrightson, Bernie, author, artist. |
  Villarrubia, José, 1961- colourist. | Thomas, Michael David, letterer.
Title: City of others / story by Steve Niles and Bernie Wrightson ; cover and
  interior art by Bernie Wrightson ; colors by Jose Villarrubia ; lettered
  by Michael David Thomas.
Description: 10th anniversary edition. | Milwaukie, OR : Dark Horse Books,
  June 2019. | "This volumes collects issues #1 through #4 of the Dark Horse
  comic-book series City of Others."
Identifiers: LCCN 2018061309 | ISBN 9781506712024 (hardback)
Subjects: LCSH: Comic books, strips, etc. | BISAC: COMICS & GRAPHIC NOVELS /
  Horror.
Classification: LCC PN6728.C584 N55 2019 | DDC 741.5/973--dc23
LC record available at https://lccn.loc.gov/2018061309

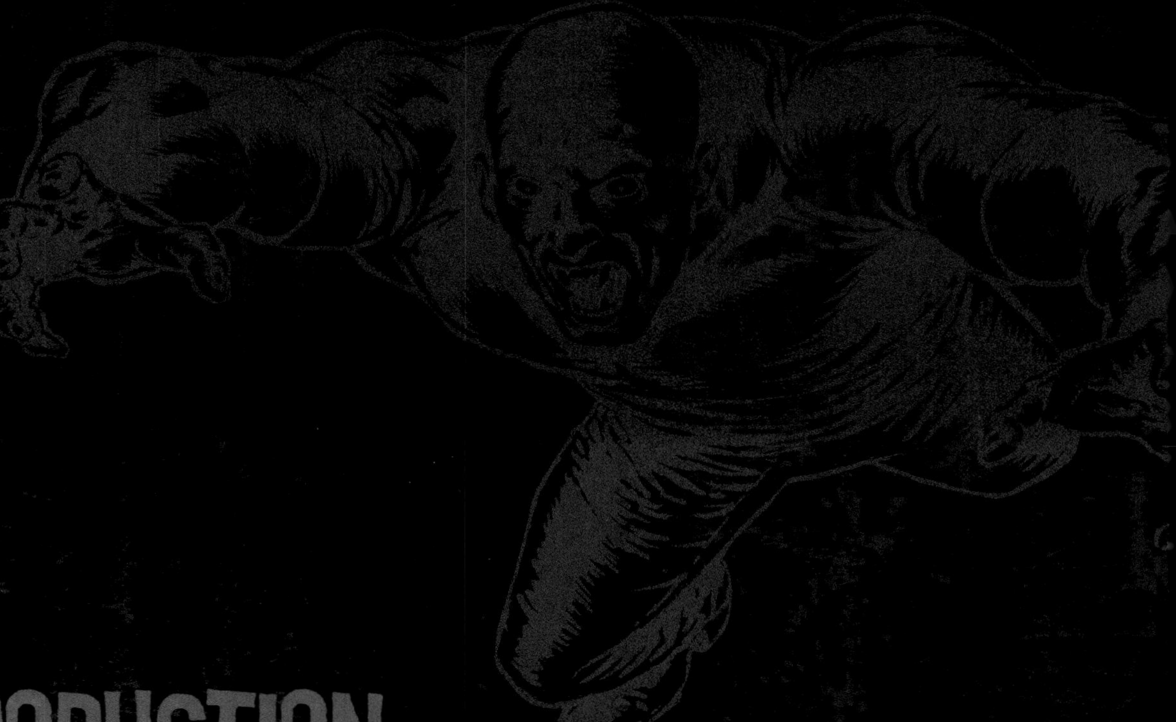

INTRODUCTION
TO THE TENTH ANNIVERSARY EDITION
BY STEVE NILES

I've been a fan of Bernie Wrightson's work practically my whole life. I remember what a thrill it was when my mother bought me the Marvel edition of his *Frankenstein* book. I'd never seen anything like it; the incredible detail of the artwork had me enthralled. I would spend hours staring at the centerfold image.

Years and years later I heard a rumor that Wrightson lived in LA, but I never actually saw him. He hadn't been doing much in the way of comics for a while. I heard he was doing illustrations for film mainly. Then one day I saw that Bernie and Len Wein had released a parody of *Swamp Thing* for The Simpsons' *Treehouse of Horror* and it looked like Wrightson was back in comics.

It was around this time that I was invited to a comic convention in Dallas, Texas. I saw on the flyer that Wrightson would be there. I was thrilled and a little nervous. The con was great, especially as I got to meet Bernie and his wife, Liz. He had no clue who I was so I weighed him down with books of mine.

It turned out that not only did Bernie live in LA, he was just a few blocks from where I lived. We'd been neighbors and never knew it.

We started hanging out immediately. We'd hang out at a place called the Concrete Beach and have beers and oysters and just talk. Bernie was a great storyteller, and I used to just sit back and listen to stories about the early days of the Studio, spending days with the likes of Richard Corben or the time he met Ditko.

I never brought up working together. I was happy to just be friends. And honestly I thought if I bugged him about doing work (because everybody did), I would scare him off.

Then one day HE brought it up. I was stunned in a really good way. He basically said, "Let's make some comics."

I didn't hesitate. I said YES before he could change his mind. He went on to describe a story idea and we just started to jam. The idea was to create our own city and populate it with monsters and their stories. What we came up with was *City of Others* and our first monster was the assassin-turned-vampire, Blud.

Bernie had one request, though. He didn't want to ink. He wanted to do detailed pencils and have the colorist work straight with the pencils. That's how José Villarrubia entered the picture and we had a team.

This was the first of five series I would do with Bernie. We would go on to populate the city, and we had a great time doing it. Bernie was a true horror fan so it was easy for us to work together. It was the most fun I've ever had working in comics.

I think about Bernie every day. I think mostly about the good times, the nights when we all got together for pizza and Scrabble and would laugh through the night. I know he is one of the greatest illustrators to ever live, but to me, he will always be my friend.

—Steve Niles
Los Angeles, December 2018

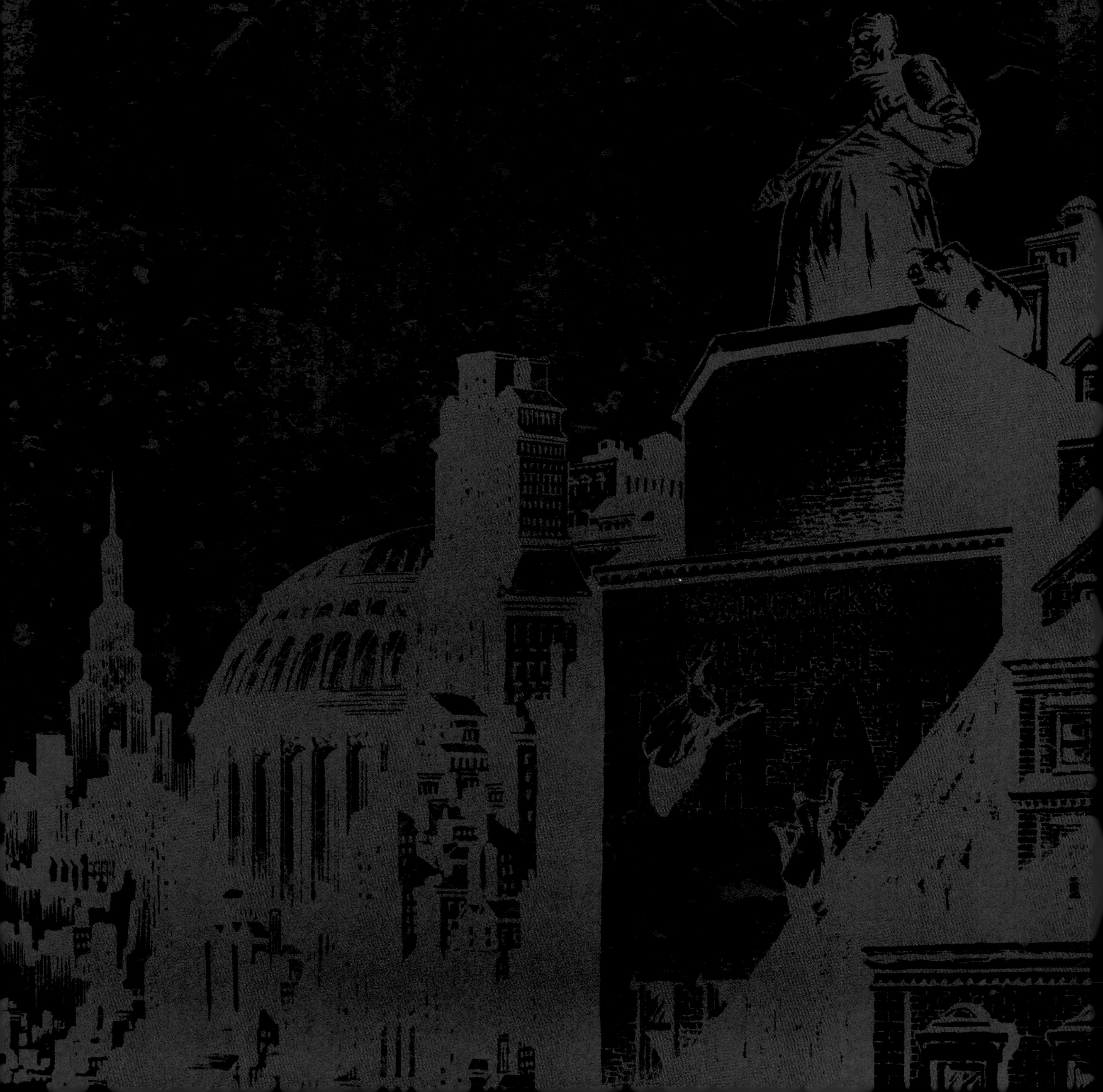

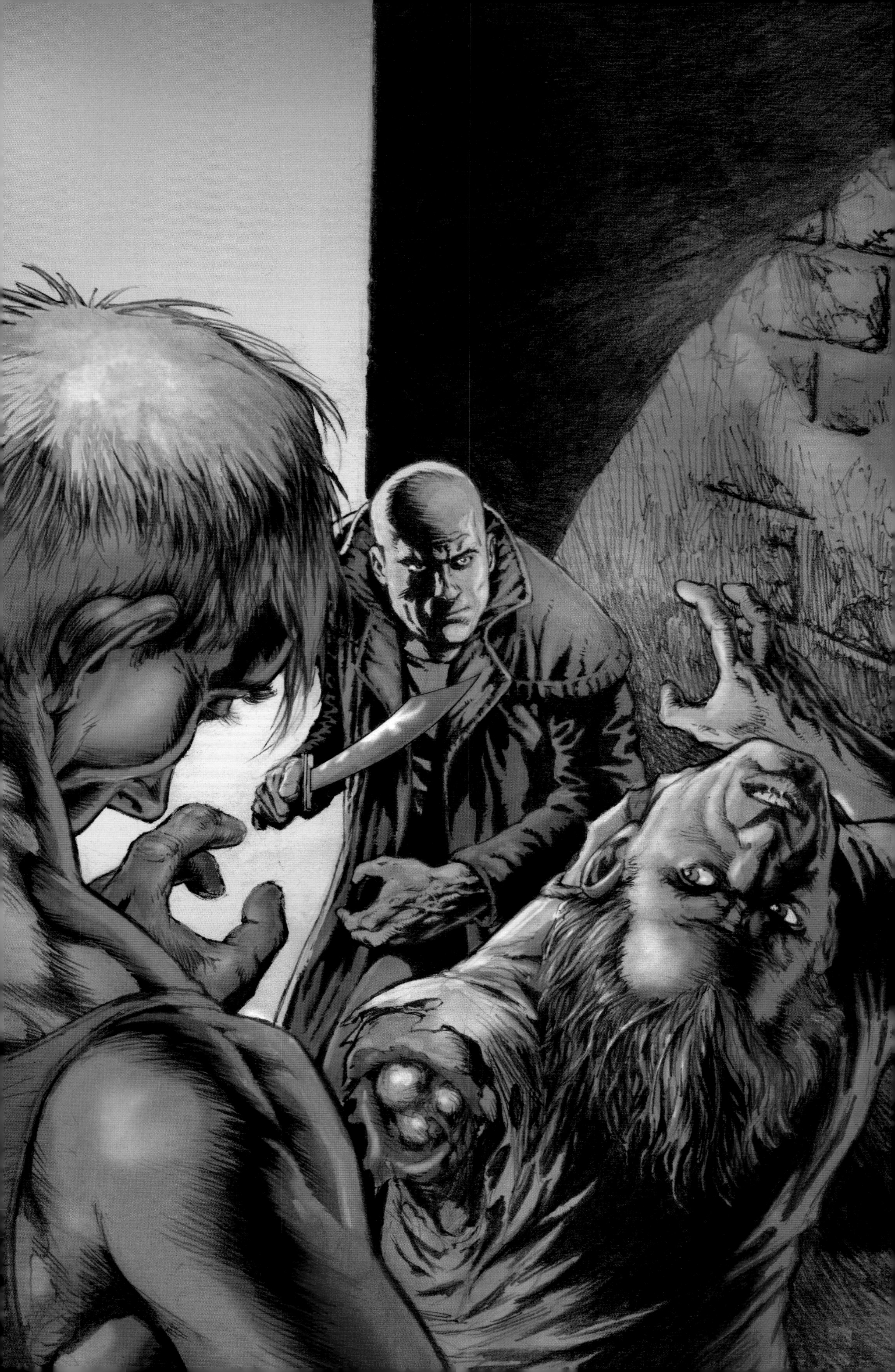

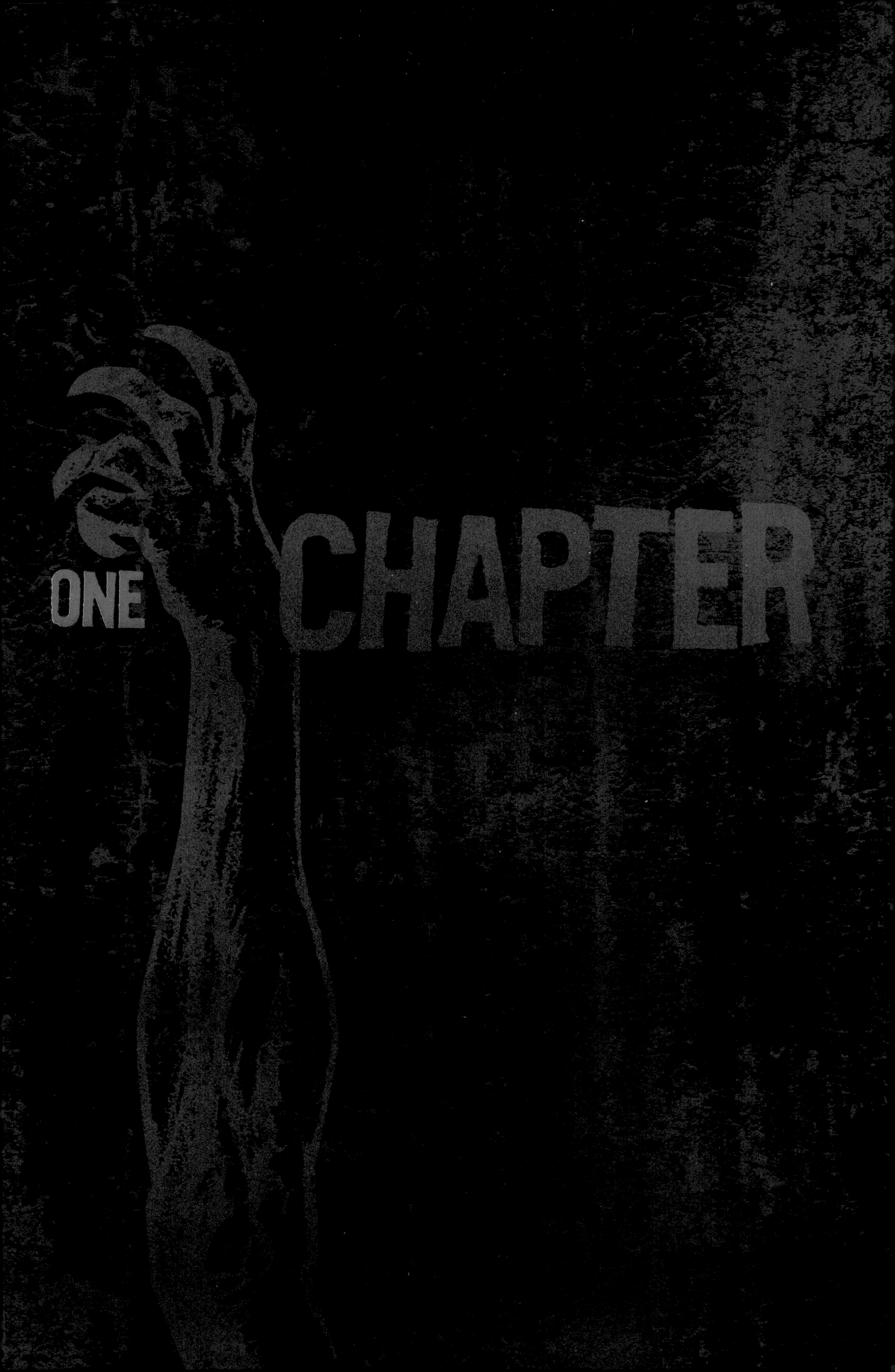

ONE CHAPTER

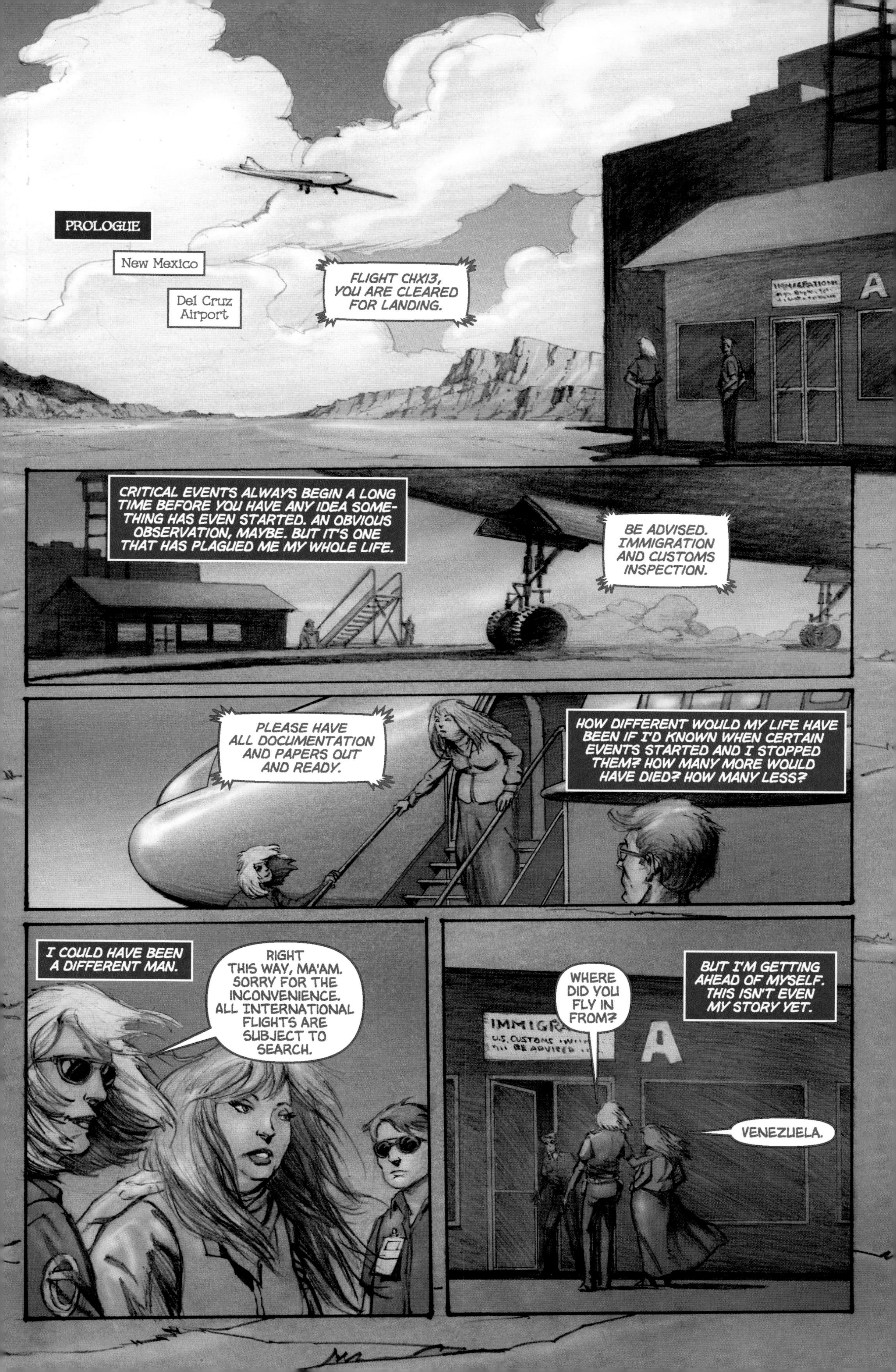
PROLOGUE
New Mexico
Del Cruz Airport
FLIGHT CHX13, YOU ARE CLEARED FOR LANDING.
CRITICAL EVENTS ALWAYS BEGIN A LONG TIME BEFORE YOU HAVE ANY IDEA SOME-THING HAS EVEN STARTED. AN OBVIOUS OBSERVATION, MAYBE. BUT IT'S ONE THAT HAS PLAGUED ME MY WHOLE LIFE.
BE ADVISED. IMMIGRATION AND CUSTOMS INSPECTION.
PLEASE HAVE ALL DOCUMENTATION AND PAPERS OUT AND READY.
HOW DIFFERENT WOULD MY LIFE HAVE BEEN IF I'D KNOWN WHEN CERTAIN EVENTS STARTED AND I STOPPED THEM? HOW MANY MORE WOULD HAVE DIED? HOW MANY LESS?
I COULD HAVE BEEN A DIFFERENT MAN.
RIGHT THIS WAY, MA'AM. SORRY FOR THE INCONVENIENCE. ALL INTERNATIONAL FLIGHTS ARE SUBJECT TO SEARCH.
WHERE DID YOU FLY IN FROM?
BUT I'M GETTING AHEAD OF MYSELF. THIS ISN'T EVEN MY STORY YET.
VENEZUELA.

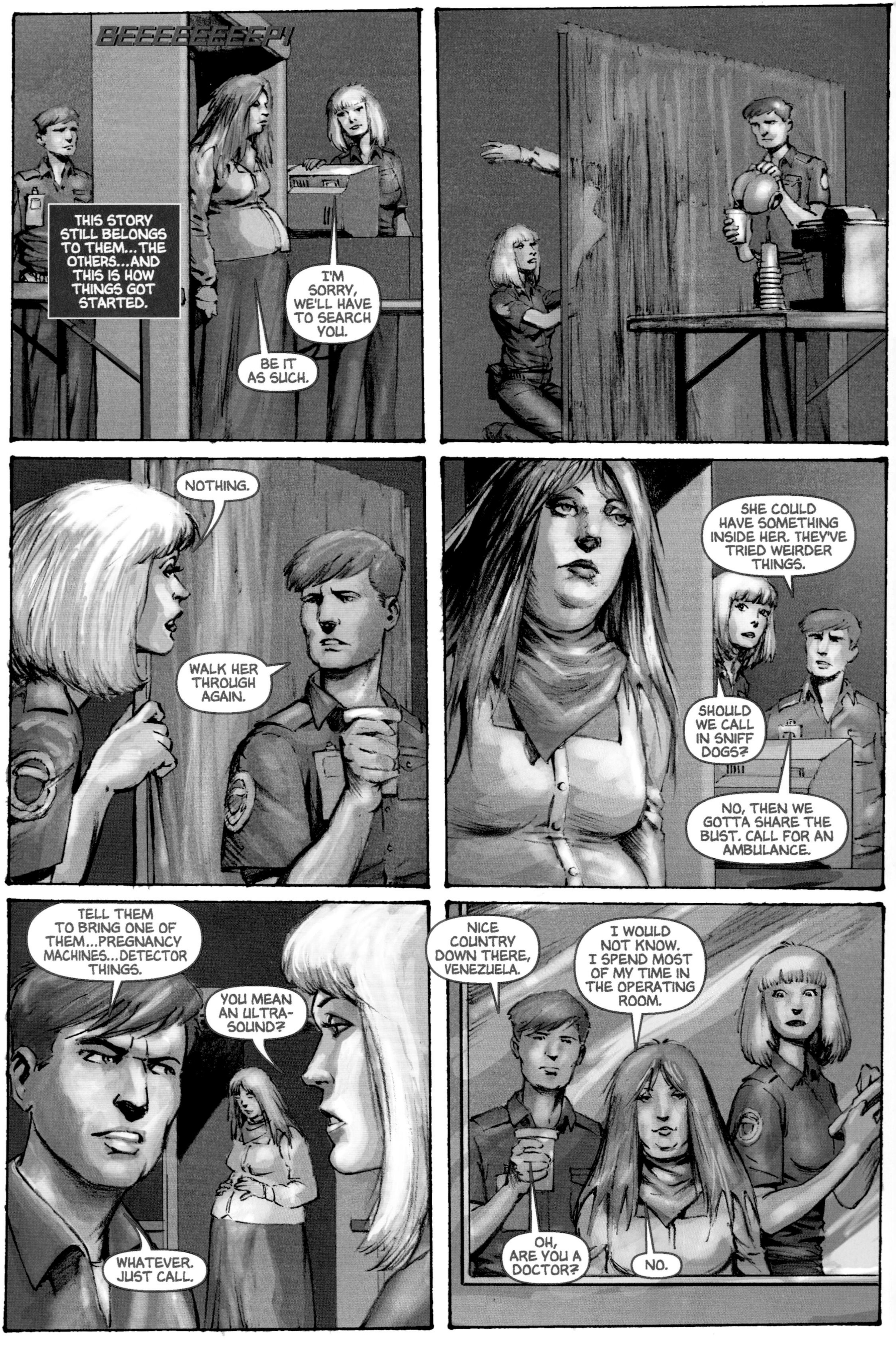
BEEEEEEEEEP!
THIS STORY STILL BELONGS TO THEM...THE OTHERS...AND THIS IS HOW THINGS GOT STARTED.
I'M SORRY, WE'LL HAVE TO SEARCH YOU.
BE IT AS SUCH.
NOTHING.
WALK HER THROUGH AGAIN.
SHE COULD HAVE SOMETHING INSIDE HER. THEY'VE TRIED WEIRDER THINGS.
SHOULD WE CALL IN SNIFF DOGS?
NO, THEN WE GOTTA SHARE THE BUST. CALL FOR AN AMBULANCE.
TELL THEM TO BRING ONE OF THEM...PREGNANCY MACHINES...DETECTOR THINGS.
YOU MEAN AN ULTRA-SOUND?
WHATEVER. JUST CALL.
NICE COUNTRY DOWN THERE, VENEZUELA.
I WOULD NOT KNOW. I SPEND MOST OF MY TIME IN THE OPERATING ROOM.
OH, ARE YOU A DOCTOR?
NO.

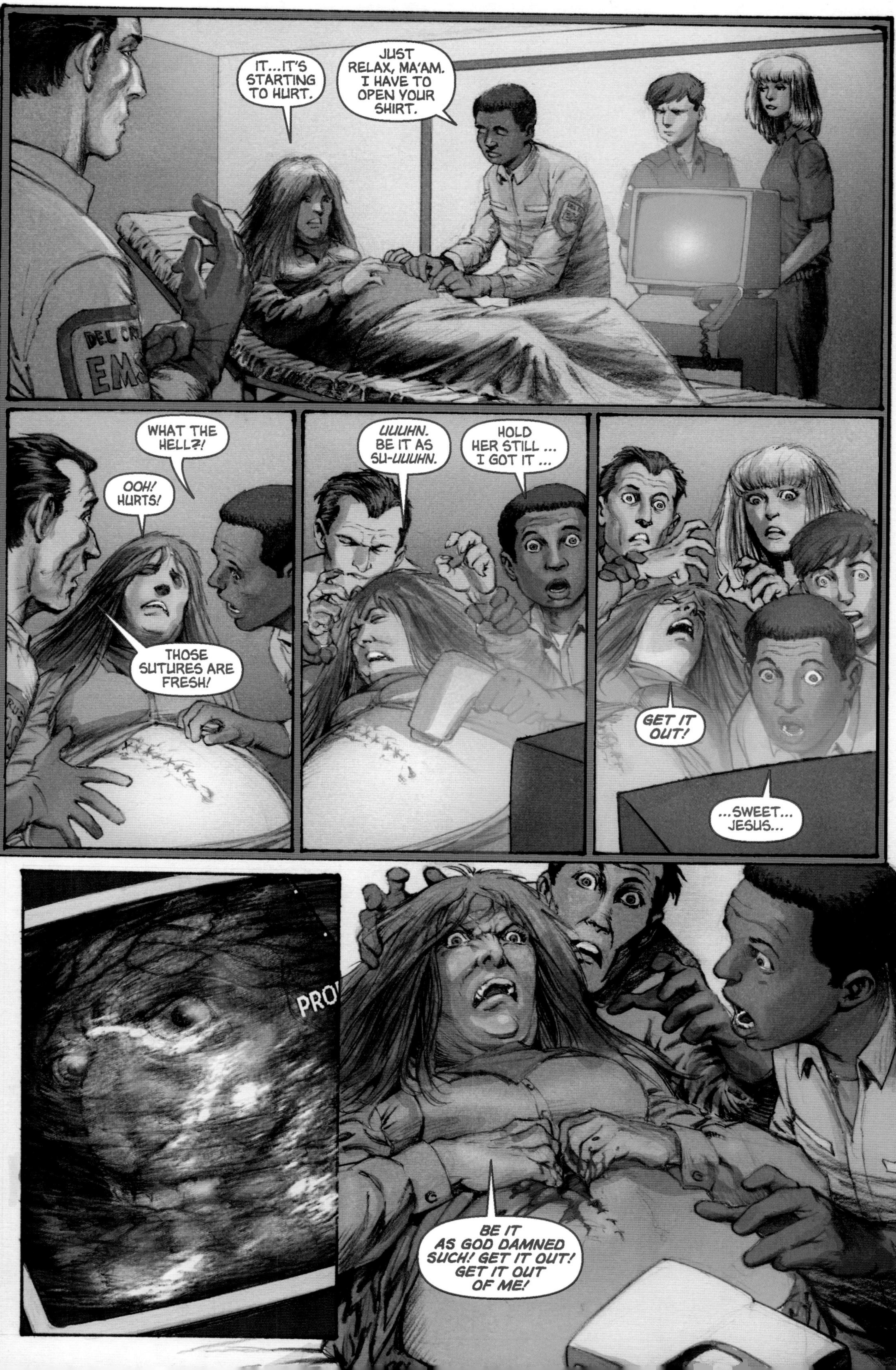
IT...IT'S STARTING TO HURT.
JUST RELAX, MA'AM. I HAVE TO OPEN YOUR SHIRT.
DEL CR
EMS
WHAT THE HELL?!
OOH! HURTS!
THOSE SUTURES ARE FRESH!
UUUHN. BE IT AS SU-UUUHN.
HOLD HER STILL ... I GOT IT ...
GET IT OUT!
...SWEET... JESUS...
PRO
BE IT AS GOD DAMNED SUCH! GET IT OUT! GET IT OUT OF ME!

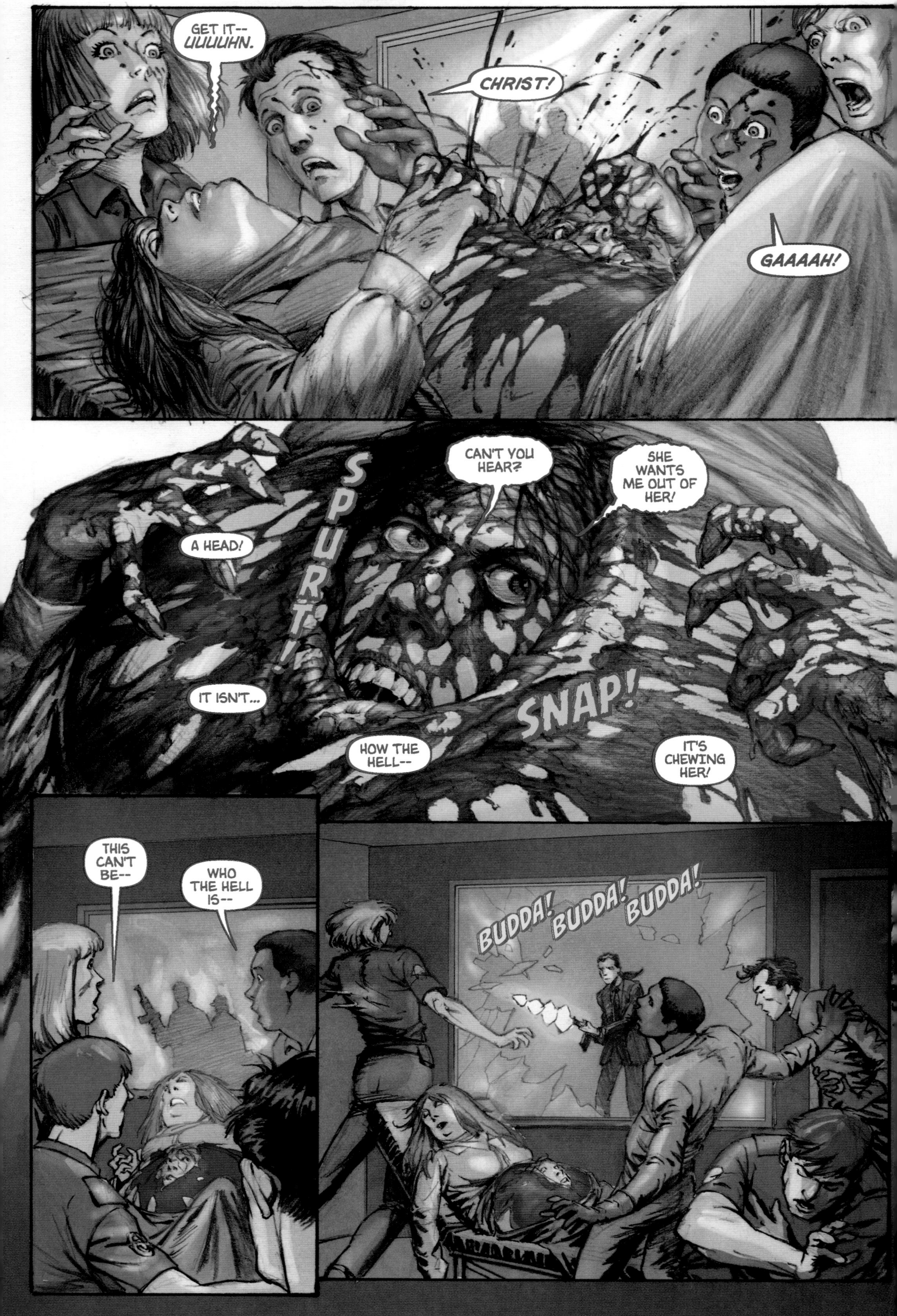
GET IT-- UUUUHN.
CHRIST!
GAAAAH!
SPURT!
CAN'T YOU HEAR?
SHE WANTS ME OUT OF HER!
A HEAD!
IT ISN'T...
SNAP!
HOW THE HELL--
IT'S CHEWING HER!
THIS CAN'T BE--
WHO THE HELL IS--
BUDDA! BUDDA! BUDDA!

SORRY WE WERE LATE, BOSS. BUTCH GOT LOST.
JEEZ, GARY. THE YAHOO MAP WAS ALL WRONG.
GENTLEMEN, PLEASE. TIME ENOUGH FOR THE FAILINGS OF MAPQUEST ...
NOW, IF YOU WOULD BE SO KIND AS TO PRY ME FROM THIS FOUL CAVITY.
I SEE YOU REMEMBERED THE MOIST TOWELETTE THIS TIME. WELL DONE.
CLICK!
AH. THANK YOU, BUTCH.
YES, MUCH BETTER.
TIME TO GO, GENTLE-MEN.
WHAT ABOUT THE WOMAN, BOSS?
BRING THE HEAD.

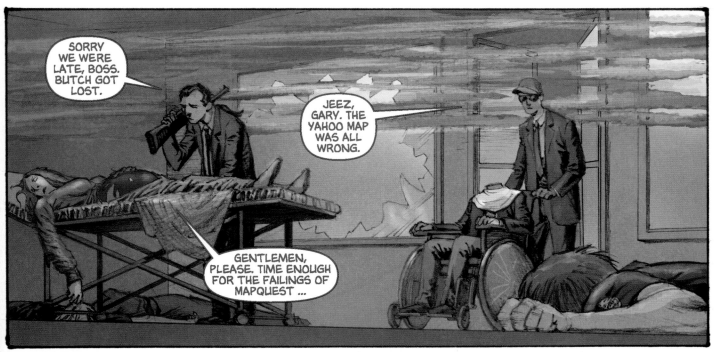

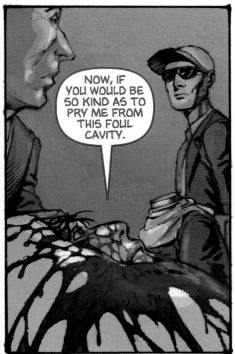

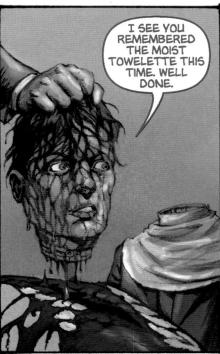

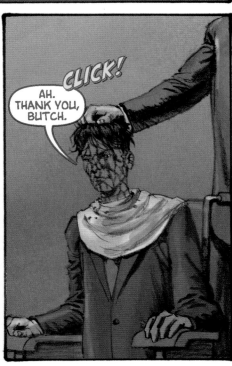

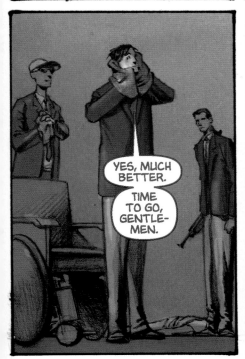

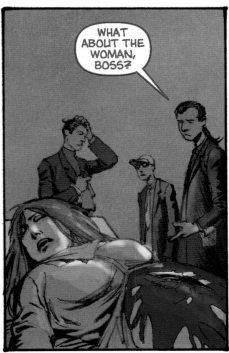

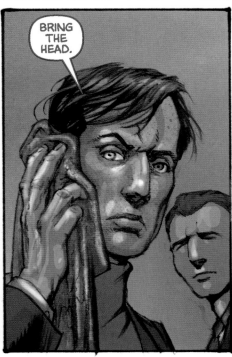

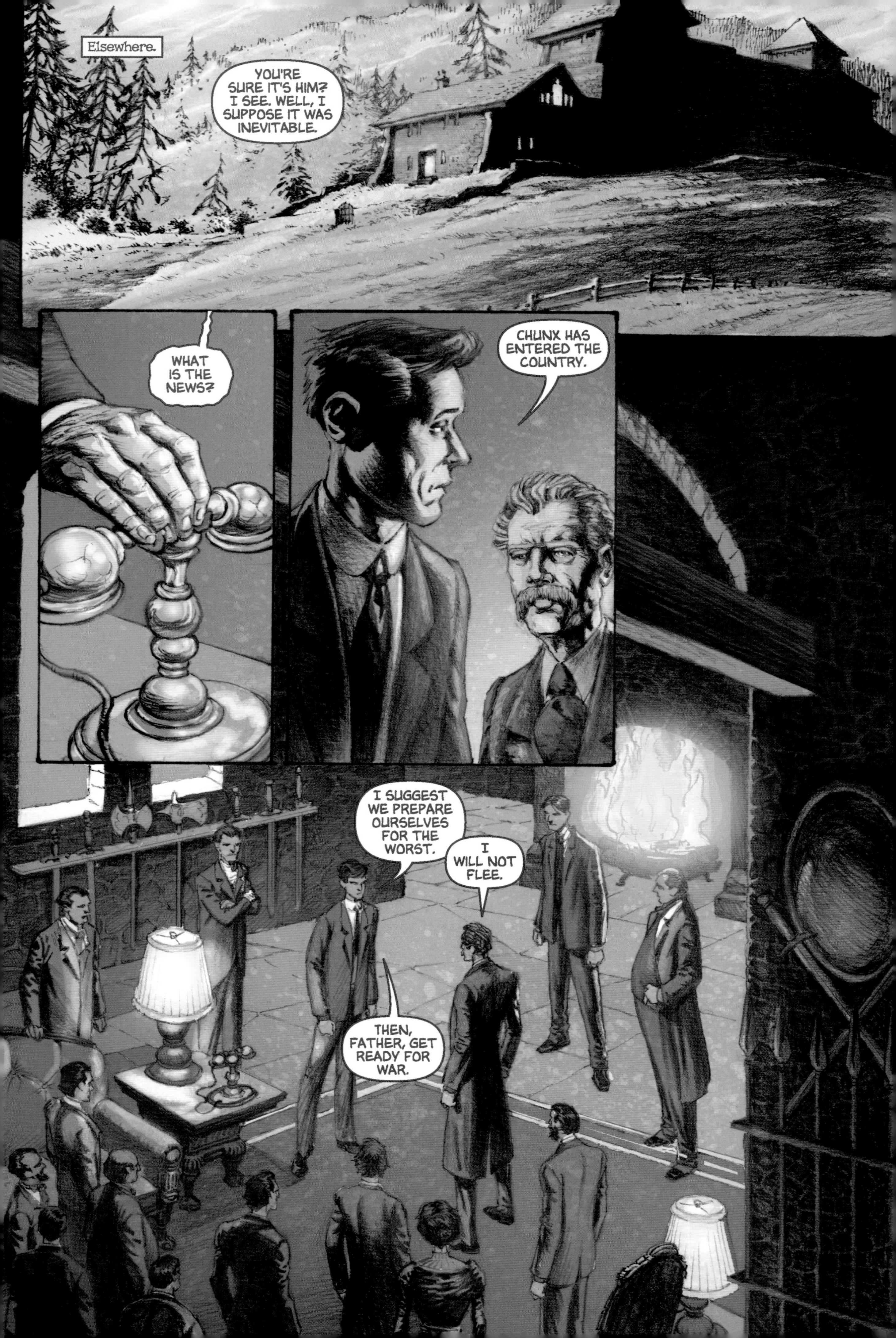
Elsewhere.
YOU'RE SURE IT'S HIM? I SEE. WELL, I SUPPOSE IT WAS INEVITABLE.
WHAT IS THE NEWS?
CHUNX HAS ENTERED THE COUNTRY.
I SUGGEST WE PREPARE OURSELVES FOR THE WORST.
I WILL NOT FLEE.
THEN, FATHER, GET READY FOR WAR.

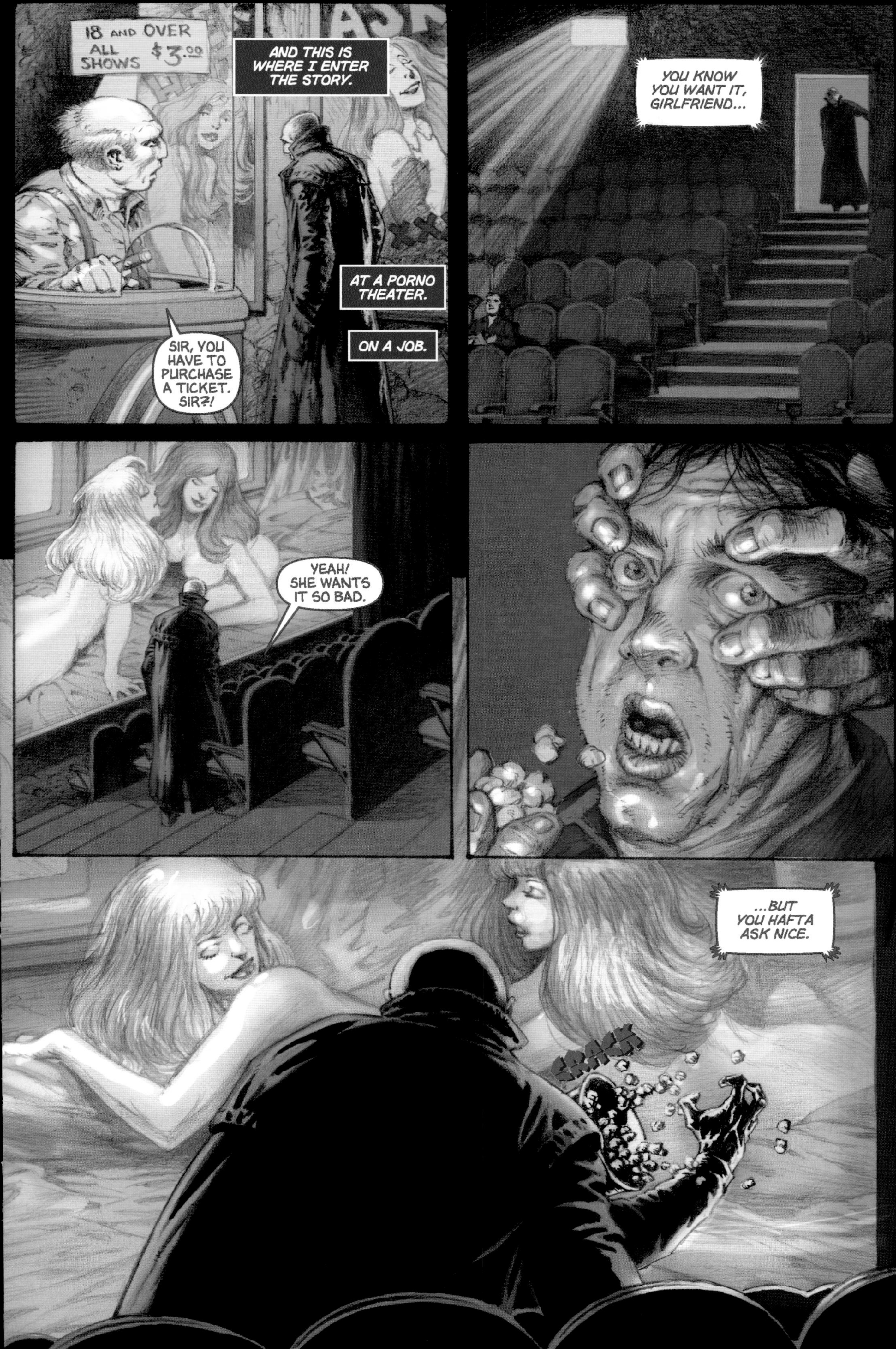
18 AND OVER
ALL SHOWS $3.00
AND THIS IS WHERE I ENTER THE STORY.
SIR, YOU HAVE TO PURCHASE A TICKET. SIR?!
AT A PORNO THEATER.
ON A JOB.
YOU KNOW YOU WANT IT, GIRLFRIEND...
YEAH! SHE WANTS IT SO BAD.
...BUT YOU HAFTA ASK NICE.

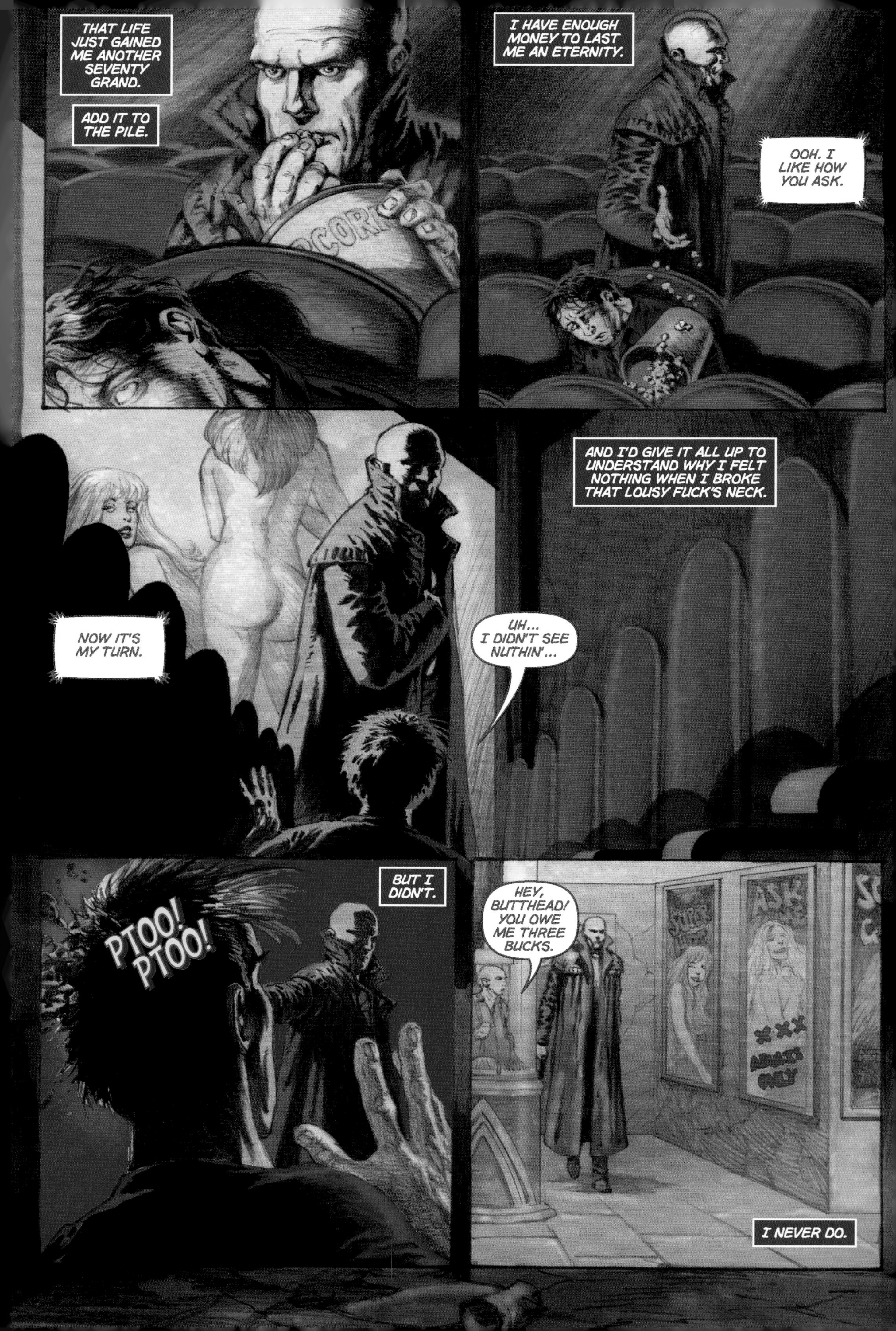
THAT LIFE JUST GAINED ME ANOTHER SEVENTY GRAND.
ADD IT TO THE PILE.
POPCORN
I HAVE ENOUGH MONEY TO LAST ME AN ETERNITY.
OOH. I LIKE HOW YOU ASK.
AND I'D GIVE IT ALL UP TO UNDERSTAND WHY I FELT NOTHING WHEN I BROKE THAT LOUSY FUCK'S NECK.
NOW IT'S MY TURN.
UH... I DIDN'T SEE NUTHIN'...
BUT I DIDN'T.
PTOO! PTOO!
HEY, BUTTHEAD! YOU OWE ME THREE BUCKS.
I NEVER DO.

CALL IT DEAD INSIDE.

THREE BUCKS!

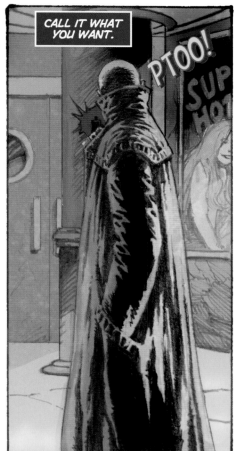

CALL IT WHAT YOU WANT.

PTOO!

IT'S THE WAY I'VE ALWAYS BEEN.

WHEN I WAS SEVEN, I KILLED MY FIRST PERSON. HIS NAME WAS TIM ROBINSON. HE SHOVED ME SO I DROWNED HIM IN A STREET PUDDLE AND CRAMMED HIM DOWN THE SEWER.

NEVER FELT A THING, JUST THE ANGER OF BEING SHOVED. NOT EVEN KILLING HIM GOT RID OF THE RAGE.

MY NAME IS BLUD. THAT'S SHORT FOR BLUDOWSKI. STOSH BLUDOWSKI BY BIRTH.

ONE GUESS WHAT I DO FOR A LIVING.

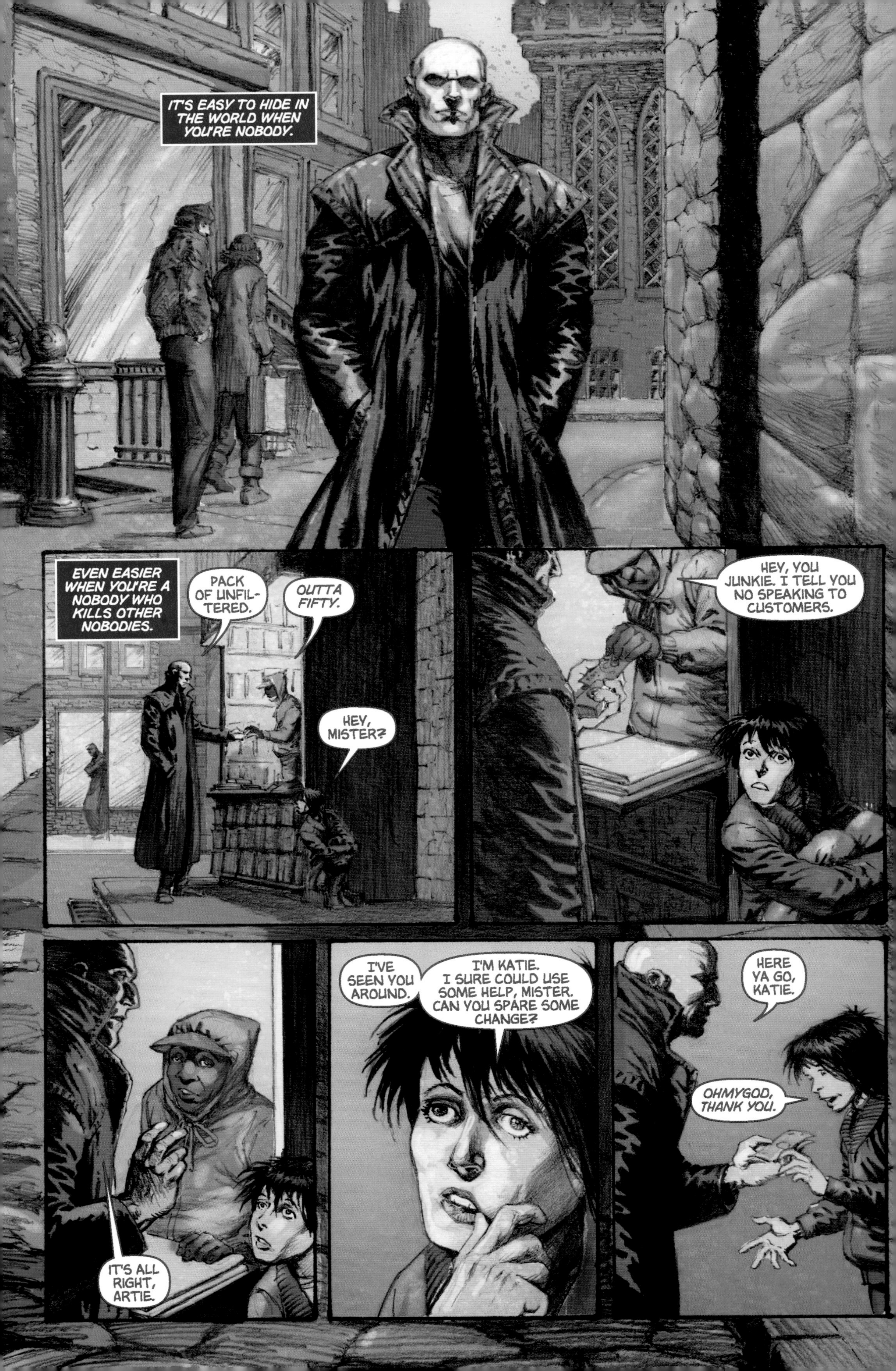
IT'S EASY TO HIDE IN THE WORLD WHEN YOU'RE NOBODY.
EVEN EASIER WHEN YOU'RE A NOBODY WHO KILLS OTHER NOBODIES.
PACK OF UNFILTERED.
OUTTA FIFTY.
HEY, MISTER?
HEY, YOU JUNKIE. I TELL YOU NO SPEAKING TO CUSTOMERS.
IT'S ALL RIGHT, ARTIE.
I'VE SEEN YOU AROUND.
I'M KATIE. I SURE COULD USE SOME HELP, MISTER. CAN YOU SPARE SOME CHANGE?
HERE YA GO, KATIE.
OHMYGOD, THANK YOU.

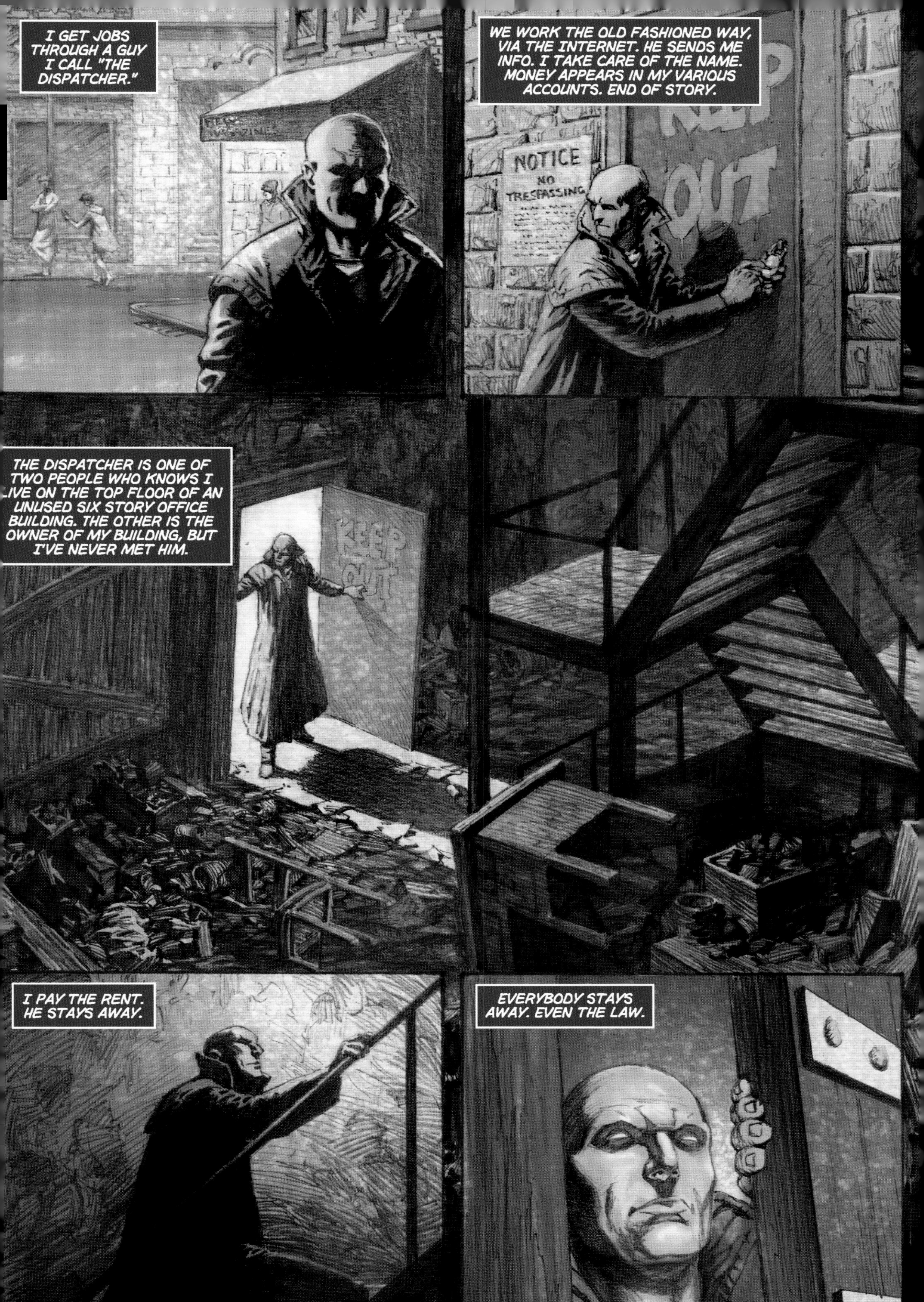
I GET JOBS THROUGH A GUY I CALL "THE DISPATCHER."
WE WORK THE OLD FASHIONED WAY, VIA THE INTERNET. HE SENDS ME INFO. I TAKE CARE OF THE NAME. MONEY APPEARS IN MY VARIOUS ACCOUNTS. END OF STORY.
NOTICE
NO TRESPASSING
OUT
THE DISPATCHER IS ONE OF TWO PEOPLE WHO KNOWS I LIVE ON THE TOP FLOOR OF AN UNUSED SIX STORY OFFICE BUILDING. THE OTHER IS THE OWNER OF MY BUILDING, BUT I'VE NEVER MET HIM.
KEEP OUT
I PAY THE RENT. HE STAYS AWAY.
EVERYBODY STAYS AWAY. EVEN THE LAW.

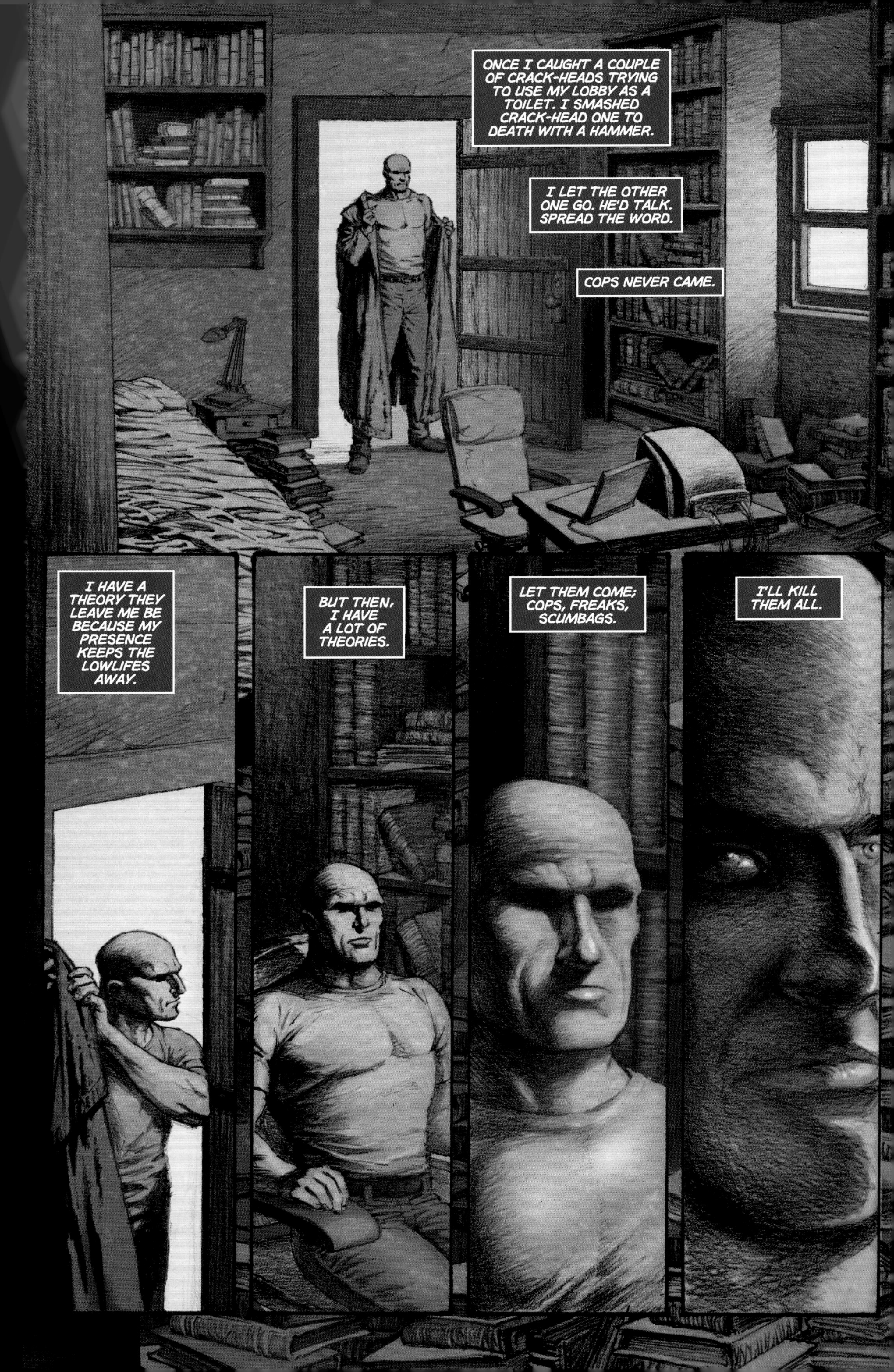

ONCE I CAUGHT A COUPLE OF CRACK-HEADS TRYING TO USE MY LOBBY AS A TOILET. I SMASHED CRACK-HEAD ONE TO DEATH WITH A HAMMER.
I LET THE OTHER ONE GO. HE'D TALK. SPREAD THE WORD.
COPS NEVER CAME.
I HAVE A THEORY THEY LEAVE ME BE BECAUSE MY PRESENCE KEEPS THE LOWLIFES AWAY.
BUT THEN, I HAVE A LOT OF THEORIES.
LET THEM COME; COPS, FREAKS, SCUMBAGS.
I'LL KILL THEM ALL.

Two hours later.

I HAVE A SMALL TV SET.

SOMETIMES I WATCH NEWS REPORTS ABOUT THE PEOPLE I'VE KILLED.

TO SEE IF I FEEL ANYTHING.

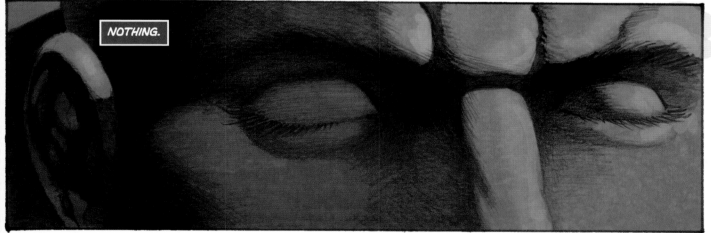

I WATCH THE HORRIFIED PEOPLE WHO FOUND THE MURDER SCENE.

I WATCH THE POLICE DESCRIBE THE BRUTALITY.

I WATCH THE FAMILY MEMBERS OF THE MURDERED CRY.

NOTHING.

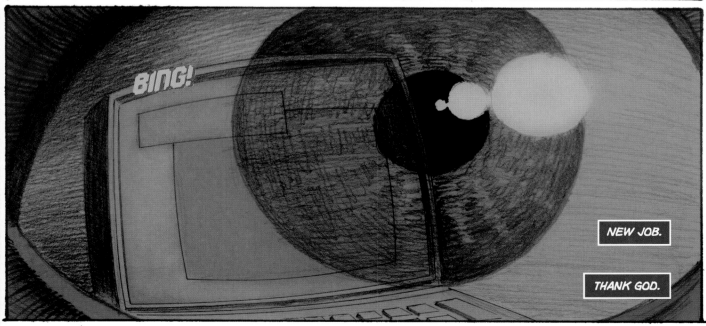

BING!

NEW JOB.

THANK GOD.

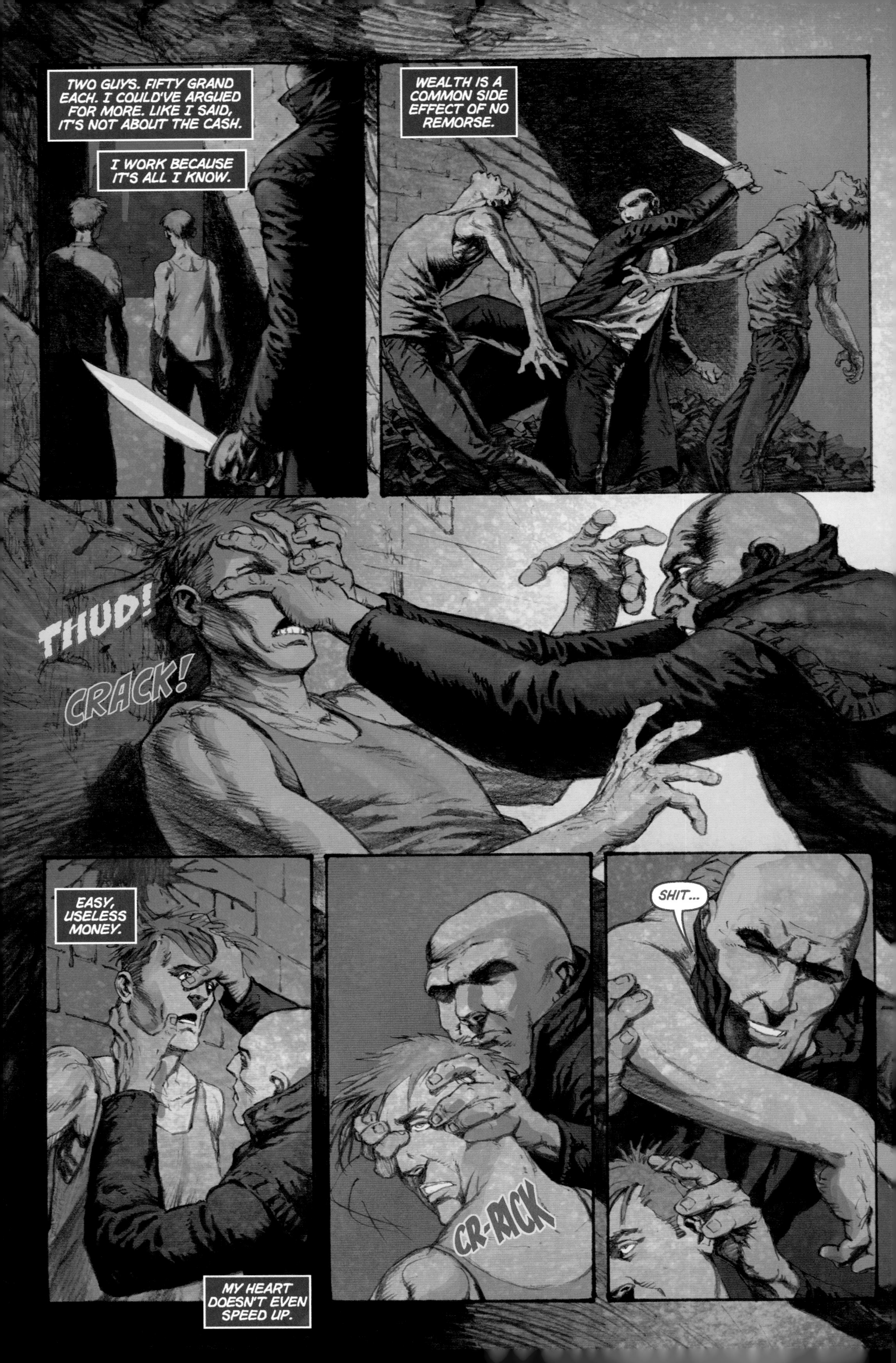
TWO GUYS. FIFTY GRAND EACH. I COULD'VE ARGUED FOR MORE. LIKE I SAID, IT'S NOT ABOUT THE CASH.
I WORK BECAUSE IT'S ALL I KNOW.
WEALTH IS A COMMON SIDE EFFECT OF NO REMORSE.
THUD!
CRACK!
EASY, USELESS MONEY.
MY HEART DOESN'T EVEN SPEED UP.
CR-RACK
SHIT...

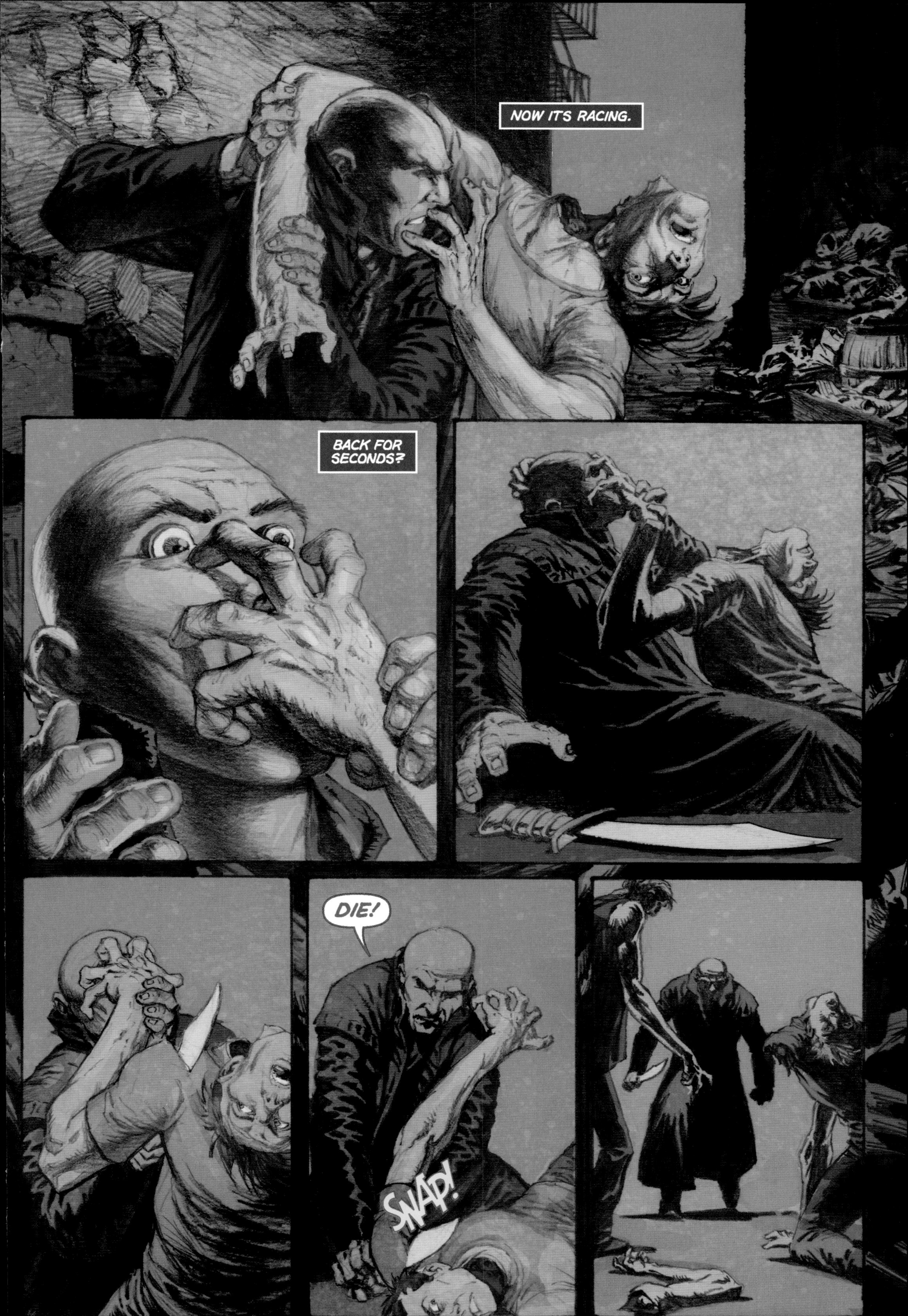
NOW IT'S RACING.
BACK FOR SECONDS?
DIE!
SNAP!

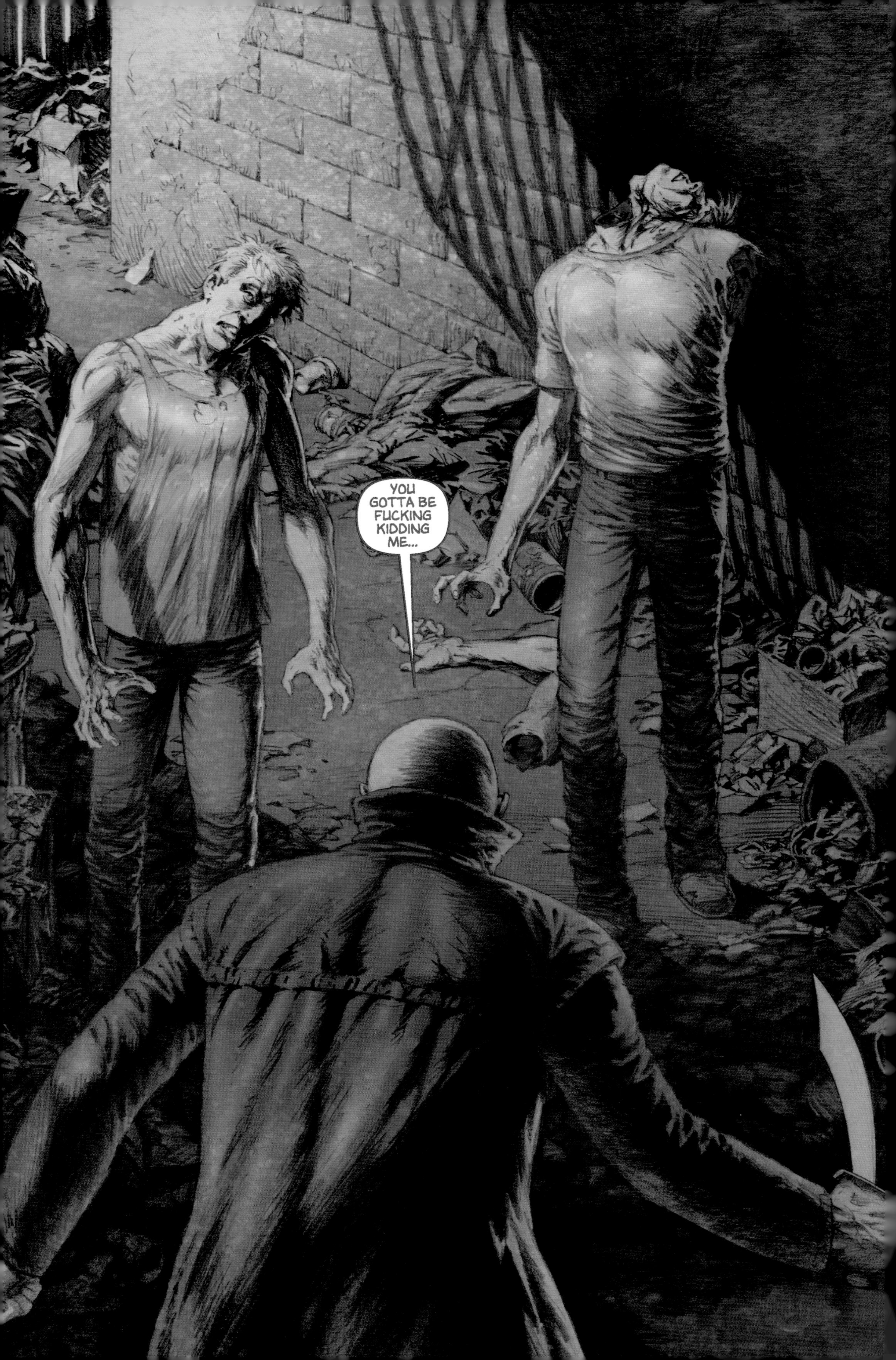
YOU GOTTA BE FUCKING KIDDING ME...

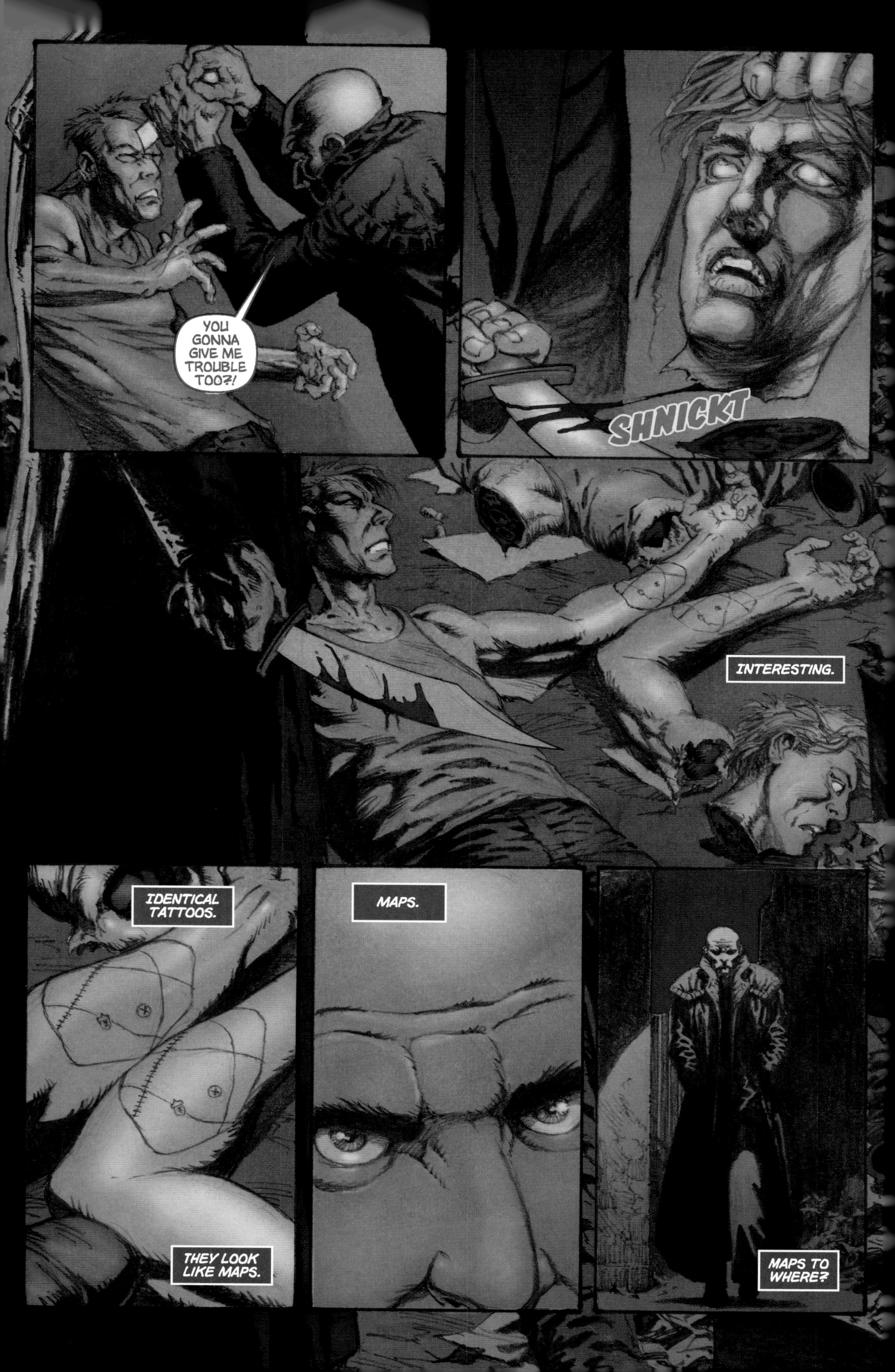
YOU GONNA GIVE ME TROUBLE TOO?!
SHNICKT
INTERESTING.
IDENTICAL TATTOOS.
THEY LOOK LIKE MAPS.
MAPS.
MAPS TO WHERE?

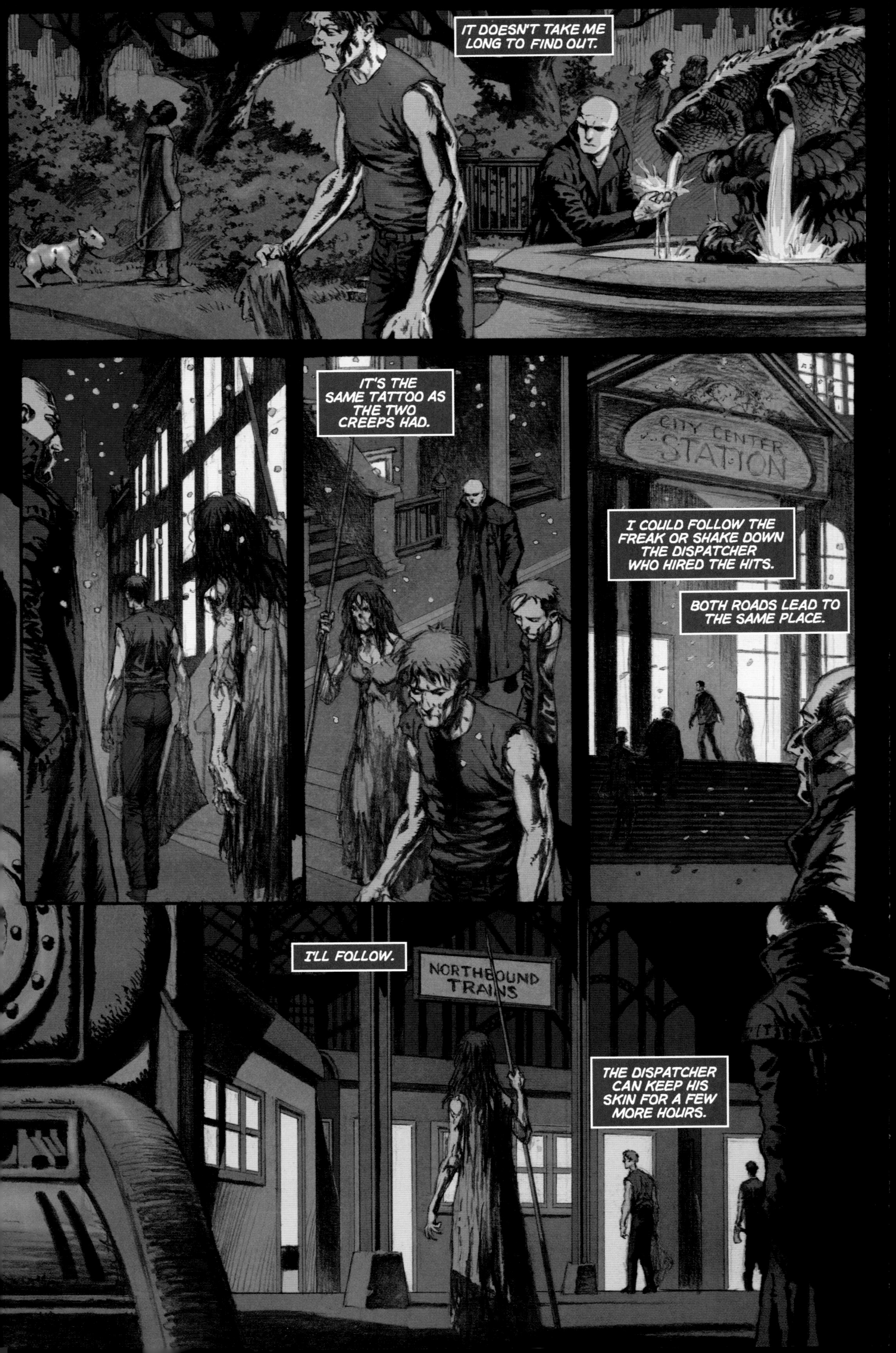
IT DOESN'T TAKE ME LONG TO FIND OUT.
IT'S THE SAME TATTOO AS THE TWO CREEPS HAD.
CITY CENTER STATION
I COULD FOLLOW THE FREAK OR SHAKE DOWN THE DISPATCHER WHO HIRED THE HITS.
BOTH ROADS LEAD TO THE SAME PLACE.
I'LL FOLLOW.
NORTHBOUND TRAINS
THE DISPATCHER CAN KEEP HIS SKIN FOR A FEW MORE HOURS.

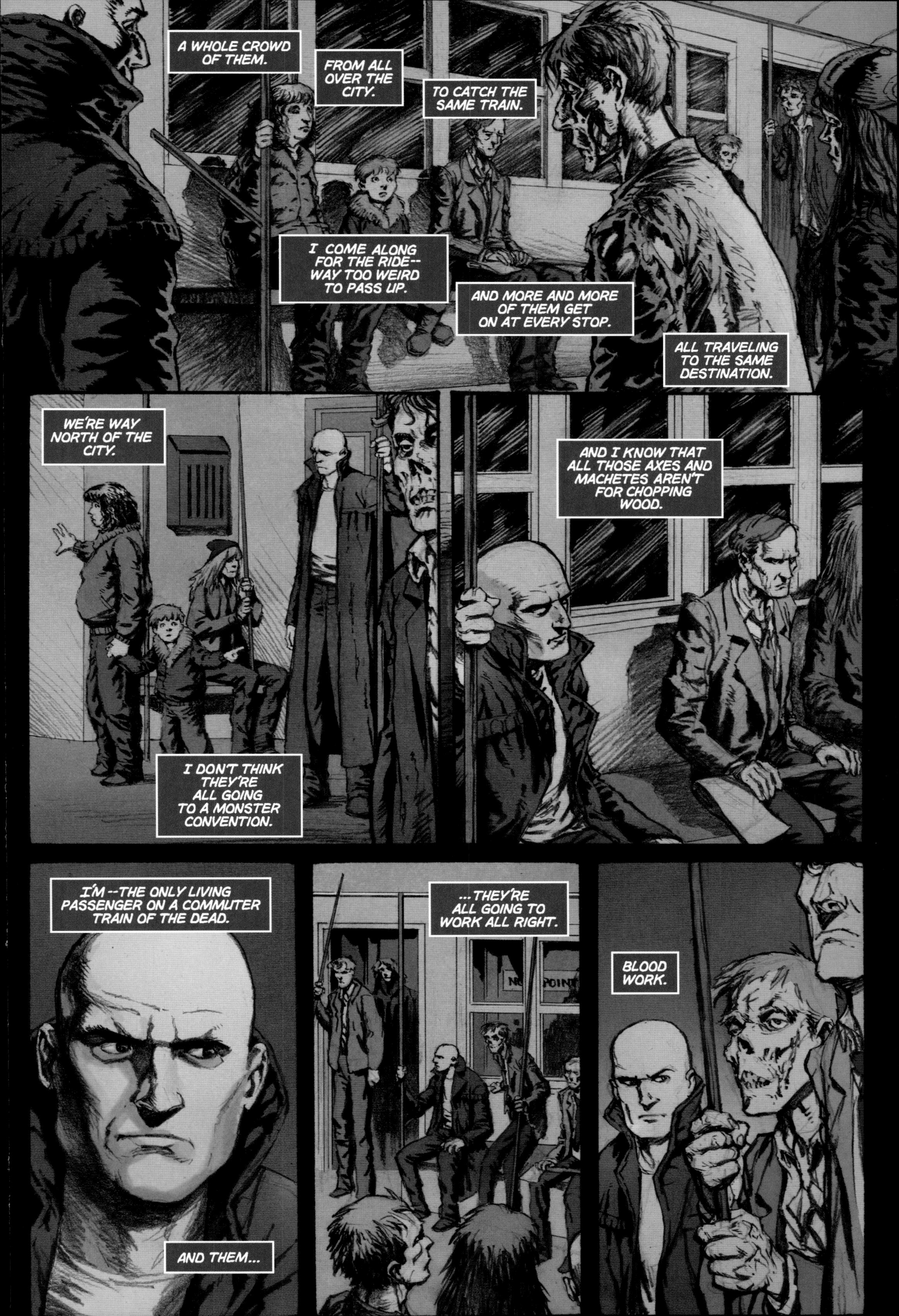
A WHOLE CROWD OF THEM.
FROM ALL OVER THE CITY.
TO CATCH THE SAME TRAIN.
I COME ALONG FOR THE RIDE-- WAY TOO WEIRD TO PASS UP.
AND MORE AND MORE OF THEM GET ON AT EVERY STOP.
ALL TRAVELING TO THE SAME DESTINATION.
WE'RE WAY NORTH OF THE CITY.
I DON'T THINK THEY'RE ALL GOING TO A MONSTER CONVENTION.
AND I KNOW THAT ALL THOSE AXES AND MACHETES AREN'T FOR CHOPPING WOOD.
I'M --THE ONLY LIVING PASSENGER ON A COMMUTER TRAIN OF THE DEAD.
AND THEM...
...THEY'RE ALL GOING TO WORK ALL RIGHT.
BLOOD WORK.

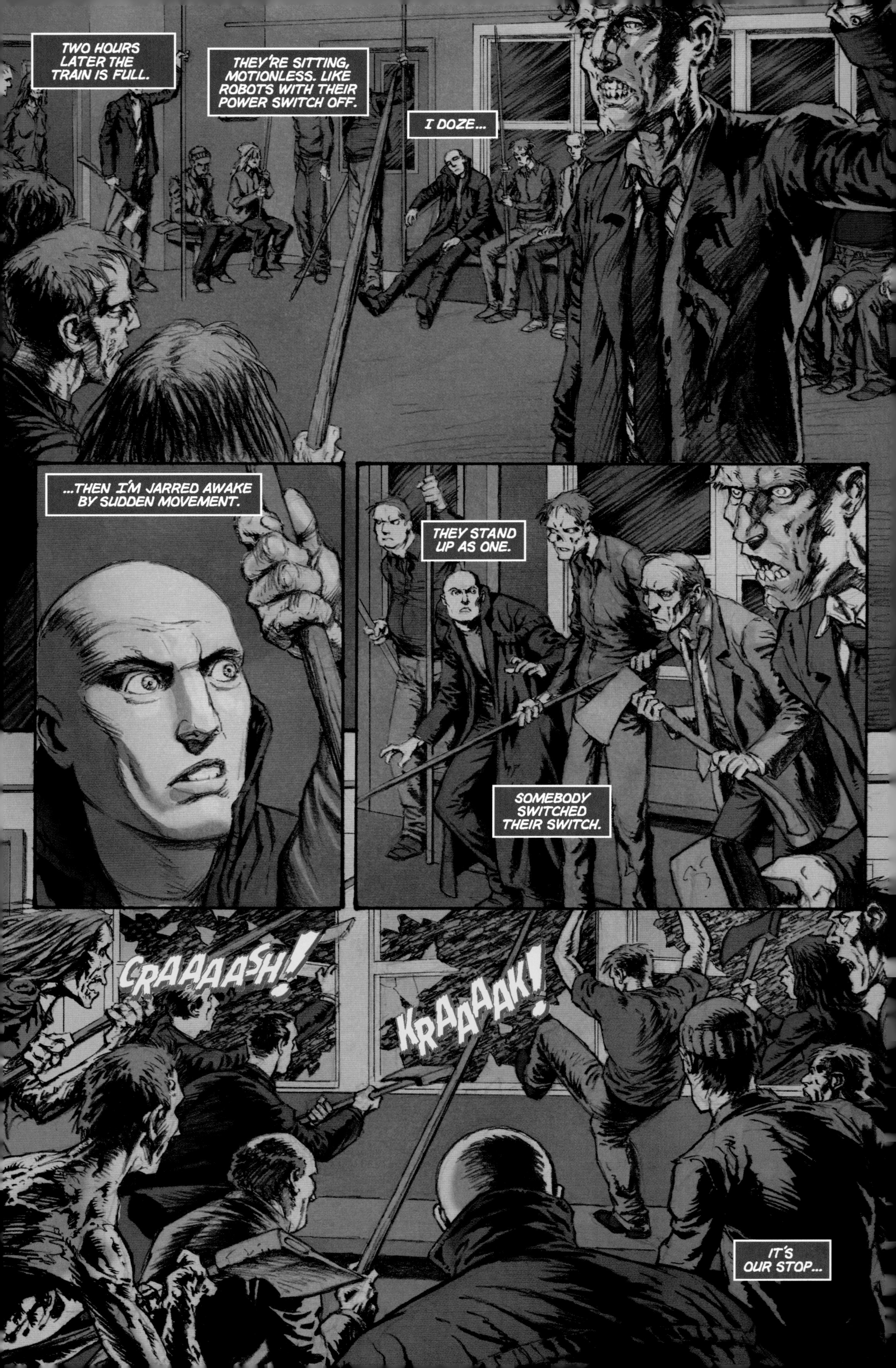
TWO HOURS LATER THE TRAIN IS FULL.
THEY'RE SITTING, MOTIONLESS. LIKE ROBOTS WITH THEIR POWER SWITCH OFF.
I DOZE...
...THEN I'M JARRED AWAKE BY SUDDEN MOVEMENT.
THEY STAND UP AS ONE.
SOMEBODY SWITCHED THEIR SWITCH.
CRAAAASH!
KRAAAK!
IT'S OUR STOP...

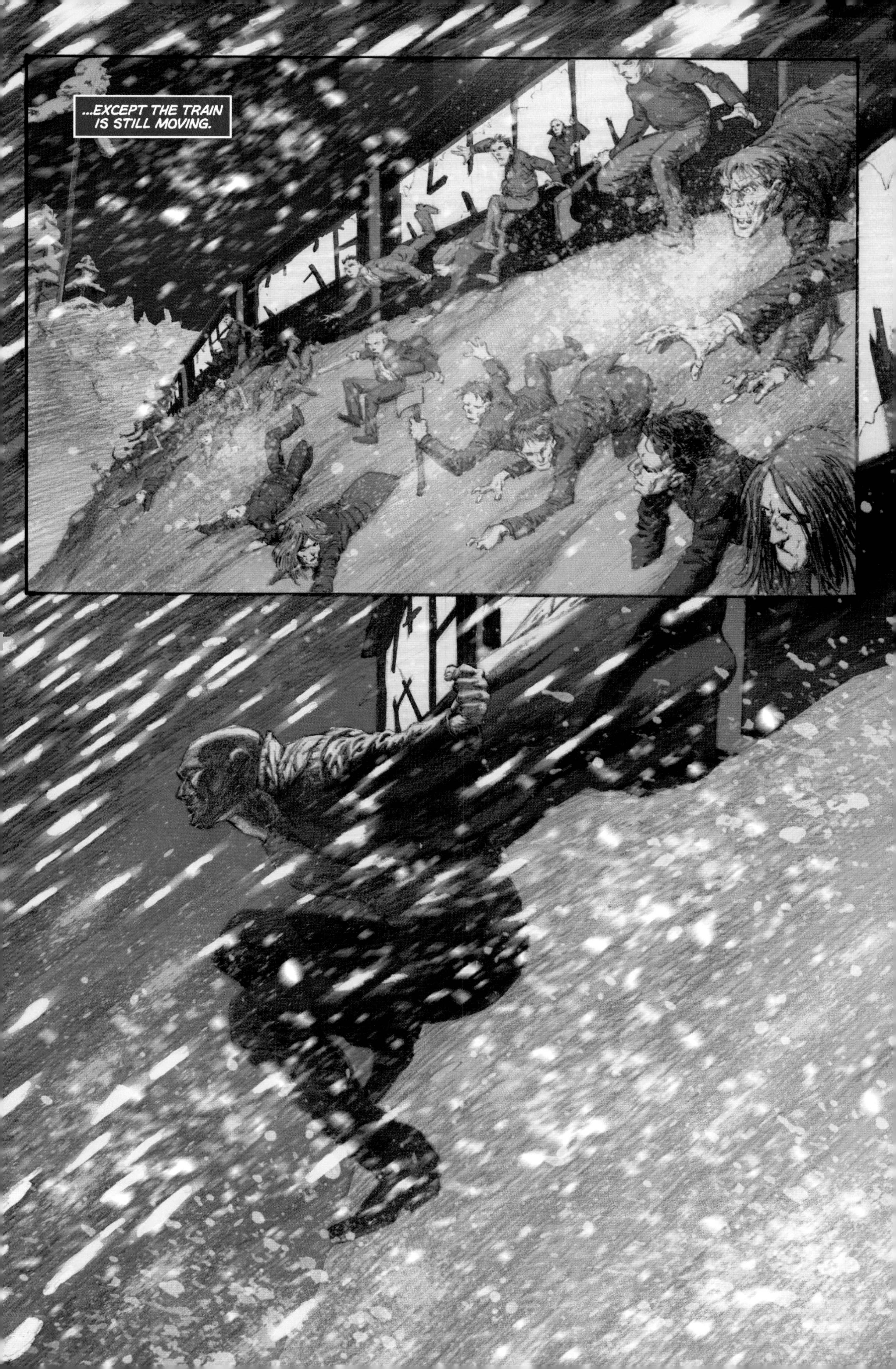
...EXCEPT THE TRAIN
IS STILL MOVING.

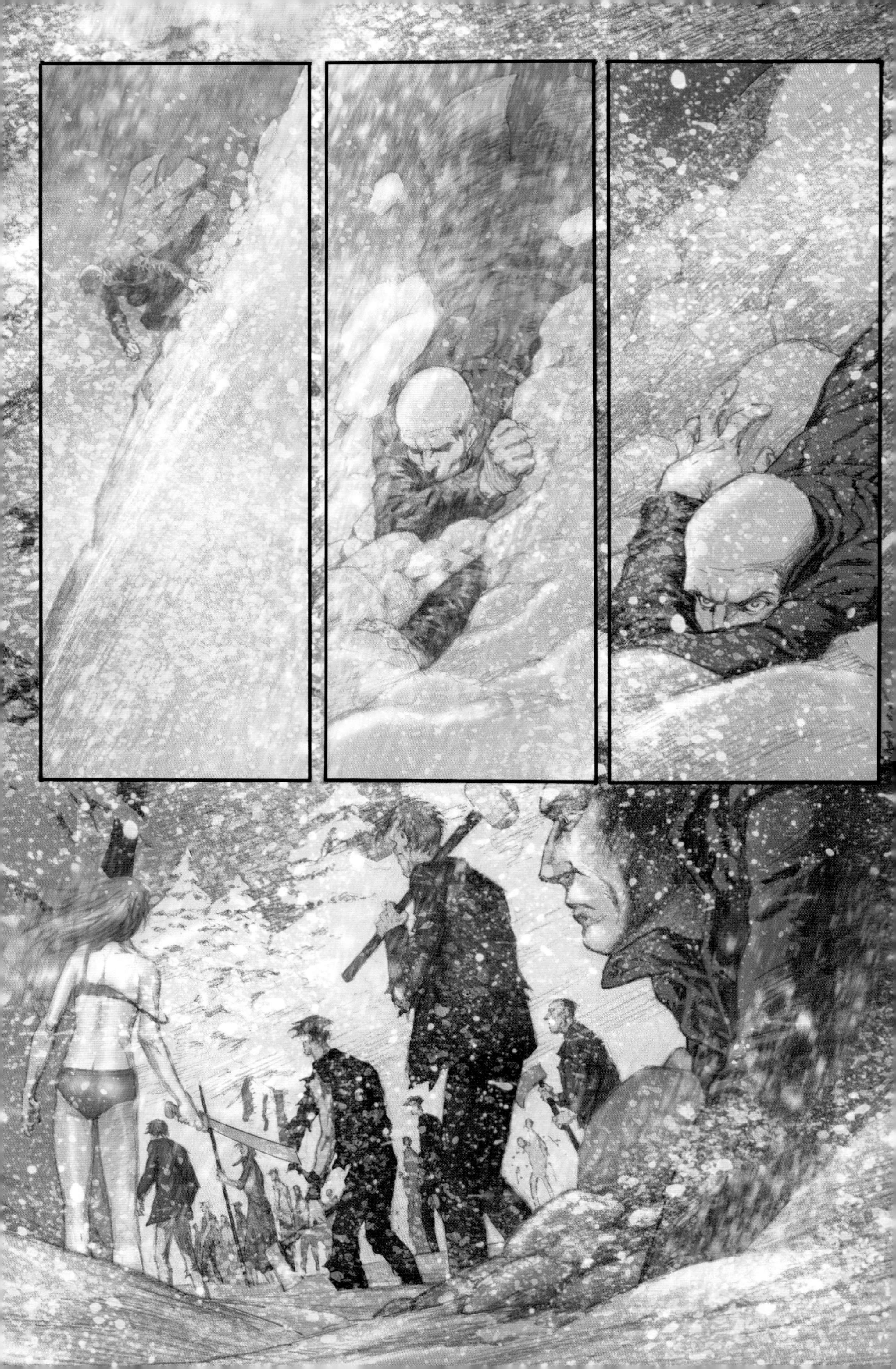

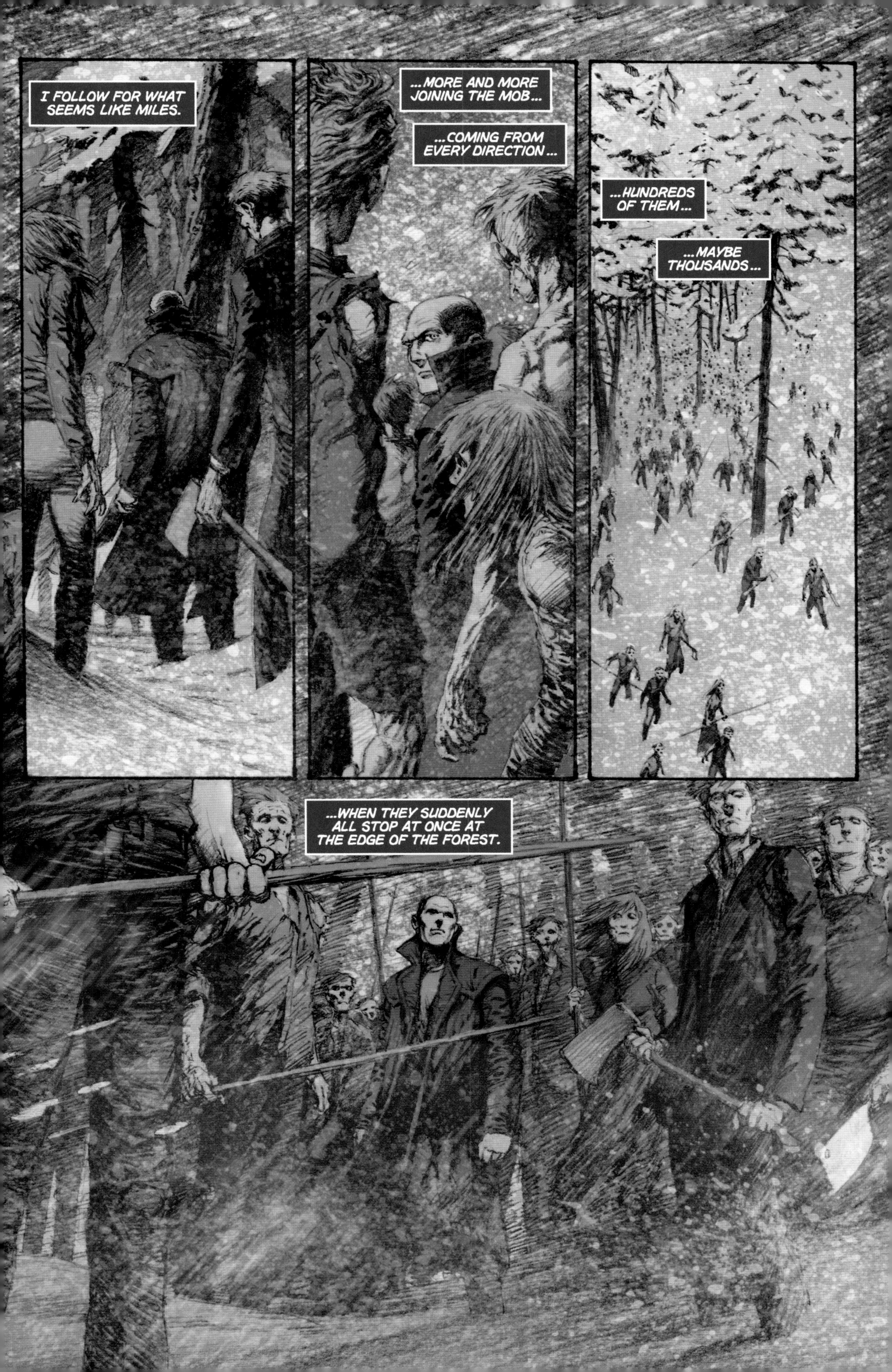

I FOLLOW FOR WHAT SEEMS LIKE MILES.
...MORE AND MORE JOINING THE MOB...
...COMING FROM EVERY DIRECTION...
...HUNDREDS OF THEM...
...MAYBE THOUSANDS...
...WHEN THEY SUDDENLY ALL STOP AT ONCE AT THE EDGE OF THE FOREST.

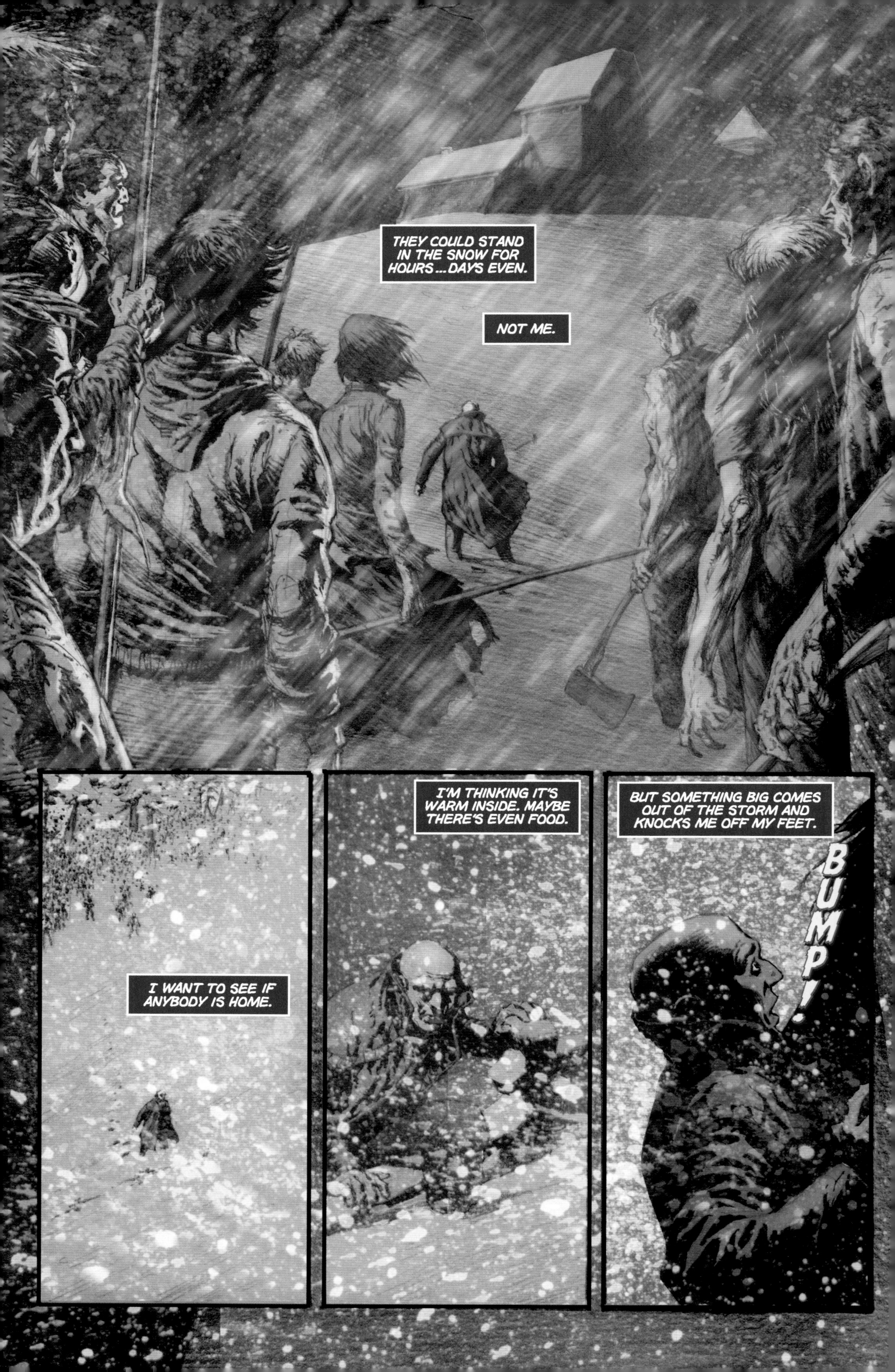
THEY COULD STAND IN THE SNOW FOR HOURS ... DAYS EVEN.
NOT ME.
I WANT TO SEE IF ANYBODY IS HOME.
I'M THINKING IT'S WARM INSIDE. MAYBE THERE'S EVEN FOOD.
BUT SOMETHING BIG COMES OUT OF THE STORM AND KNOCKS ME OFF MY FEET.
BUMP!

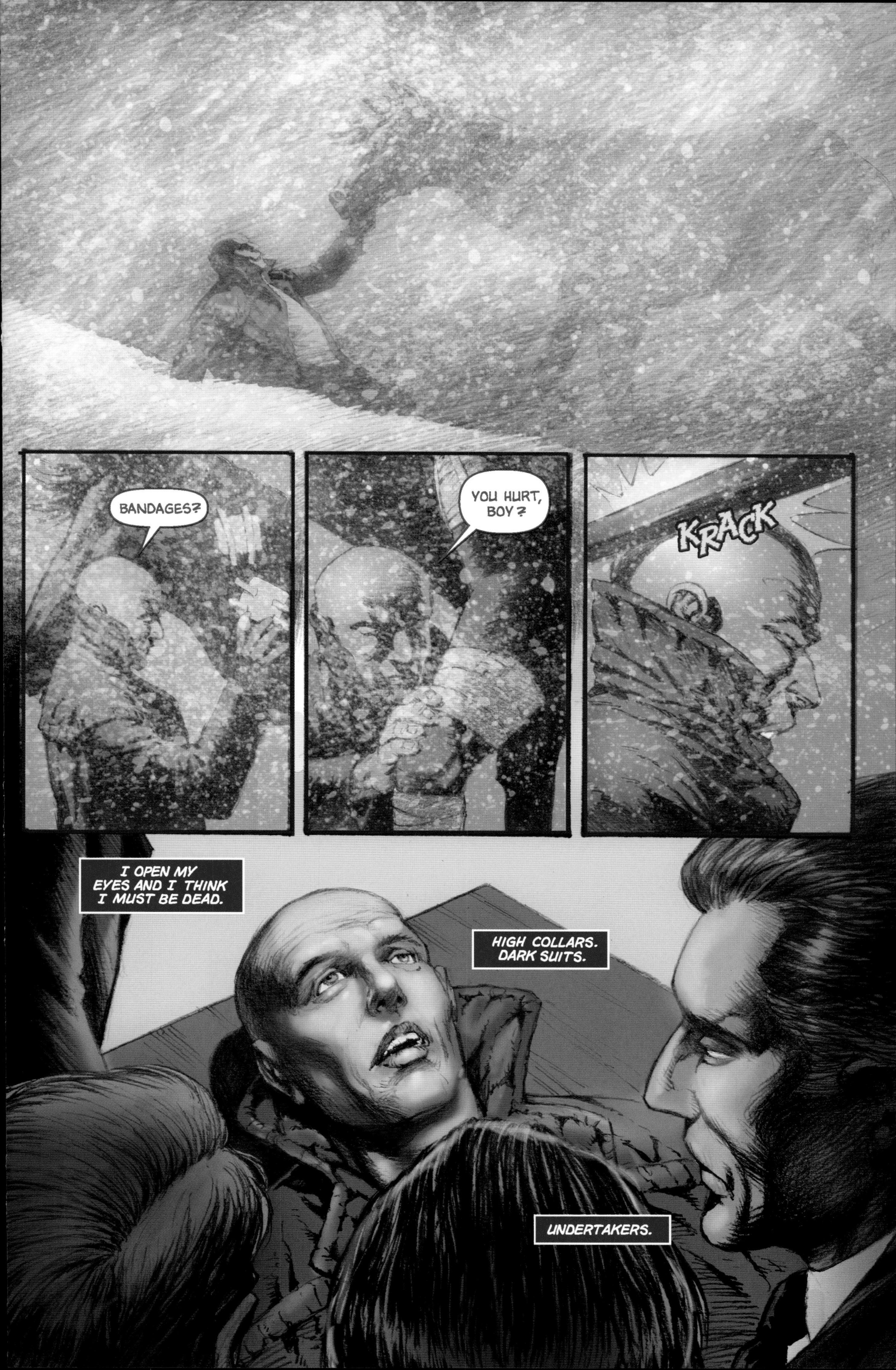
BANDAGES?
YOU HURT, BOY?
KRACK
I OPEN MY EYES AND I THINK I MUST BE DEAD.
HIGH COLLARS. DARK SUITS.
UNDERTAKERS.

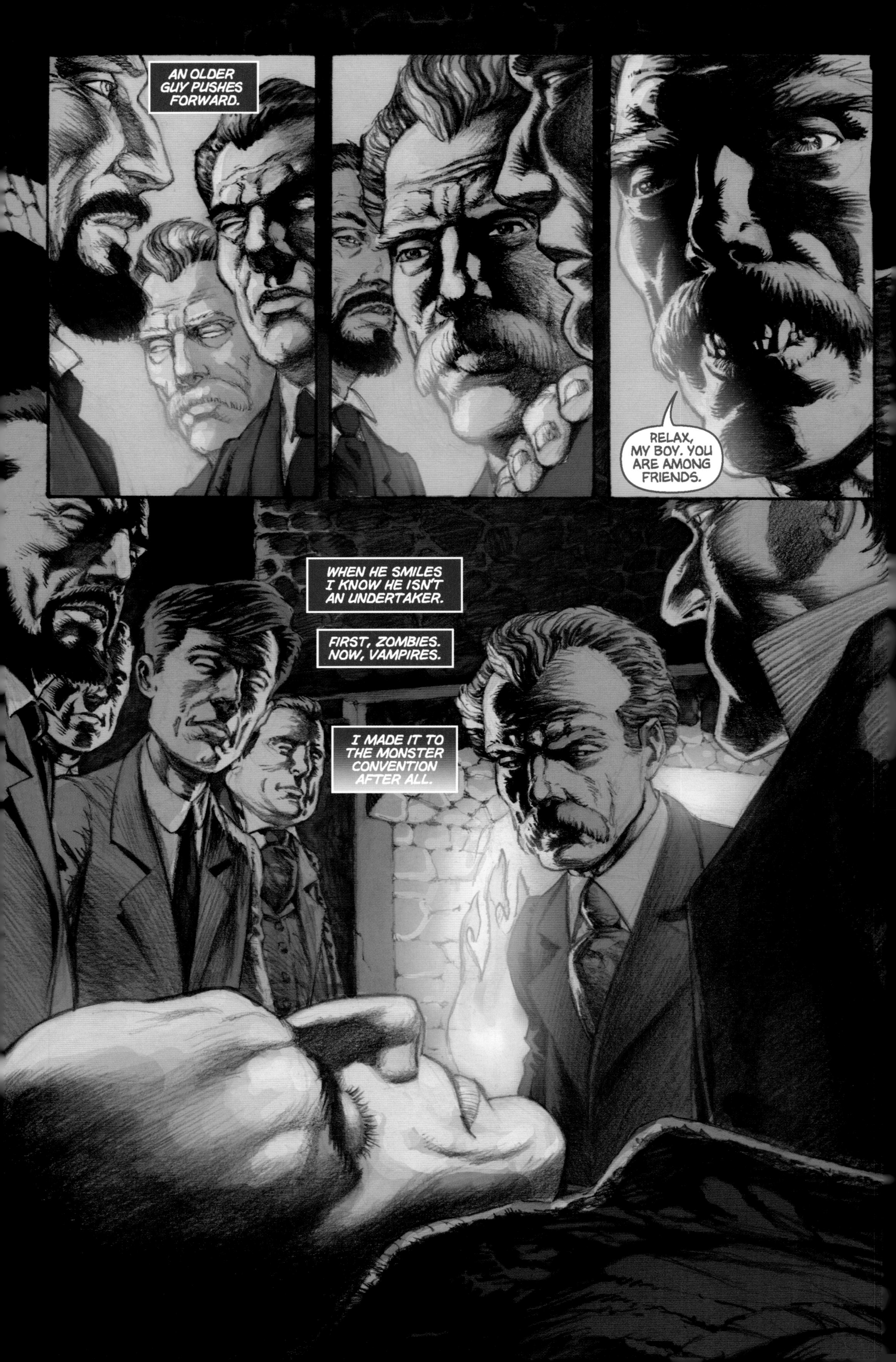
AN OLDER GUY PUSHES FORWARD.
RELAX, MY BOY. YOU ARE AMONG FRIENDS.
WHEN HE SMILES I KNOW HE ISN'T AN UNDERTAKER.
FIRST, ZOMBIES. NOW, VAMPIRES.
I MADE IT TO THE MONSTER CONVENTION AFTER ALL.

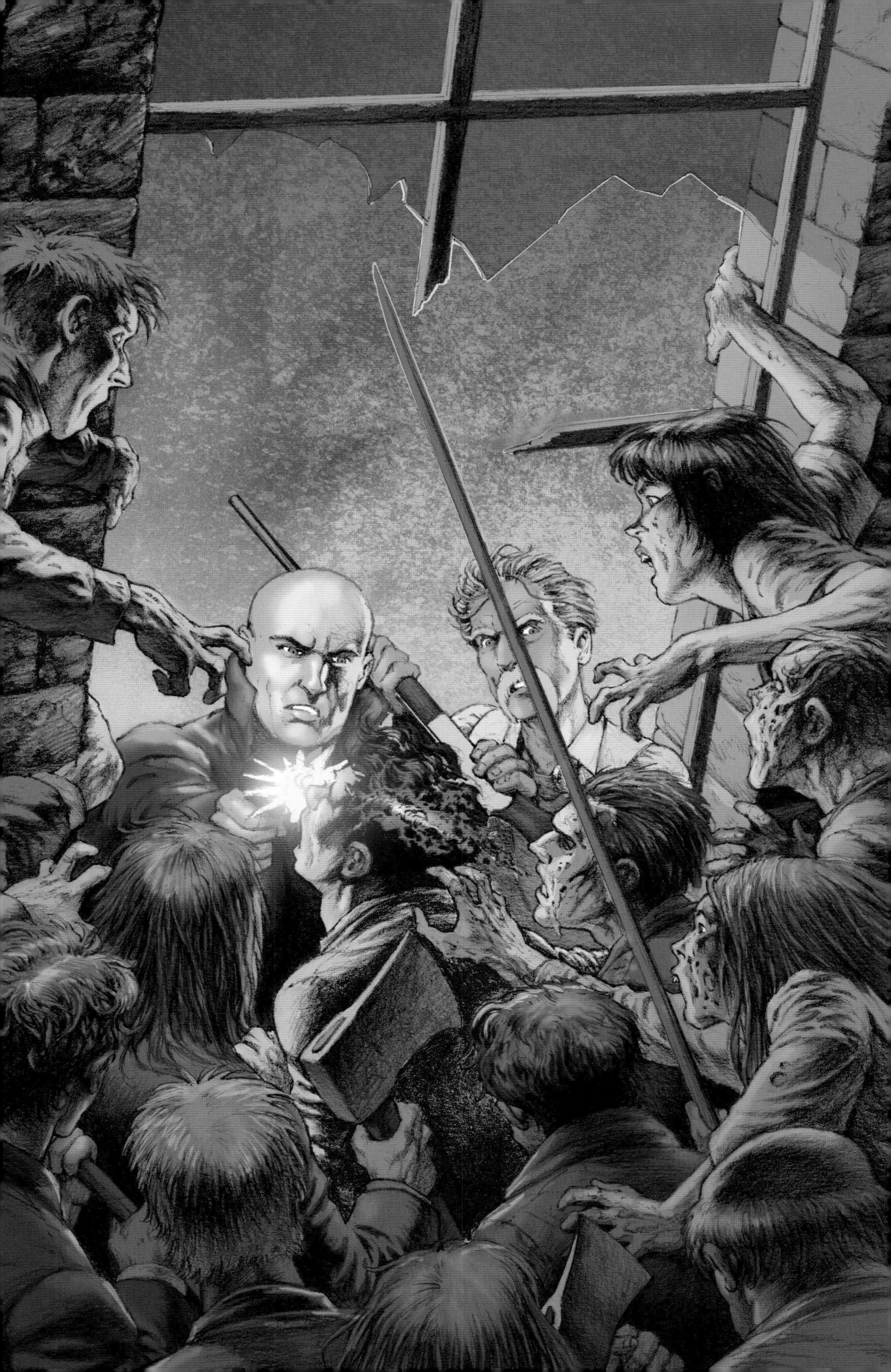

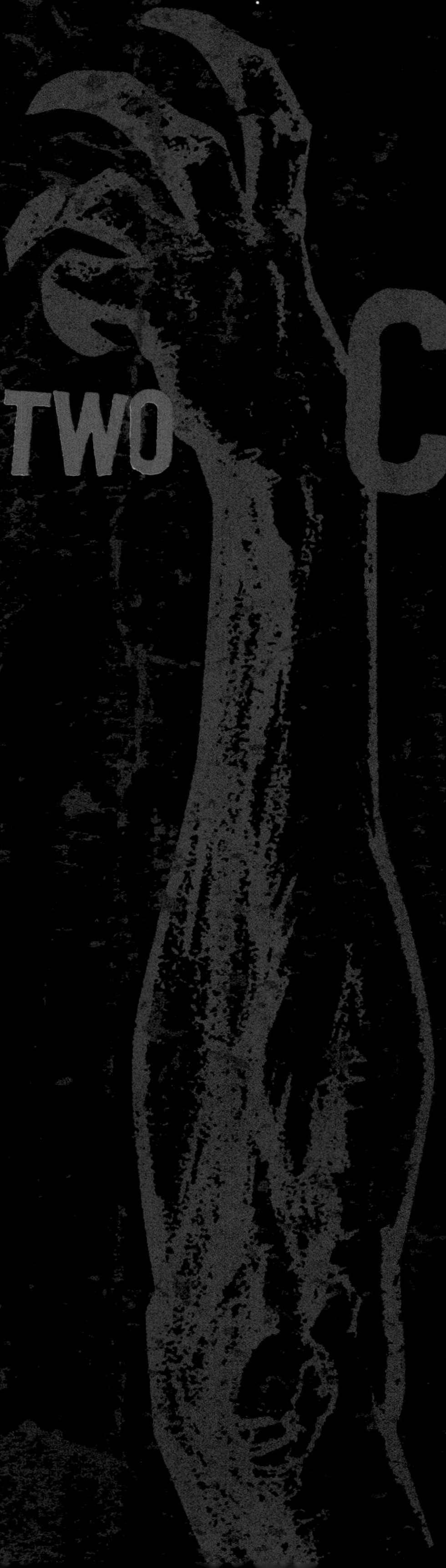

CHAPTER TWO

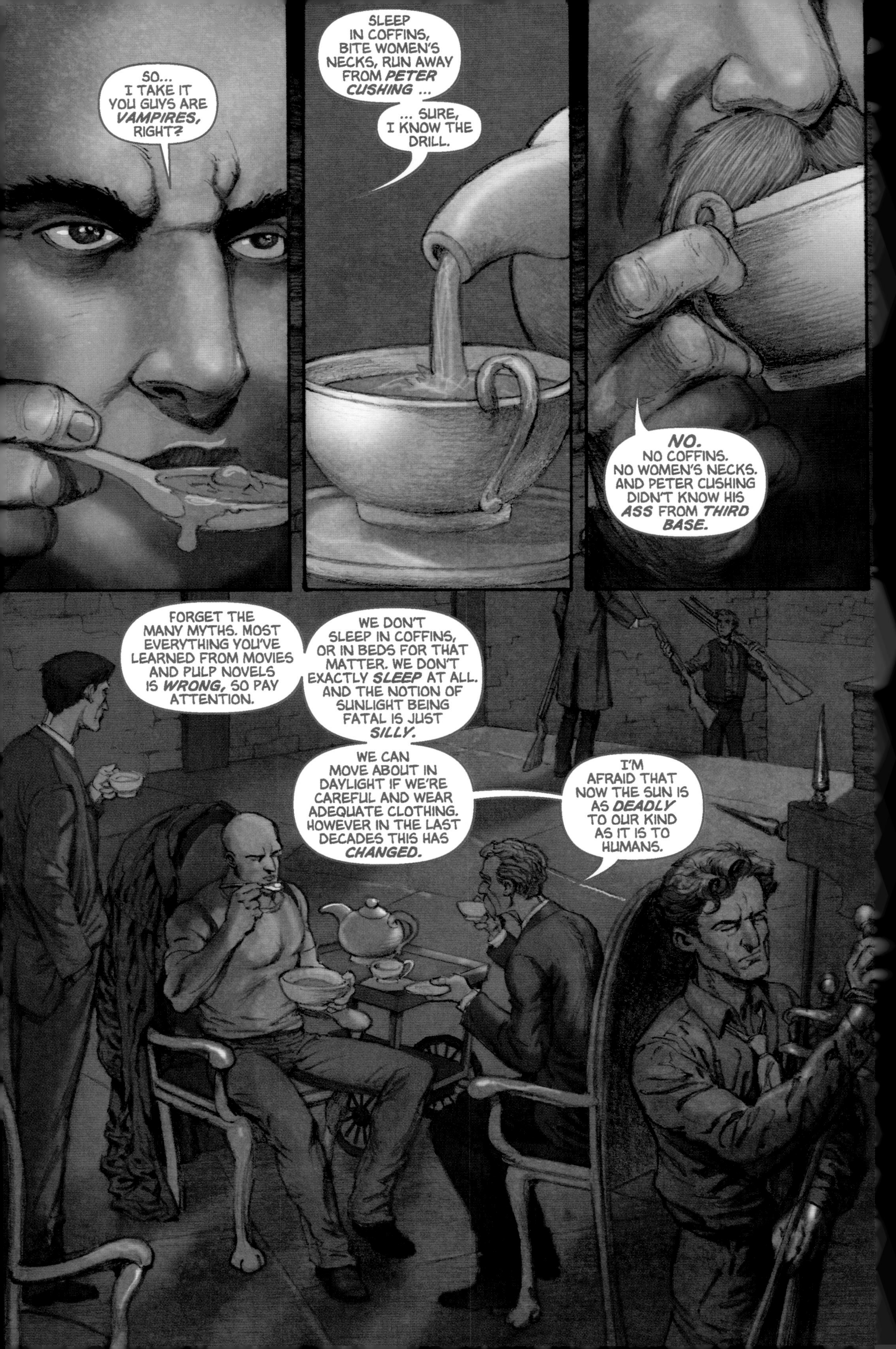
SO... I TAKE IT YOU GUYS ARE VAMPIRES, RIGHT?
SLEEP IN COFFINS, BITE WOMEN'S NECKS, RUN AWAY FROM PETER CUSHING ...
... SURE, I KNOW THE DRILL.
NO. NO COFFINS. NO WOMEN'S NECKS. AND PETER CUSHING DIDN'T KNOW HIS ASS FROM THIRD BASE.
FORGET THE MANY MYTHS. MOST EVERYTHING YOU'VE LEARNED FROM MOVIES AND PULP NOVELS IS WRONG, SO PAY ATTENTION.
WE DON'T SLEEP IN COFFINS, OR IN BEDS FOR THAT MATTER. WE DON'T EXACTLY SLEEP AT ALL. AND THE NOTION OF SUNLIGHT BEING FATAL IS JUST SILLY.
WE CAN MOVE ABOUT IN DAYLIGHT IF WE'RE CAREFUL AND WEAR ADEQUATE CLOTHING. HOWEVER IN THE LAST DECADES THIS HAS CHANGED.
I'M AFRAID THAT NOW THE SUN IS AS DEADLY TO OUR KIND AS IT IS TO HUMANS.

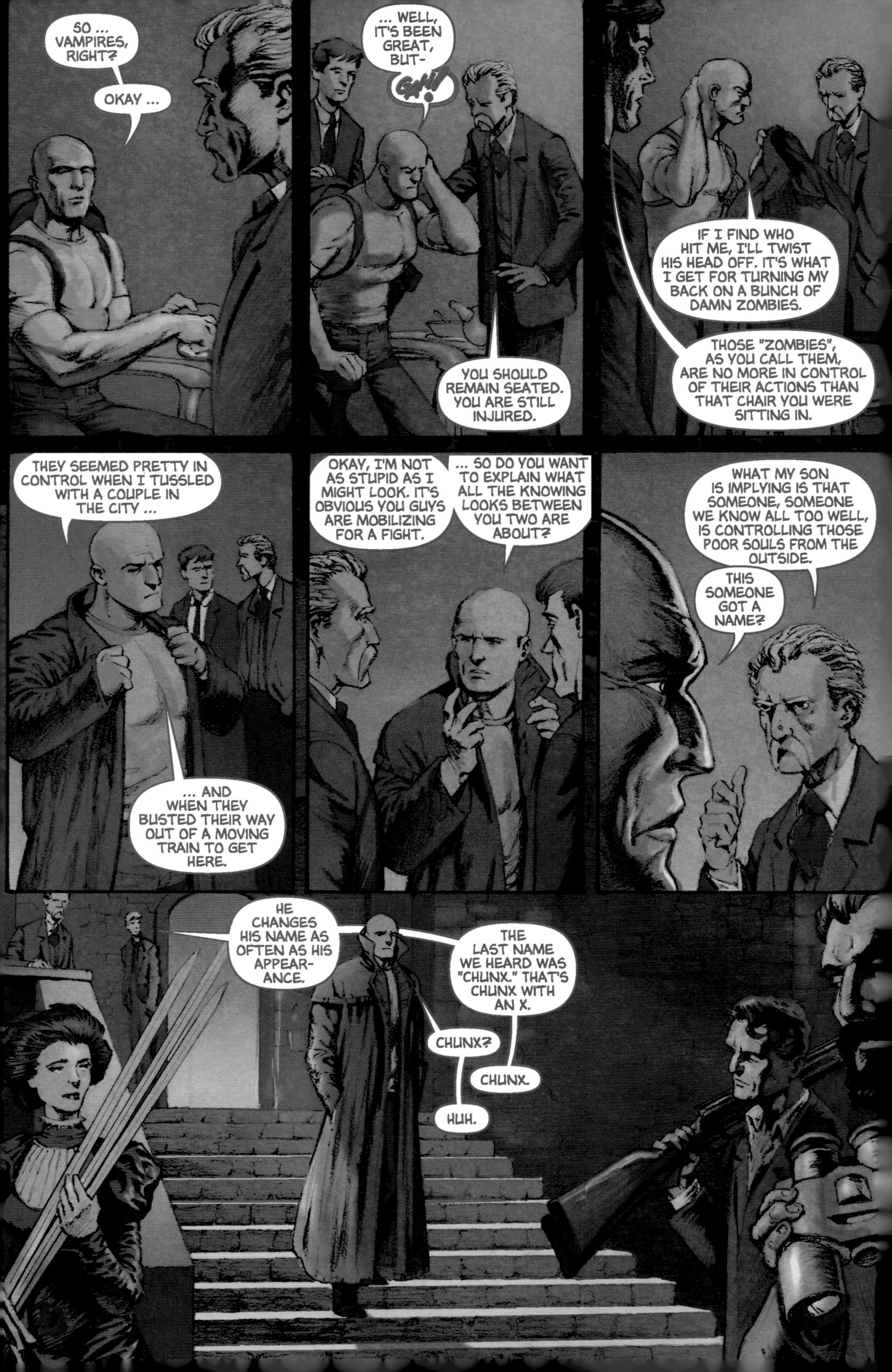

SO ... VAMPIRES, RIGHT?
OKAY ...
... WELL, IT'S BEEN GREAT, BUT-
GAH!
YOU SHOULD REMAIN SEATED. YOU ARE STILL INJURED.
IF I FIND WHO HIT ME, I'LL TWIST HIS HEAD OFF. IT'S WHAT I GET FOR TURNING MY BACK ON A BUNCH OF DAMN ZOMBIES.
THOSE "ZOMBIES", AS YOU CALL THEM, ARE NO MORE IN CONTROL OF THEIR ACTIONS THAN THAT CHAIR YOU WERE SITTING IN.
THEY SEEMED PRETTY IN CONTROL WHEN I TUSSLED WITH A COUPLE IN THE CITY ...
... AND WHEN THEY BUSTED THEIR WAY OUT OF A MOVING TRAIN TO GET HERE.
OKAY, I'M NOT AS STUPID AS I MIGHT LOOK. IT'S OBVIOUS YOU GUYS ARE MOBILIZING FOR A FIGHT.
... SO DO YOU WANT TO EXPLAIN WHAT ALL THE KNOWING LOOKS BETWEEN YOU TWO ARE ABOUT?
WHAT MY SON IS IMPLYING IS THAT SOMEONE, SOMEONE WE KNOW ALL TOO WELL, IS CONTROLLING THOSE POOR SOULS FROM THE OUTSIDE.
THIS SOMEONE GOT A NAME?
HE CHANGES HIS NAME AS OFTEN AS HIS APPEAR-ANCE.
THE LAST NAME WE HEARD WAS "CHUNX." THAT'S CHUNX WITH AN X.
CHUNX?
CHUNX.
HUH.

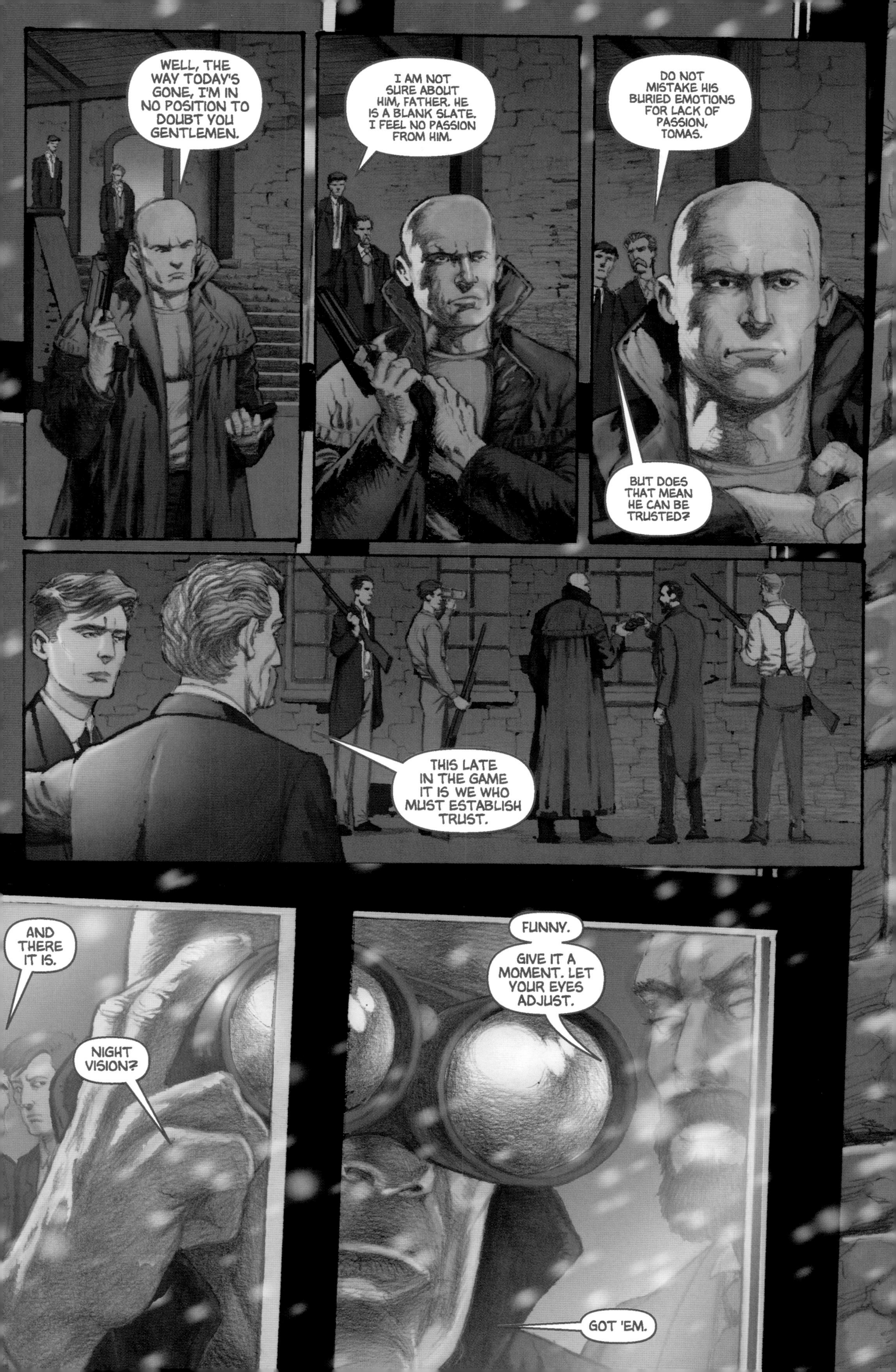
WELL, THE WAY TODAY'S GONE, I'M IN NO POSITION TO DOUBT YOU GENTLEMEN.
I AM NOT SURE ABOUT HIM, FATHER. HE IS A BLANK SLATE. I FEEL NO PASSION FROM HIM.
DO NOT MISTAKE HIS BURIED EMOTIONS FOR LACK OF PASSION, TOMAS.
BUT DOES THAT MEAN HE CAN BE TRUSTED?
THIS LATE IN THE GAME IT IS WE WHO MUST ESTABLISH TRUST.
AND THERE IT IS.
NIGHT VISION?
FUNNY.
GIVE IT A MOMENT. LET YOUR EYES ADJUST.
GOT 'EM.

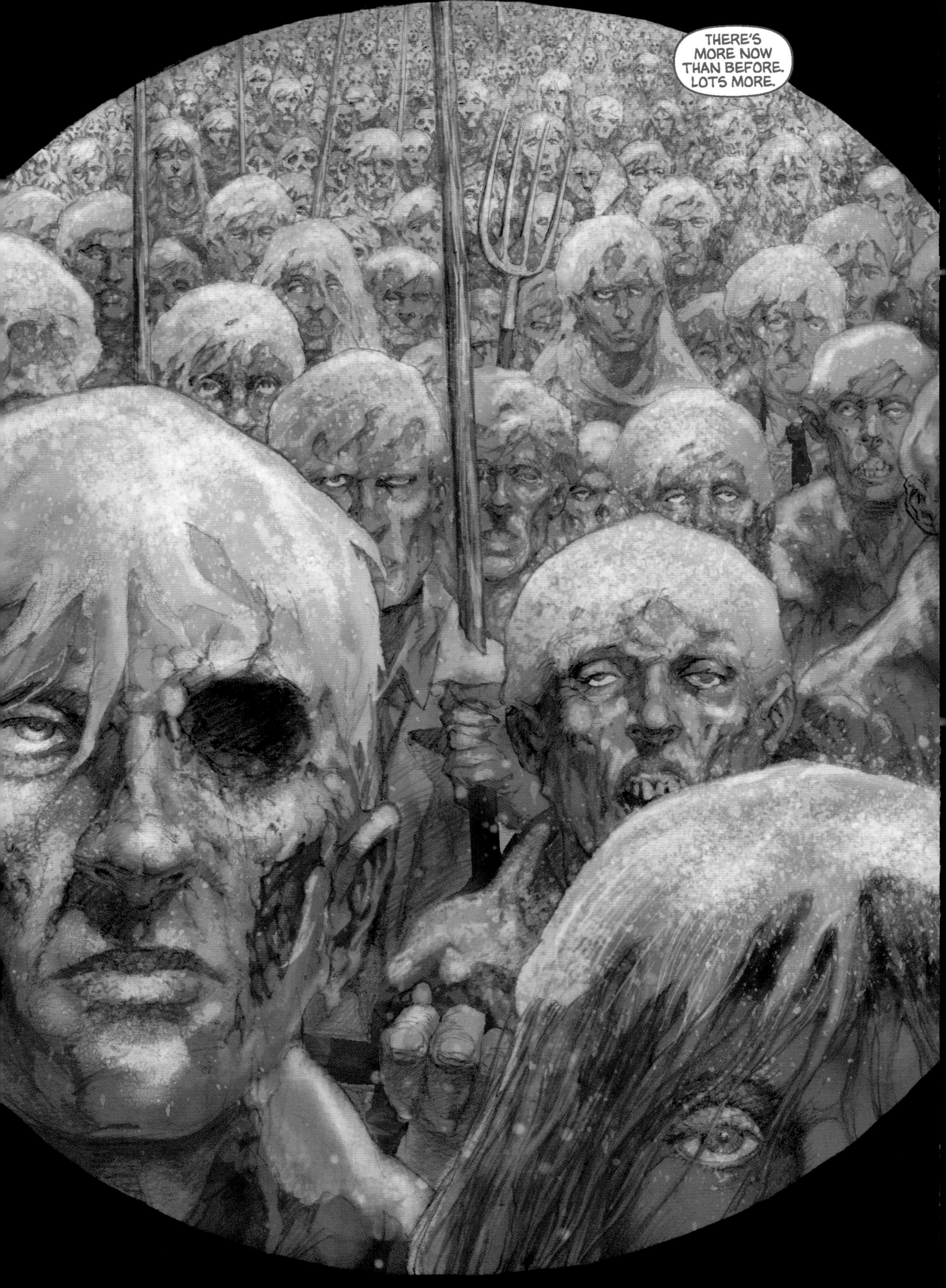
THERE'S MORE NOW THAN BEFORE. LOTS MORE.

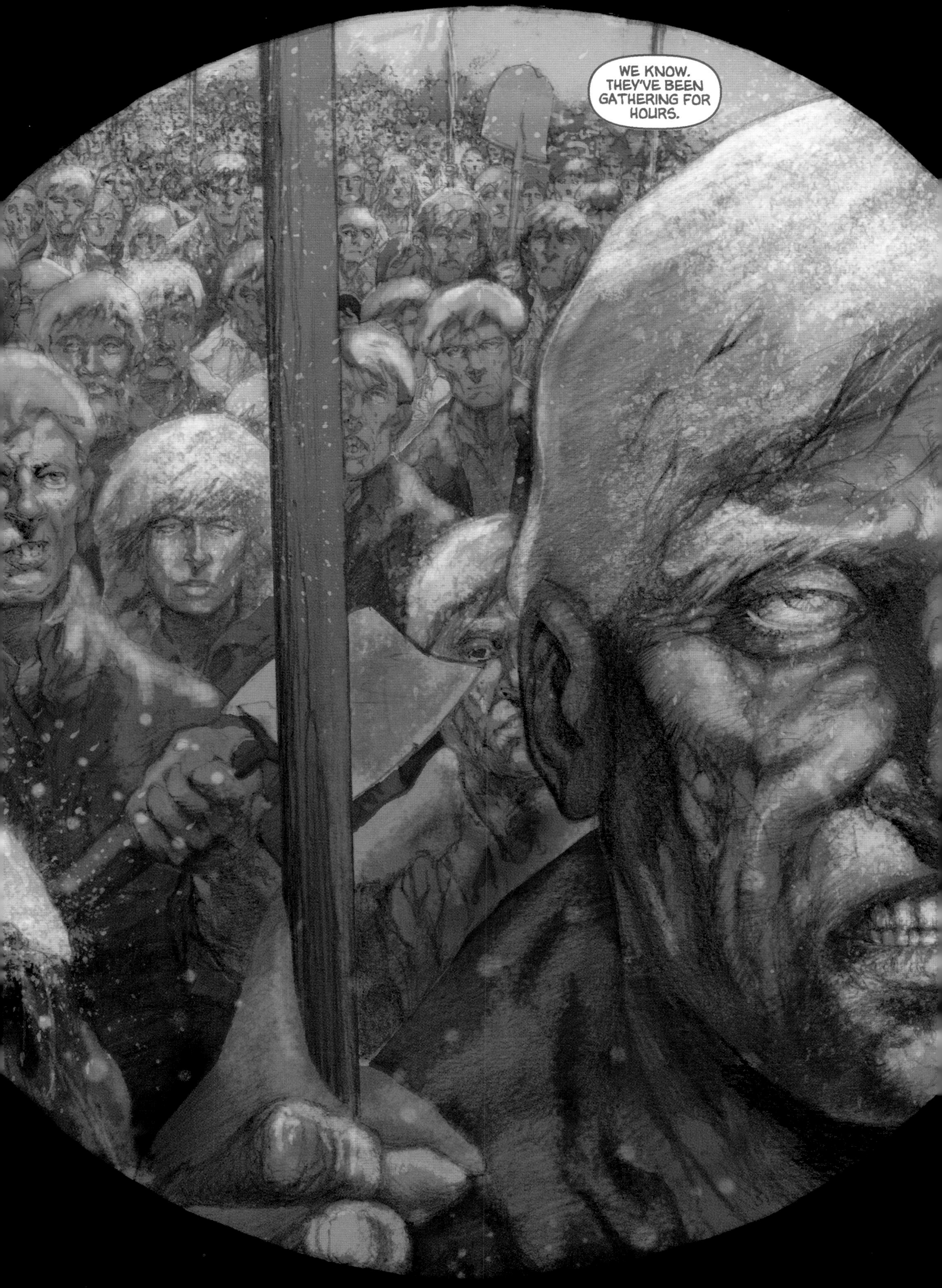
WE KNOW.
THEY'VE BEEN GATHERING FOR HOURS.

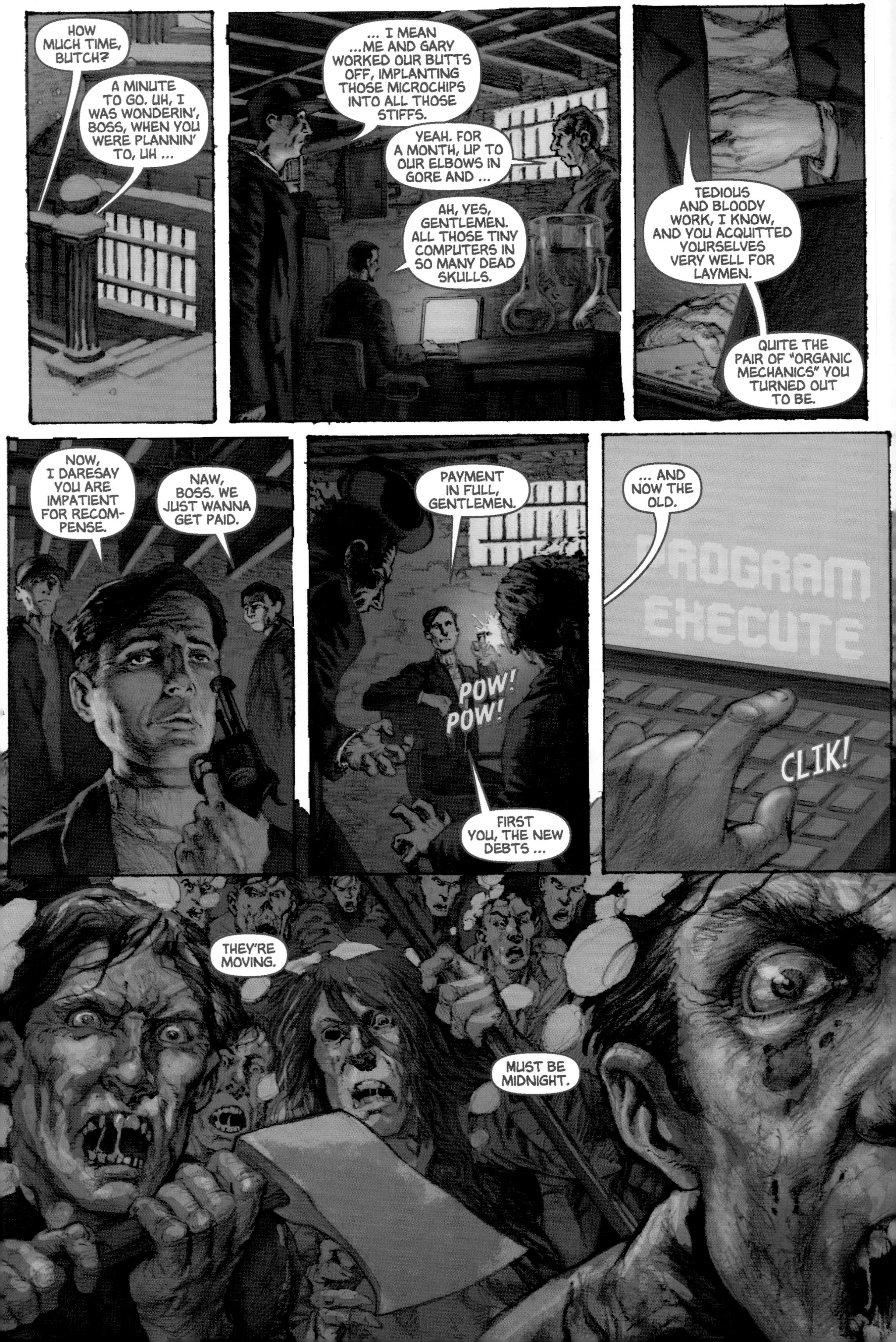
HOW MUCH TIME, BUTCH?
A MINUTE TO GO. UH, I WAS WONDERIN', BOSS, WHEN YOU WERE PLANNIN' TO, UH ...
... I MEAN ...ME AND GARY WORKED OUR BUTTS OFF, IMPLANTING THOSE MICROCHIPS INTO ALL THOSE STIFFS.
YEAH. FOR A MONTH, UP TO OUR ELBOWS IN GORE AND ...
AH, YES, GENTLEMEN. ALL THOSE TINY COMPUTERS IN SO MANY DEAD SKULLS.
TEDIOUS AND BLOODY WORK, I KNOW, AND YOU ACQUITTED YOURSELVES VERY WELL FOR LAYMEN.
QUITE THE PAIR OF "ORGANIC MECHANICS" YOU TURNED OUT TO BE.
NOW, I DARESAY YOU ARE IMPATIENT FOR RECOM-PENSE.
NAW, BOSS. WE JUST WANNA GET PAID.
PAYMENT IN FULL, GENTLEMEN.
POW! POW!
FIRST YOU, THE NEW DEBTS ...
... AND NOW THE OLD.
PROGRAM EXECUTE
CLIK!
THEY'RE MOVING.
MUST BE MIDNIGHT.

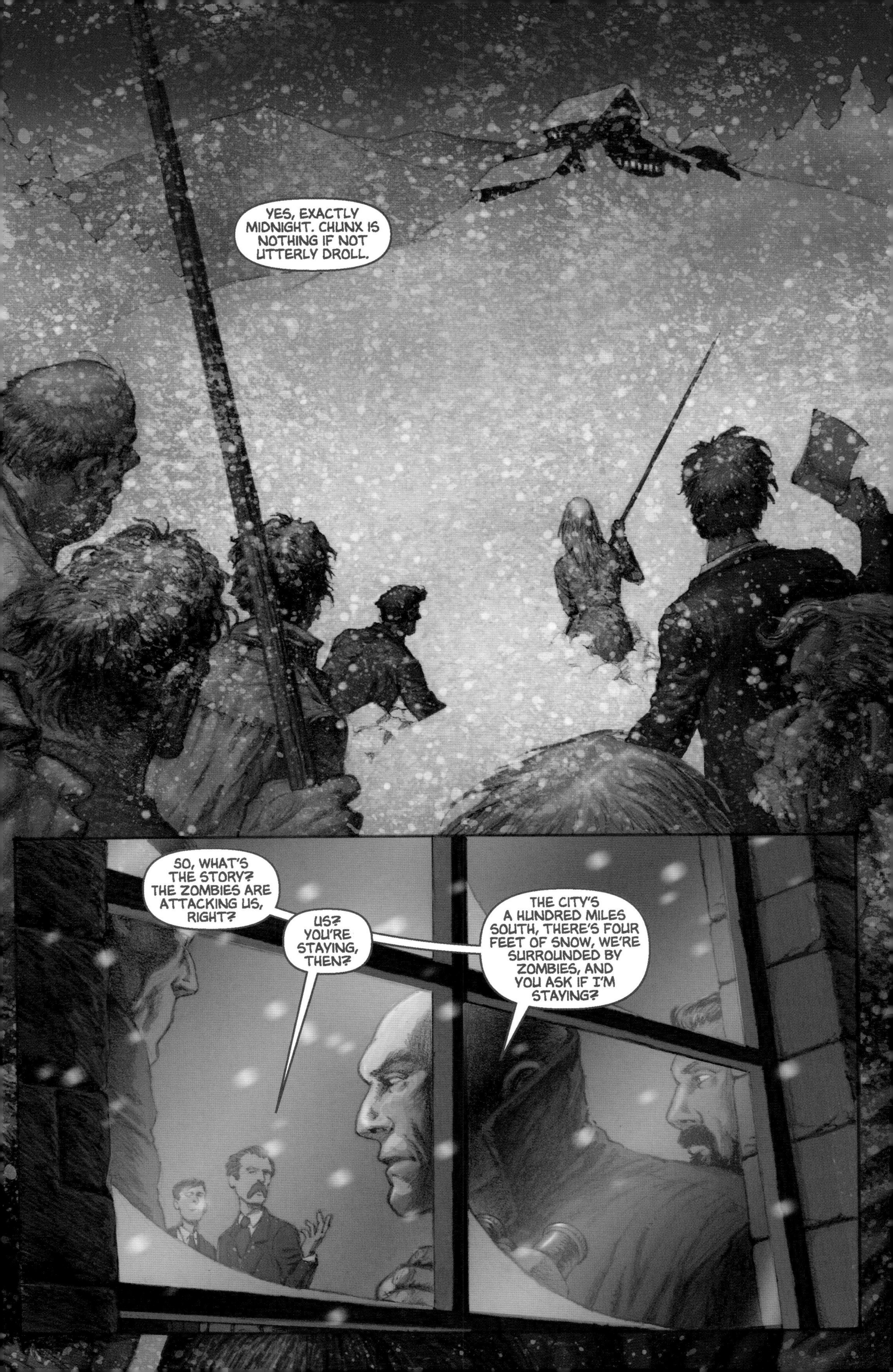
YES, EXACTLY MIDNIGHT. CHUNX IS NOTHING IF NOT UTTERLY DROLL.
SO, WHAT'S THE STORY? THE ZOMBIES ARE ATTACKING US, RIGHT?
US? YOU'RE STAYING, THEN?
THE CITY'S A HUNDRED MILES SOUTH, THERE'S FOUR FEET OF SNOW, WE'RE SURROUNDED BY ZOMBIES, AND YOU ASK IF I'M STAYING?

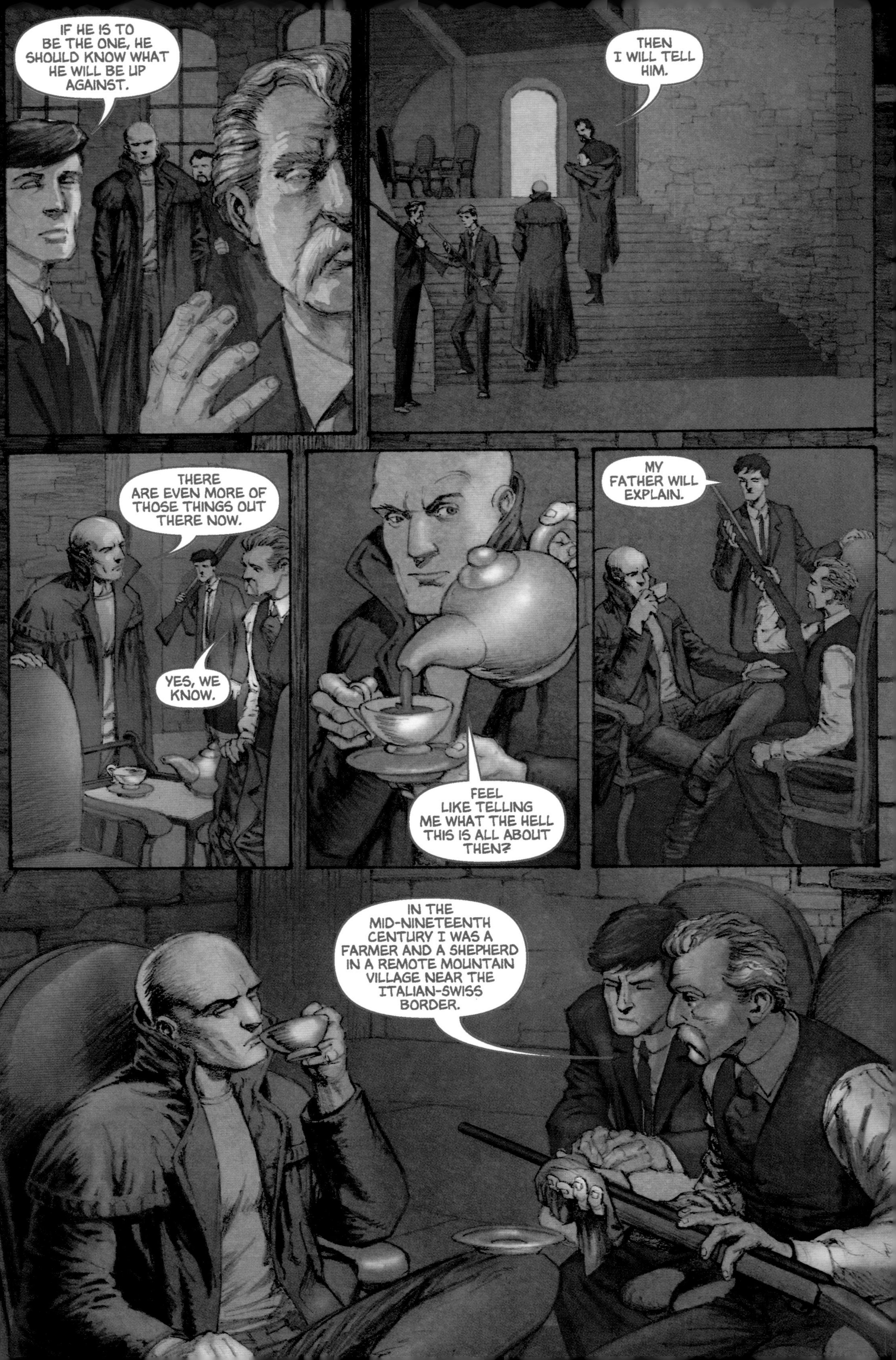
IF HE IS TO BE THE ONE, HE SHOULD KNOW WHAT HE WILL BE UP AGAINST.
THEN I WILL TELL HIM.
THERE ARE EVEN MORE OF THOSE THINGS OUT THERE NOW.
YES, WE KNOW.
FEEL LIKE TELLING ME WHAT THE HELL THIS IS ALL ABOUT THEN?
MY FATHER WILL EXPLAIN.
IN THE MID-NINETEENTH CENTURY I WAS A FARMER AND A SHEPHERD IN A REMOTE MOUNTAIN VILLAGE NEAR THE ITALIAN-SWISS BORDER.

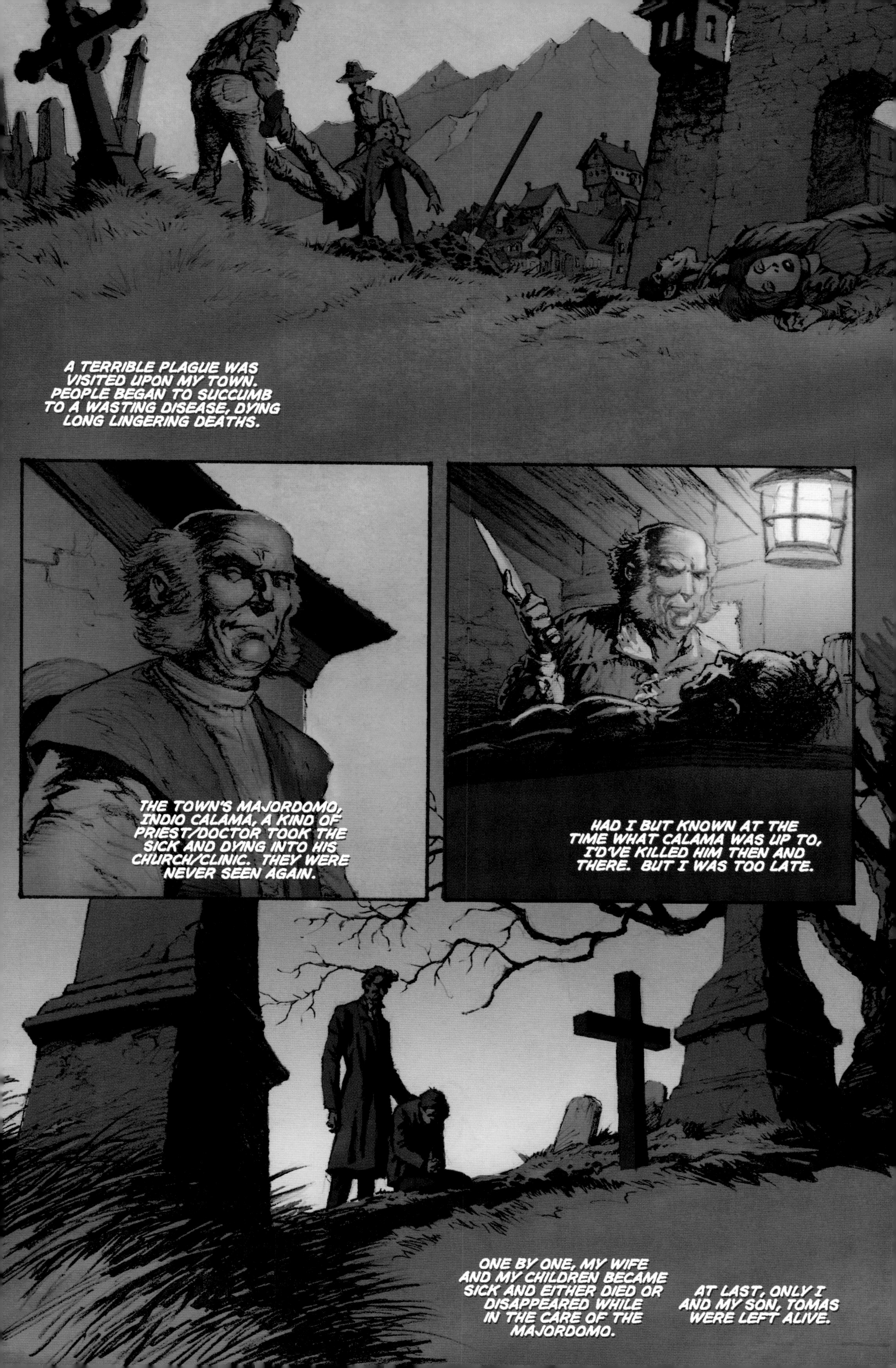
A TERRIBLE PLAGUE WAS VISITED UPON MY TOWN. PEOPLE BEGAN TO SUCCUMB TO A WASTING DISEASE, DYING LONG LINGERING DEATHS.
THE TOWN'S MAJORDOMO, INDIO CALAMA, A KIND OF PRIEST/DOCTOR TOOK THE SICK AND DYING INTO HIS CHURCH/CLINIC. THEY WERE NEVER SEEN AGAIN.
HAD I BUT KNOWN AT THE TIME WHAT CALAMA WAS UP TO, I'D'VE KILLED HIM THEN AND THERE. BUT I WAS TOO LATE.
ONE BY ONE, MY WIFE AND MY CHILDREN BECAME SICK AND EITHER DIED OR DISAPPEARED WHILE IN THE CARE OF THE MAJORDOMO.
AT LAST, ONLY I AND MY SON, TOMAS WERE LEFT ALIVE.

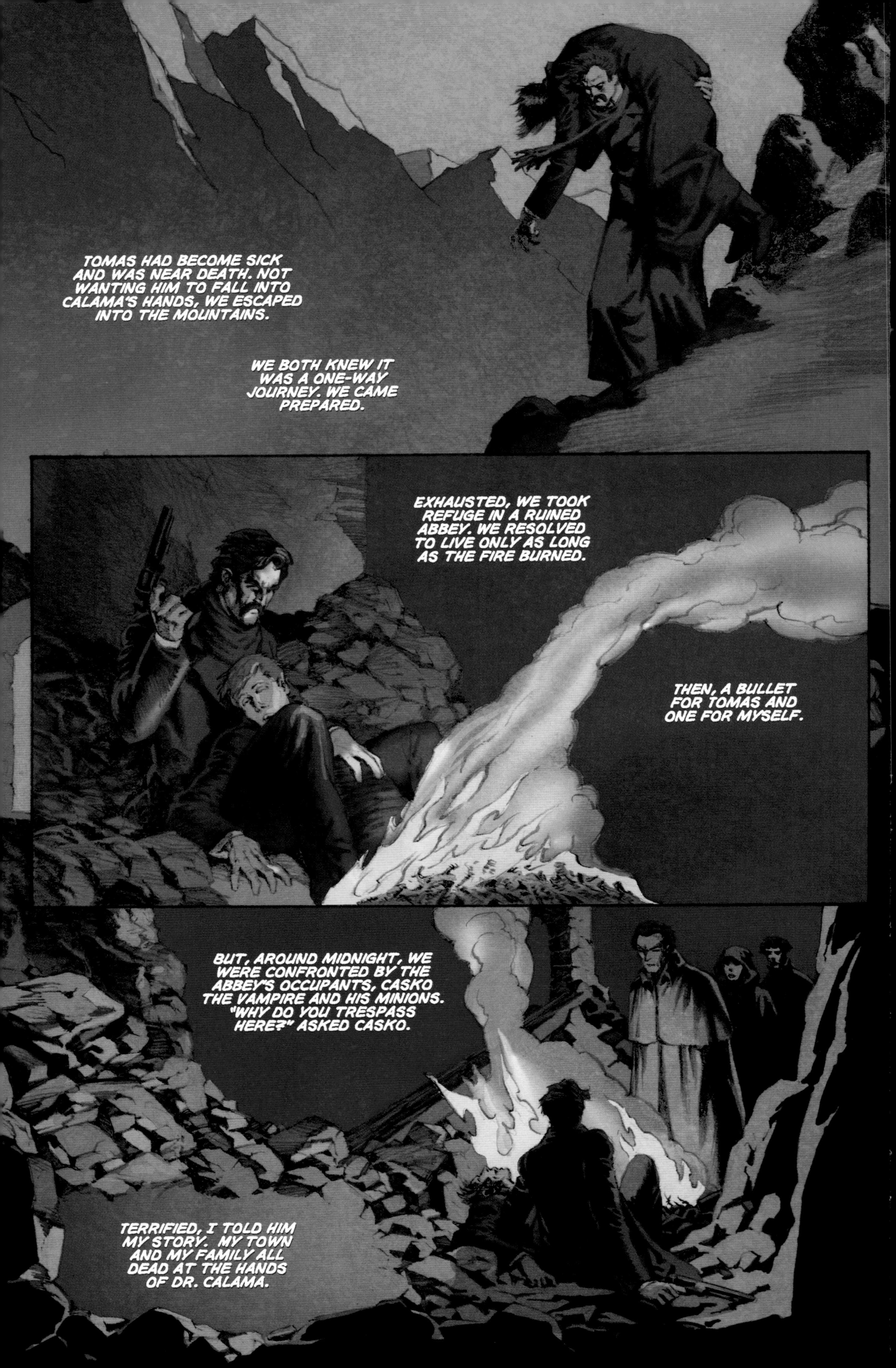
TOMAS HAD BECOME SICK AND WAS NEAR DEATH. NOT WANTING HIM TO FALL INTO CALAMA'S HANDS, WE ESCAPED INTO THE MOUNTAINS.
WE BOTH KNEW IT WAS A ONE-WAY JOURNEY. WE CAME PREPARED.
EXHAUSTED, WE TOOK REFUGE IN A RUINED ABBEY. WE RESOLVED TO LIVE ONLY AS LONG AS THE FIRE BURNED.
THEN, A BULLET FOR TOMAS AND ONE FOR MYSELF.
BUT, AROUND MIDNIGHT, WE WERE CONFRONTED BY THE ABBEY'S OCCUPANTS, CASKO THE VAMPIRE AND HIS MINIONS. "WHY DO YOU TRESPASS HERE?" ASKED CASKO.
TERRIFIED, I TOLD HIM MY STORY. MY TOWN AND MY FAMILY ALL DEAD AT THE HANDS OF DR. CALAMA.

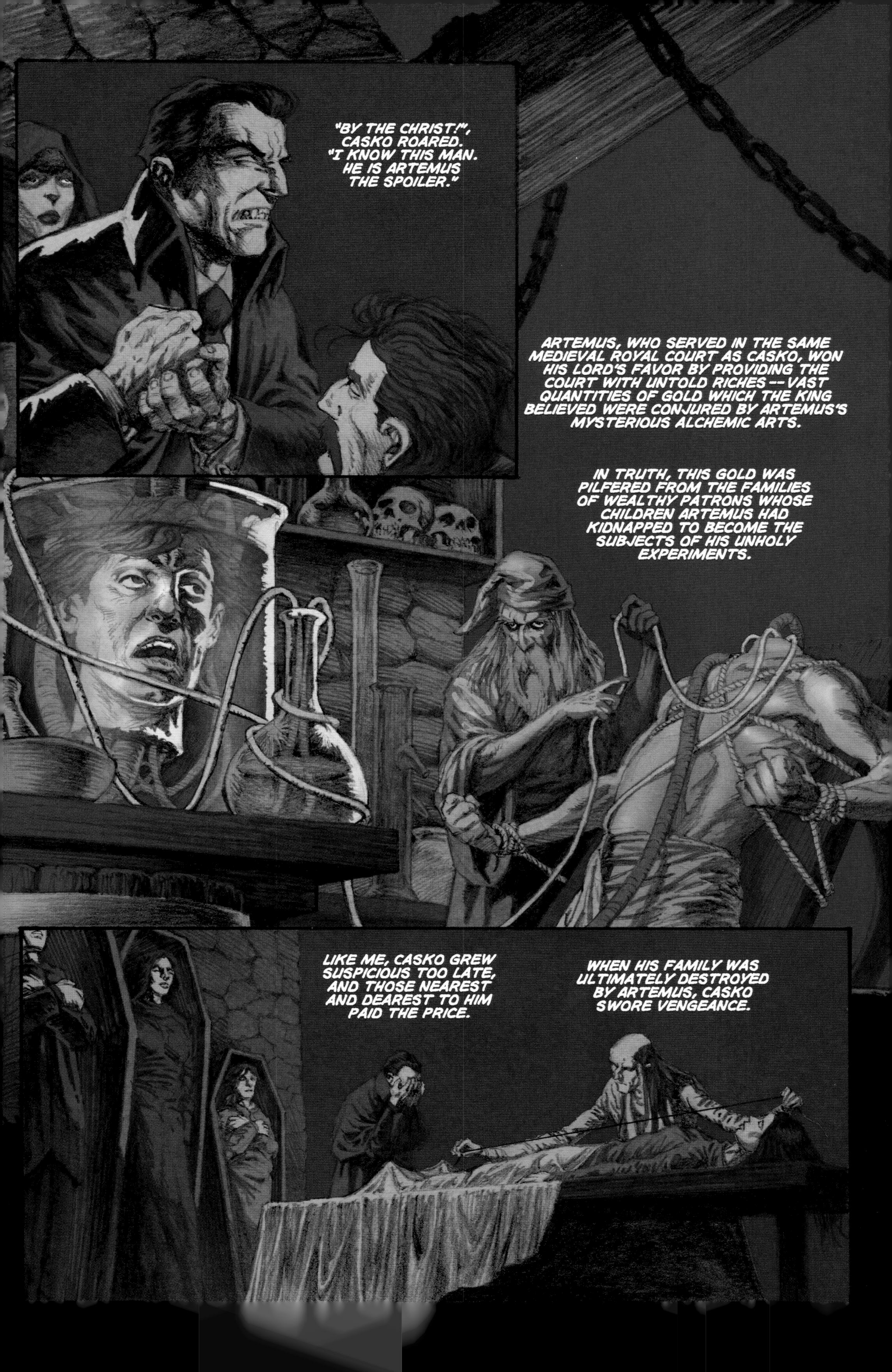
"BY THE CHRIST!", CASKO ROARED. "I KNOW THIS MAN. HE IS ARTEMUS THE SPOILER."
ARTEMUS, WHO SERVED IN THE SAME MEDIEVAL ROYAL COURT AS CASKO, WON HIS LORD'S FAVOR BY PROVIDING THE COURT WITH UNTOLD RICHES--VAST QUANTITIES OF GOLD WHICH THE KING BELIEVED WERE CONJURED BY ARTEMUS'S MYSTERIOUS ALCHEMIC ARTS.
IN TRUTH, THIS GOLD WAS PILFERED FROM THE FAMILIES OF WEALTHY PATRONS WHOSE CHILDREN ARTEMUS HAD KIDNAPPED TO BECOME THE SUBJECTS OF HIS UNHOLY EXPERIMENTS.
LIKE ME, CASKO GREW SUSPICIOUS TOO LATE, AND THOSE NEAREST AND DEAREST TO HIM PAID THE PRICE.
WHEN HIS FAMILY WAS ULTIMATELY DESTROYED BY ARTEMUS, CASKO SWORE VENGEANCE.

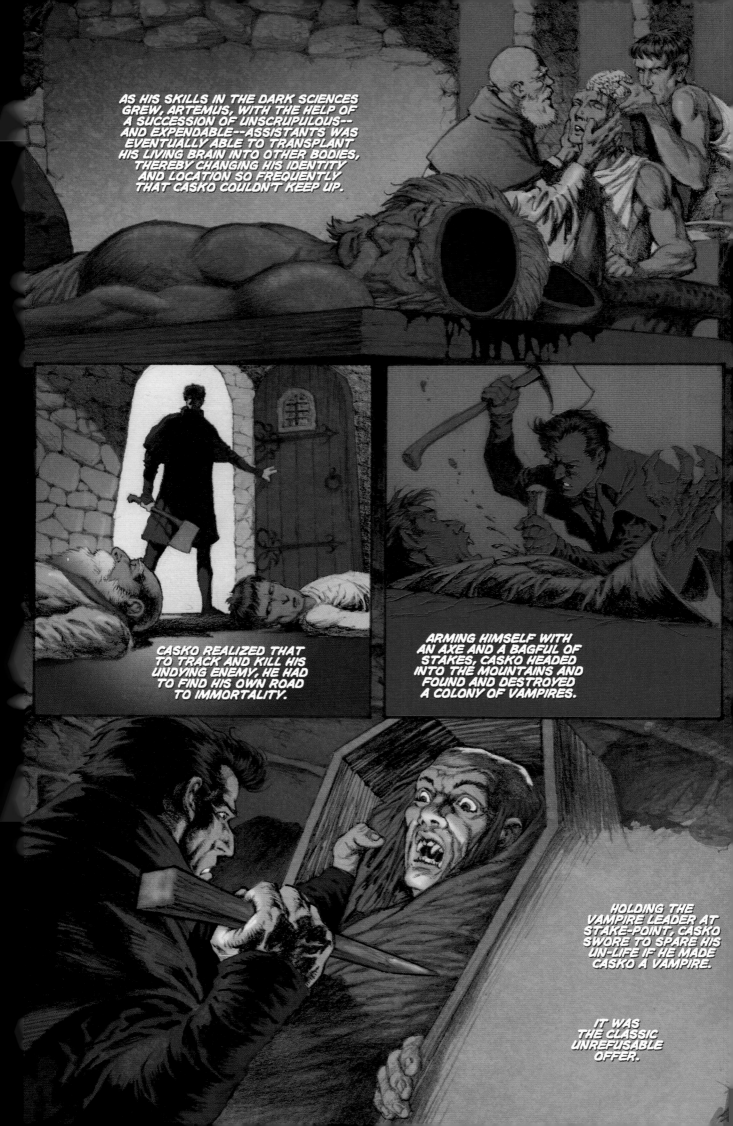

AS HIS SKILLS IN THE DARK SCIENCES GREW, ARTEMUS, WITH THE HELP OF A SUCCESSION OF UNSCRUPULOUS-- AND EXPENDABLE--ASSISTANTS WAS EVENTUALLY ABLE TO TRANSPLANT HIS LIVING BRAIN INTO OTHER BODIES, THEREBY CHANGING HIS IDENTITY AND LOCATION SO FREQUENTLY THAT CASKO COULDN'T KEEP UP.

CASKO REALIZED THAT TO TRACK AND KILL HIS UNDYING ENEMY, HE HAD TO FIND HIS OWN ROAD TO IMMORTALITY.

ARMING HIMSELF WITH AN AXE AND A BAGFUL OF STAKES, CASKO HEADED INTO THE MOUNTAINS AND FOUND AND DESTROYED A COLONY OF VAMPIRES.

HOLDING THE VAMPIRE LEADER AT STAKE-POINT, CASKO SWORE TO SPARE HIS UN-LIFE IF HE MADE CASKO A VAMPIRE.

IT WAS THE CLASSIC UNREFUSABLE OFFER.

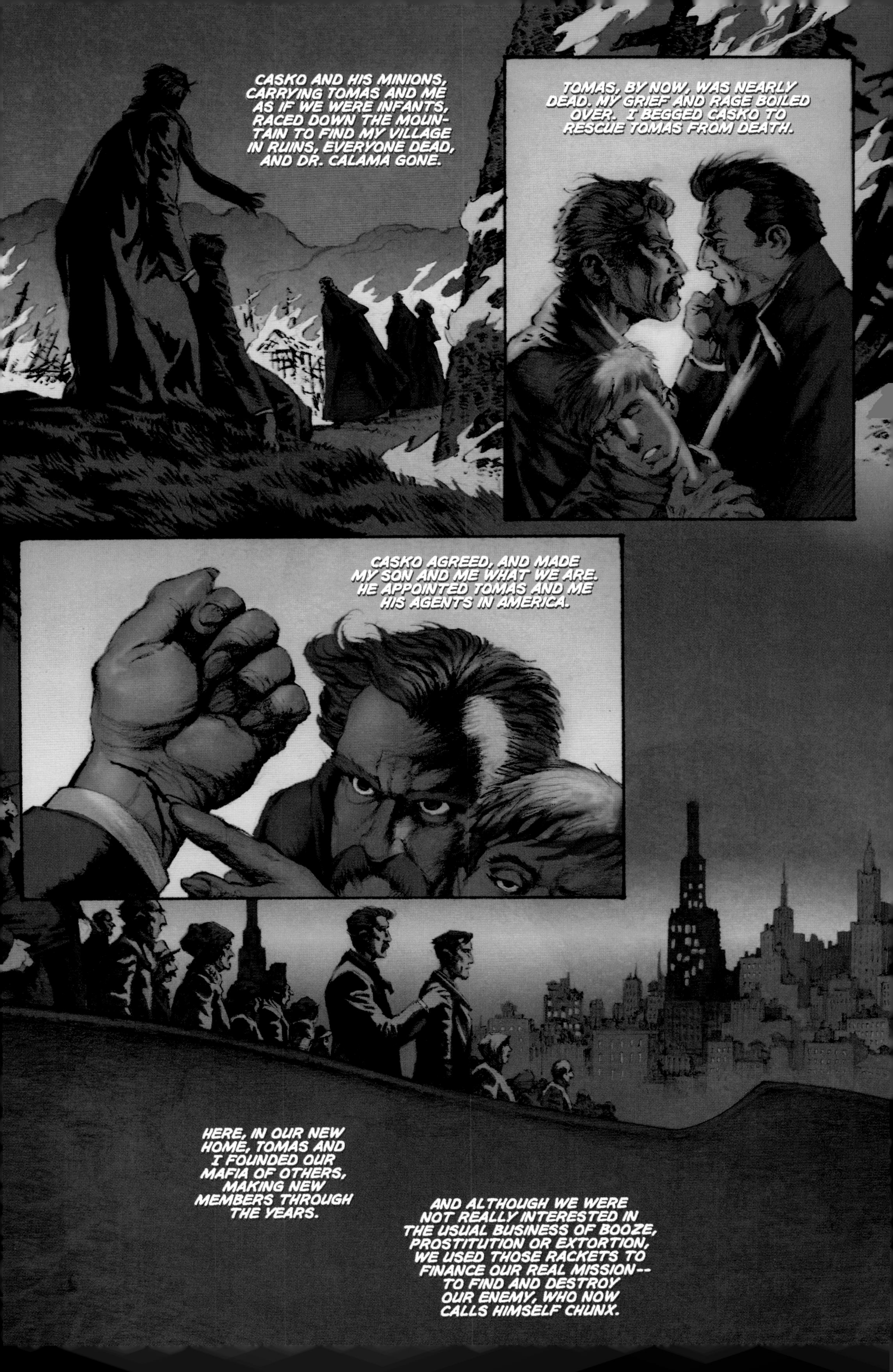
CASKO AND HIS MINIONS, CARRYING TOMAS AND ME AS IF WE WERE INFANTS, RACED DOWN THE MOUNTAIN TO FIND MY VILLAGE IN RUINS, EVERYONE DEAD, AND DR. CALAMA GONE.
TOMAS, BY NOW, WAS NEARLY DEAD. MY GRIEF AND RAGE BOILED OVER. I BEGGED CASKO TO RESCUE TOMAS FROM DEATH.
CASKO AGREED, AND MADE MY SON AND ME WHAT WE ARE. HE APPOINTED TOMAS AND ME HIS AGENTS IN AMERICA.
HERE, IN OUR NEW HOME, TOMAS AND I FOUNDED OUR MAFIA OF OTHERS, MAKING NEW MEMBERS THROUGH THE YEARS.
AND ALTHOUGH WE WERE NOT REALLY INTERESTED IN THE USUAL BUSINESS OF BOOZE, PROSTITUTION OR EXTORTION, WE USED THOSE RACKETS TO FINANCE OUR REAL MISSION-- TO FIND AND DESTROY OUR ENEMY, WHO NOW CALLS HIMSELF CHUNX.

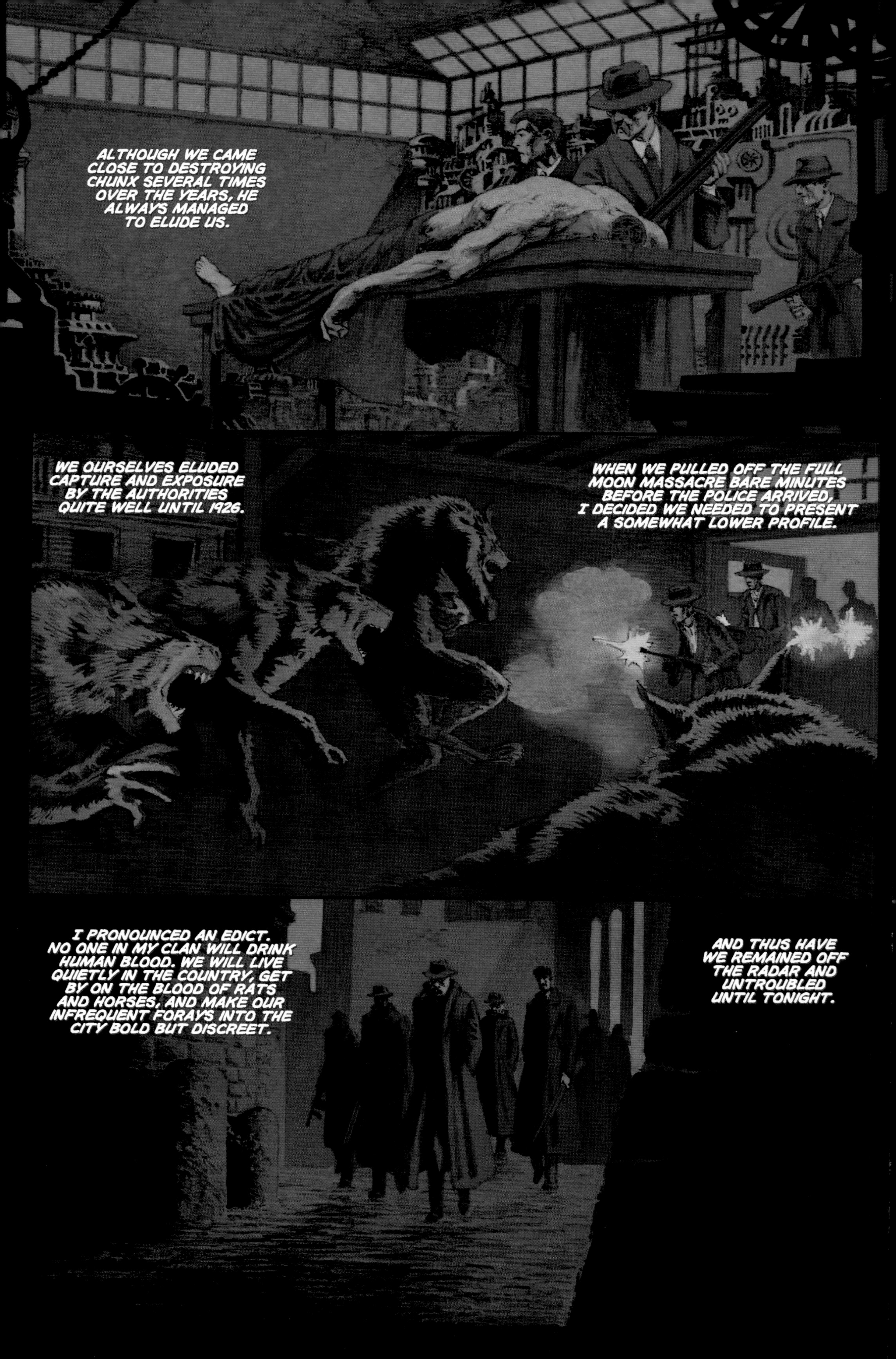
ALTHOUGH WE CAME CLOSE TO DESTROYING CHUNX SEVERAL TIMES OVER THE YEARS, HE ALWAYS MANAGED TO ELUDE US.
WE OURSELVES ELUDED CAPTURE AND EXPOSURE BY THE AUTHORITIES QUITE WELL UNTIL 1926.
WHEN WE PULLED OFF THE FULL MOON MASSACRE BARE MINUTES BEFORE THE POLICE ARRIVED, I DECIDED WE NEEDED TO PRESENT A SOMEWHAT LOWER PROFILE.
I PRONOUNCED AN EDICT. NO ONE IN MY CLAN WILL DRINK HUMAN BLOOD. WE WILL LIVE QUIETLY IN THE COUNTRY, GET BY ON THE BLOOD OF RATS AND HORSES, AND MAKE OUR INFREQUENT FORAYS INTO THE CITY BOLD BUT DISCREET.
AND THUS HAVE WE REMAINED OFF THE RADAR AND UNTROUBLED UNTIL TONIGHT.

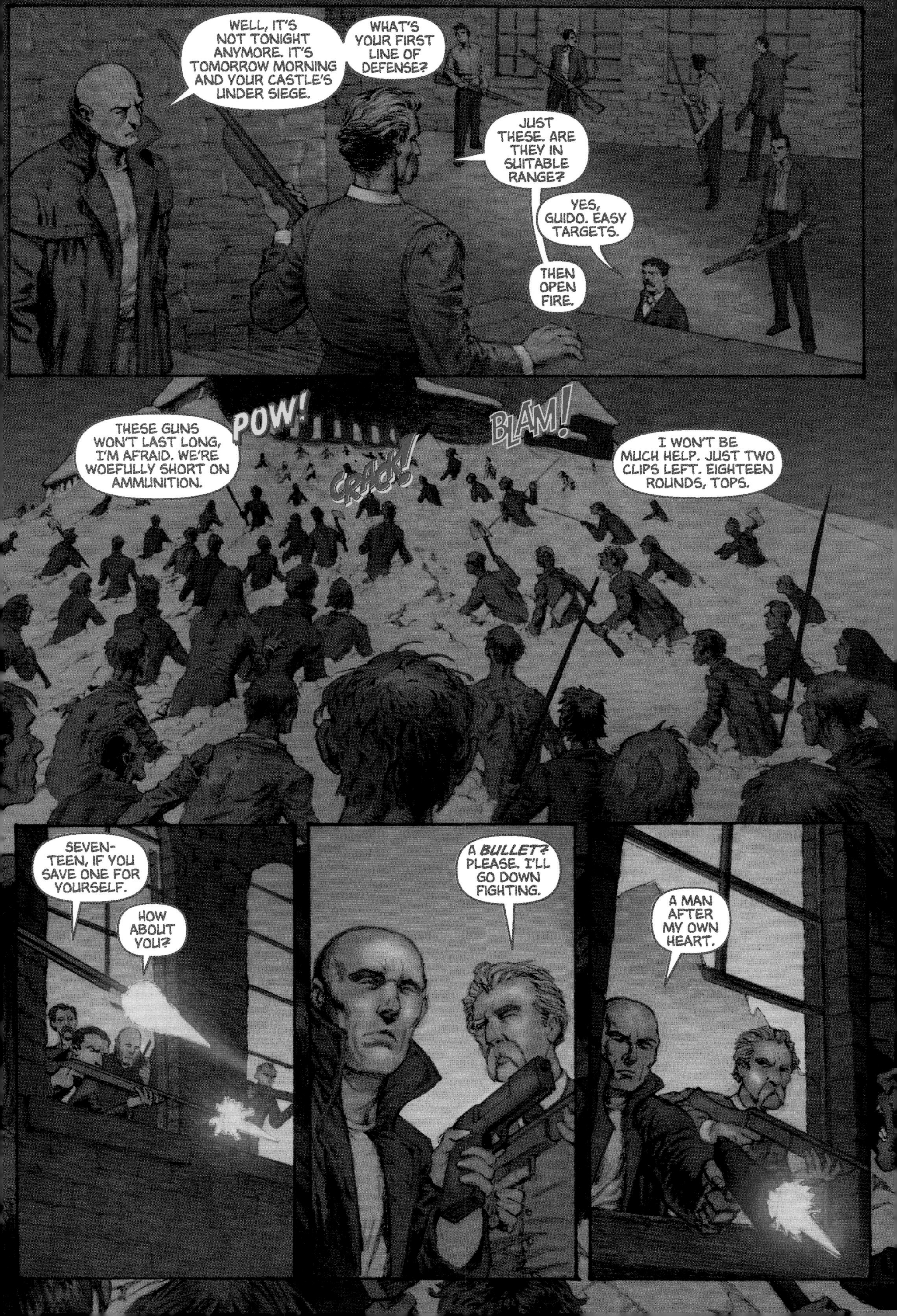
WELL, IT'S NOT TONIGHT ANYMORE. IT'S TOMORROW MORNING AND YOUR CASTLE'S UNDER SIEGE.
WHAT'S YOUR FIRST LINE OF DEFENSE?
JUST THESE. ARE THEY IN SUITABLE RANGE?
YES, GUIDO. EASY TARGETS.
THEN OPEN FIRE.
POW!
BLAM!
CRACK!
THESE GUNS WON'T LAST LONG, I'M AFRAID. WE'RE WOEFULLY SHORT ON AMMUNITION.
I WON'T BE MUCH HELP. JUST TWO CLIPS LEFT. EIGHTEEN ROUNDS, TOPS.
SEVEN-TEEN, IF YOU SAVE ONE FOR YOURSELF.
HOW ABOUT YOU?
A BULLET? PLEASE. I'LL GO DOWN FIGHTING.
A MAN AFTER MY OWN HEART.

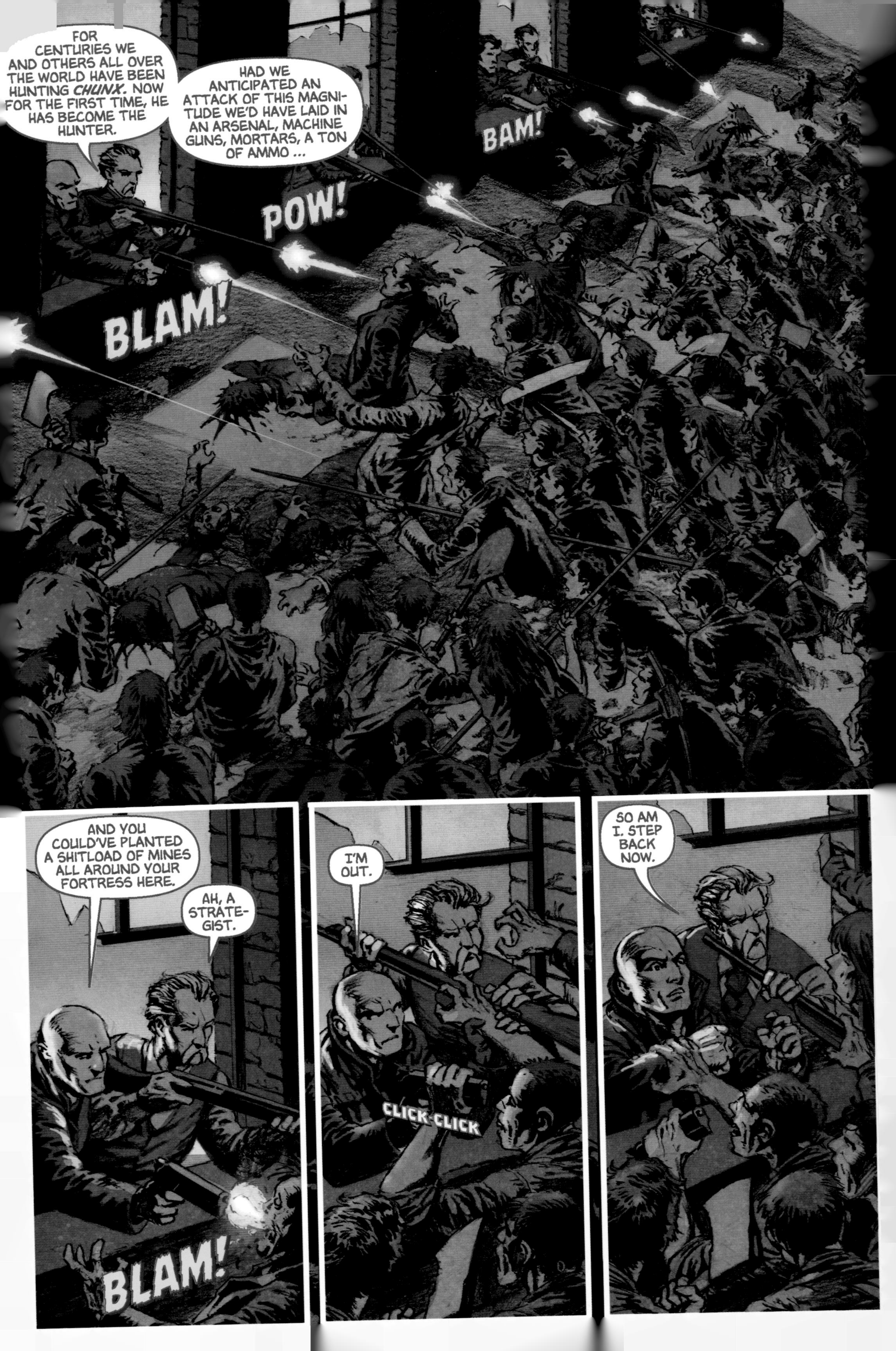
FOR CENTURIES WE AND OTHERS ALL OVER THE WORLD HAVE BEEN HUNTING CHUNX. NOW FOR THE FIRST TIME, HE HAS BECOME THE HUNTER.
HAD WE ANTICIPATED AN ATTACK OF THIS MAGNITUDE WE'D HAVE LAID IN AN ARSENAL, MACHINE GUNS, MORTARS, A TON OF AMMO ...
BAM!
POW!
BLAM!
AND YOU COULD'VE PLANTED A SHITLOAD OF MINES ALL AROUND YOUR FORTRESS HERE.
AH, A STRATEGIST.
BLAM!
I'M OUT.
CLICK-CLICK
SO AM I. STEP BACK NOW.

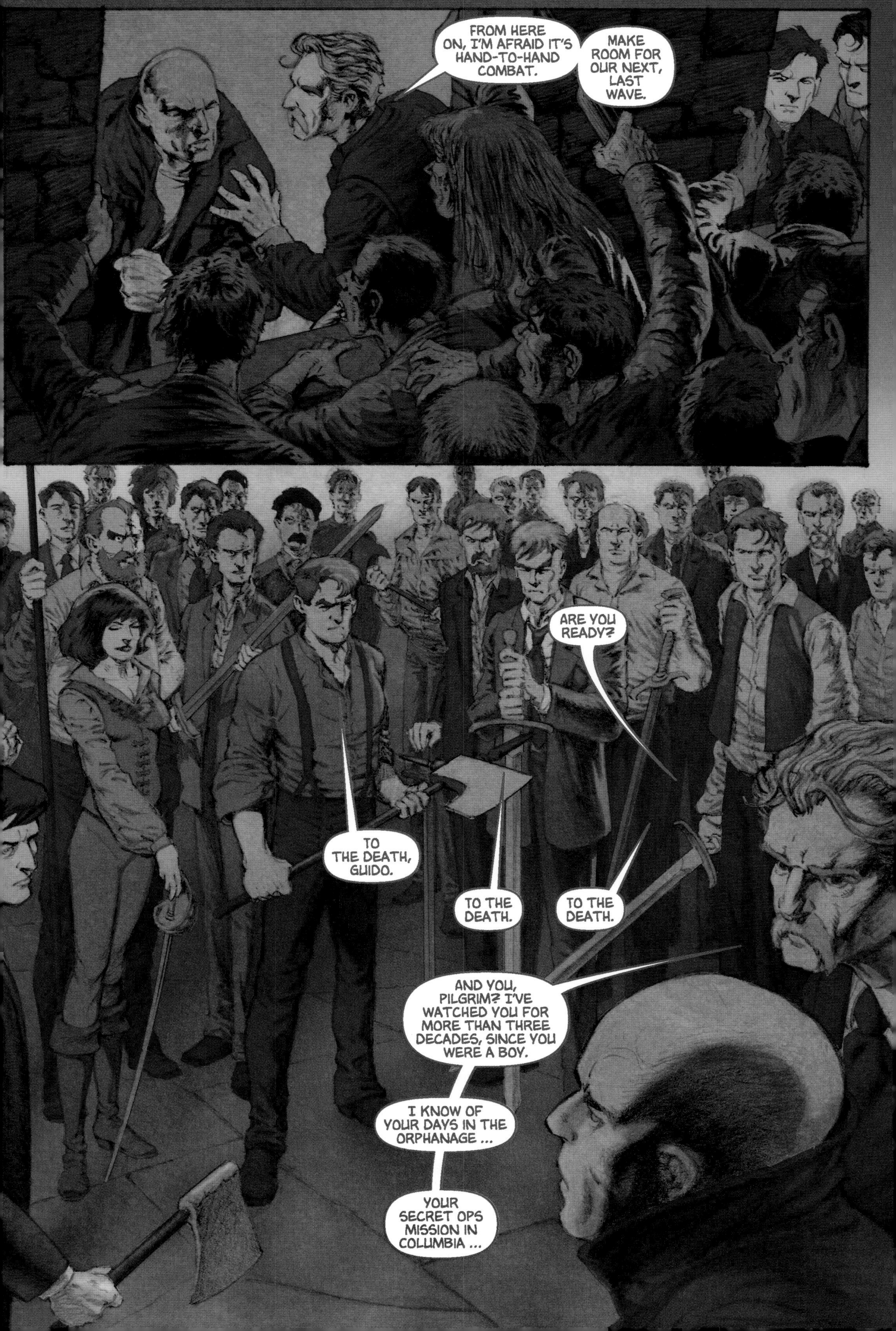
FROM HERE ON, I'M AFRAID IT'S HAND-TO-HAND COMBAT.
MAKE ROOM FOR OUR NEXT, LAST WAVE.
ARE YOU READY?
TO THE DEATH, GUIDO.
TO THE DEATH.
TO THE DEATH.
AND YOU, PILGRIM? I'VE WATCHED YOU FOR MORE THAN THREE DECADES, SINCE YOU WERE A BOY.
I KNOW OF YOUR DAYS IN THE ORPHANAGE ...
YOUR SECRET OPS MISSION IN COLUMBIA ...

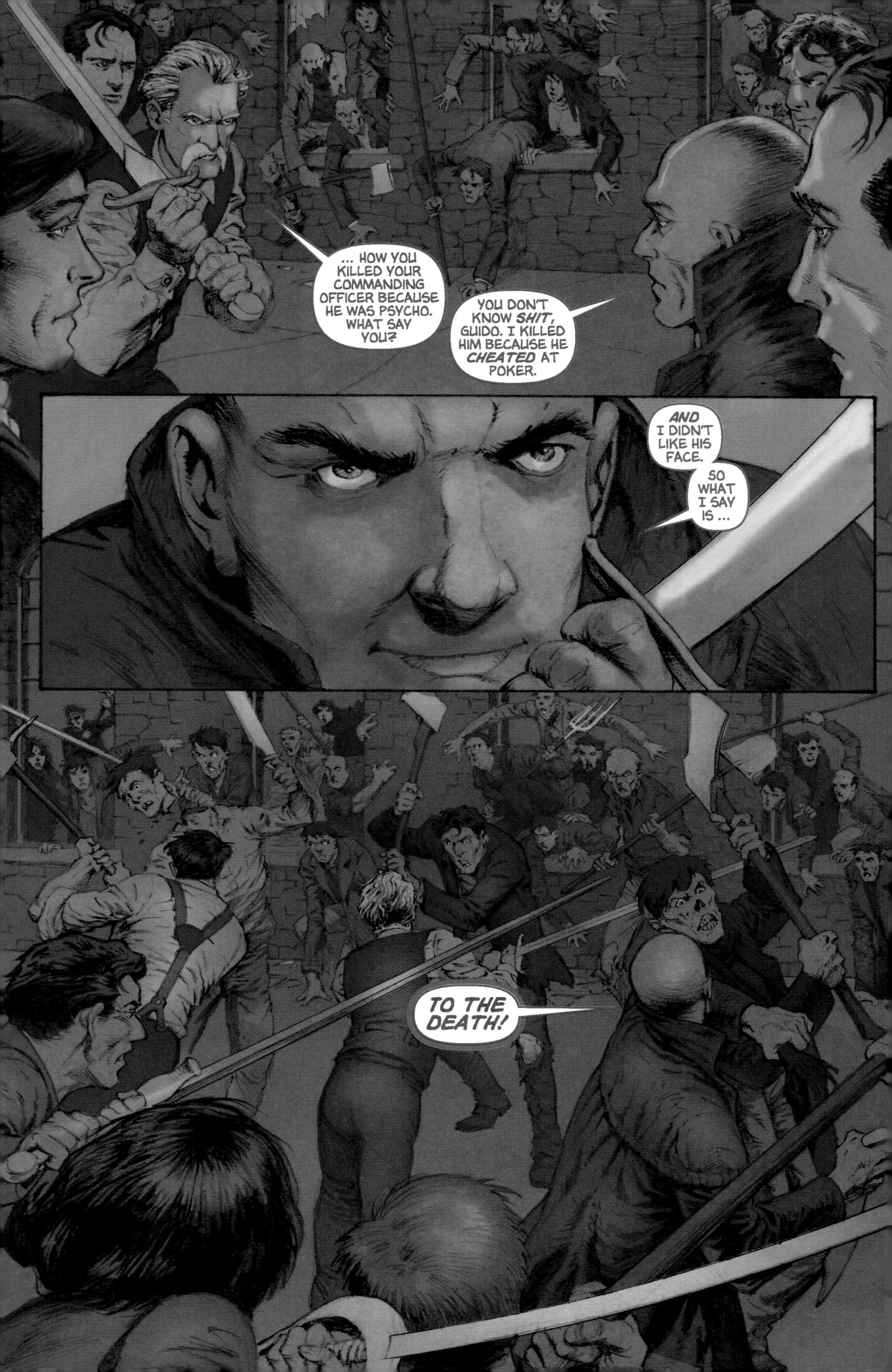
... HOW YOU KILLED YOUR COMMANDING OFFICER BECAUSE HE WAS PSYCHO. WHAT SAY YOU?
YOU DON'T KNOW *SHIT*, GUIDO. I KILLED HIM BECAUSE HE *CHEATED* AT POKER.
AND I DIDN'T LIKE HIS FACE.
SO WHAT I SAY IS ...
TO THE DEATH!

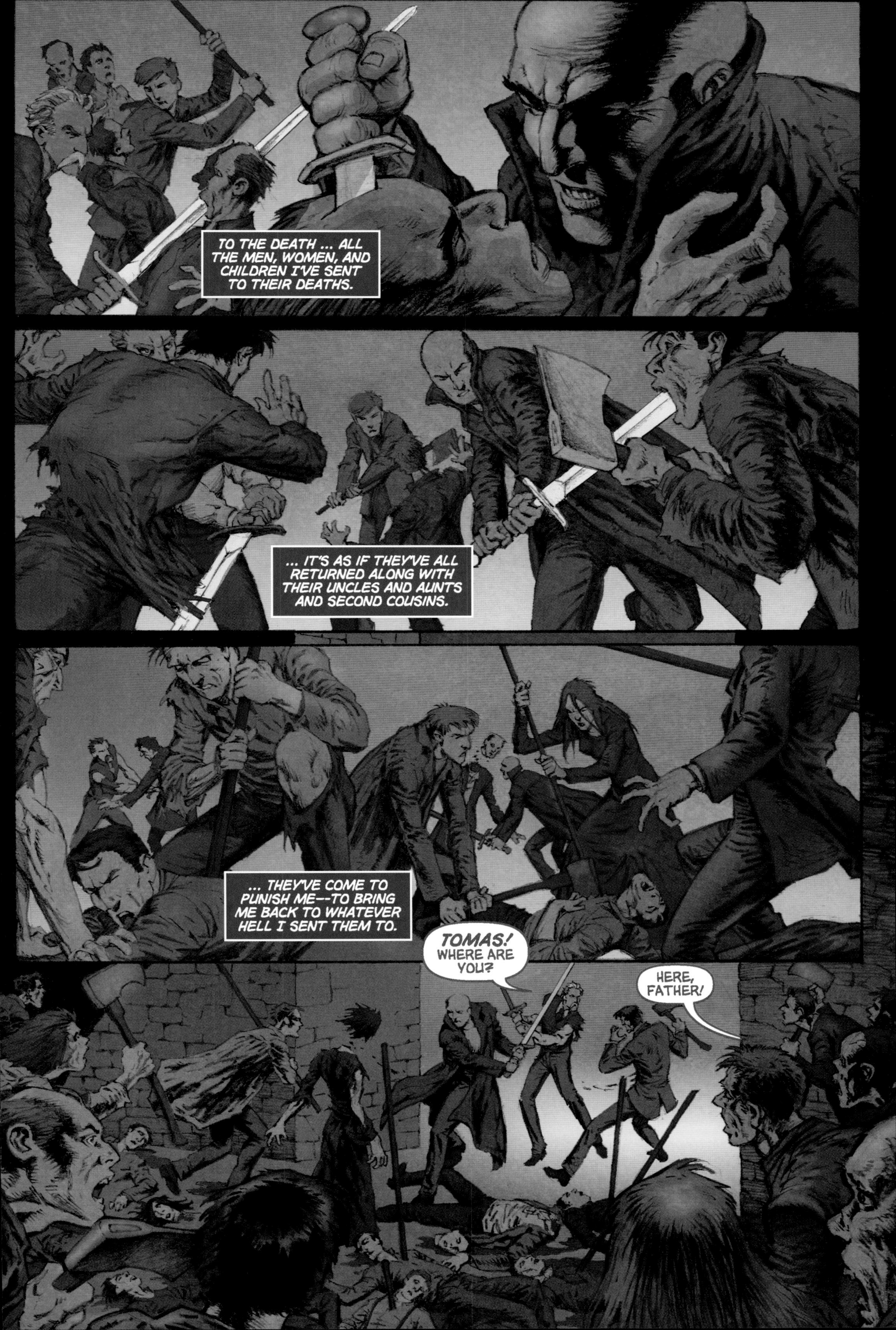
TO THE DEATH ... ALL THE MEN, WOMEN, AND CHILDREN I'VE SENT TO THEIR DEATHS.
... IT'S AS IF THEY'VE ALL RETURNED ALONG WITH THEIR UNCLES AND AUNTS AND SECOND COUSINS.
... THEY'VE COME TO PUNISH ME--TO BRING ME BACK TO WHATEVER HELL I SENT THEM TO.
TOMAS! WHERE ARE YOU?
HERE, FATHER!

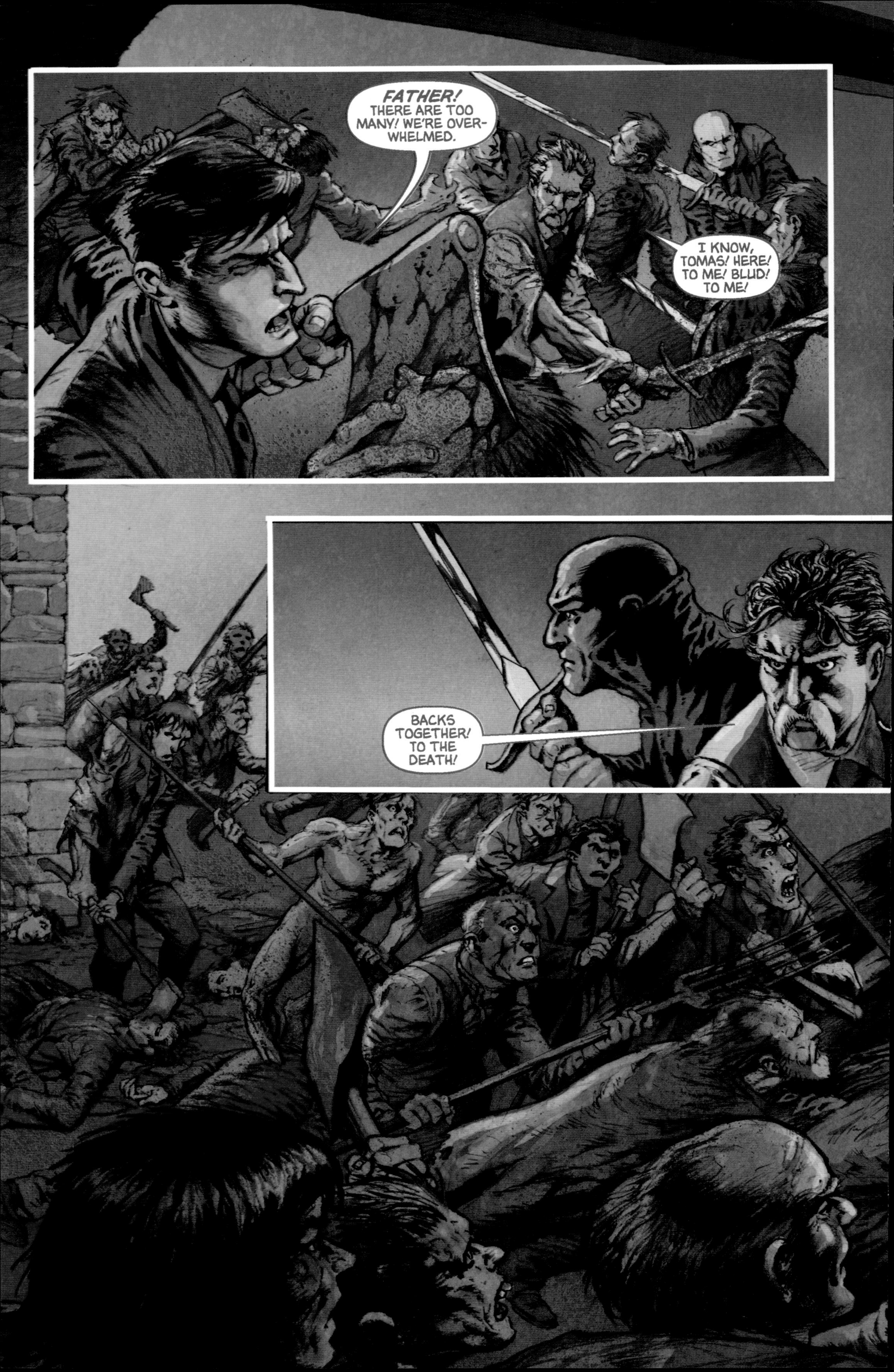
FATHER! THERE ARE TOO MANY! WE'RE OVER-WHELMED.
I KNOW, TOMAS! HERE! TO ME! BLUD! TO ME!
BACKS TOGETHER! TO THE DEATH!

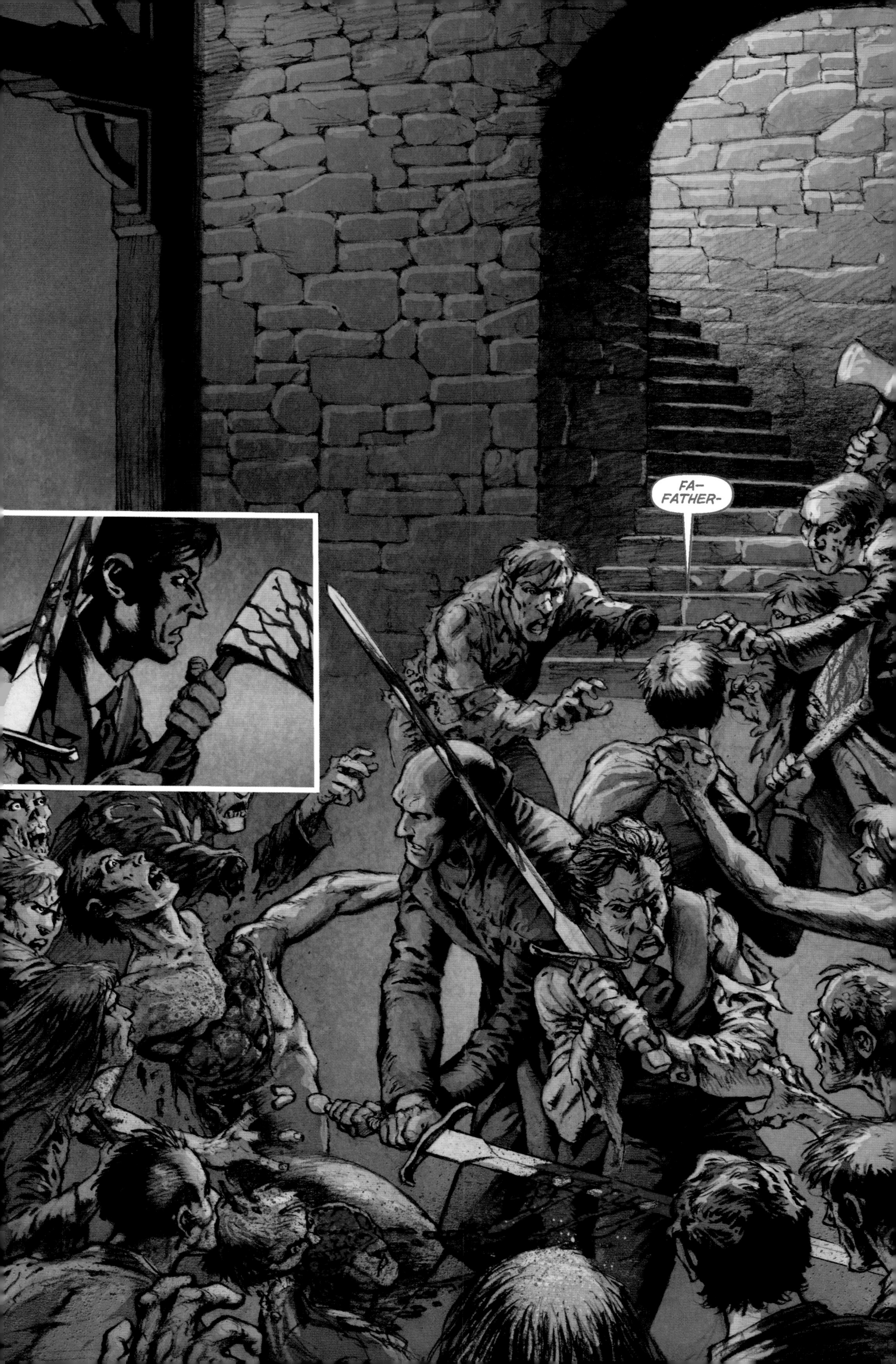
FA–
FATHER-

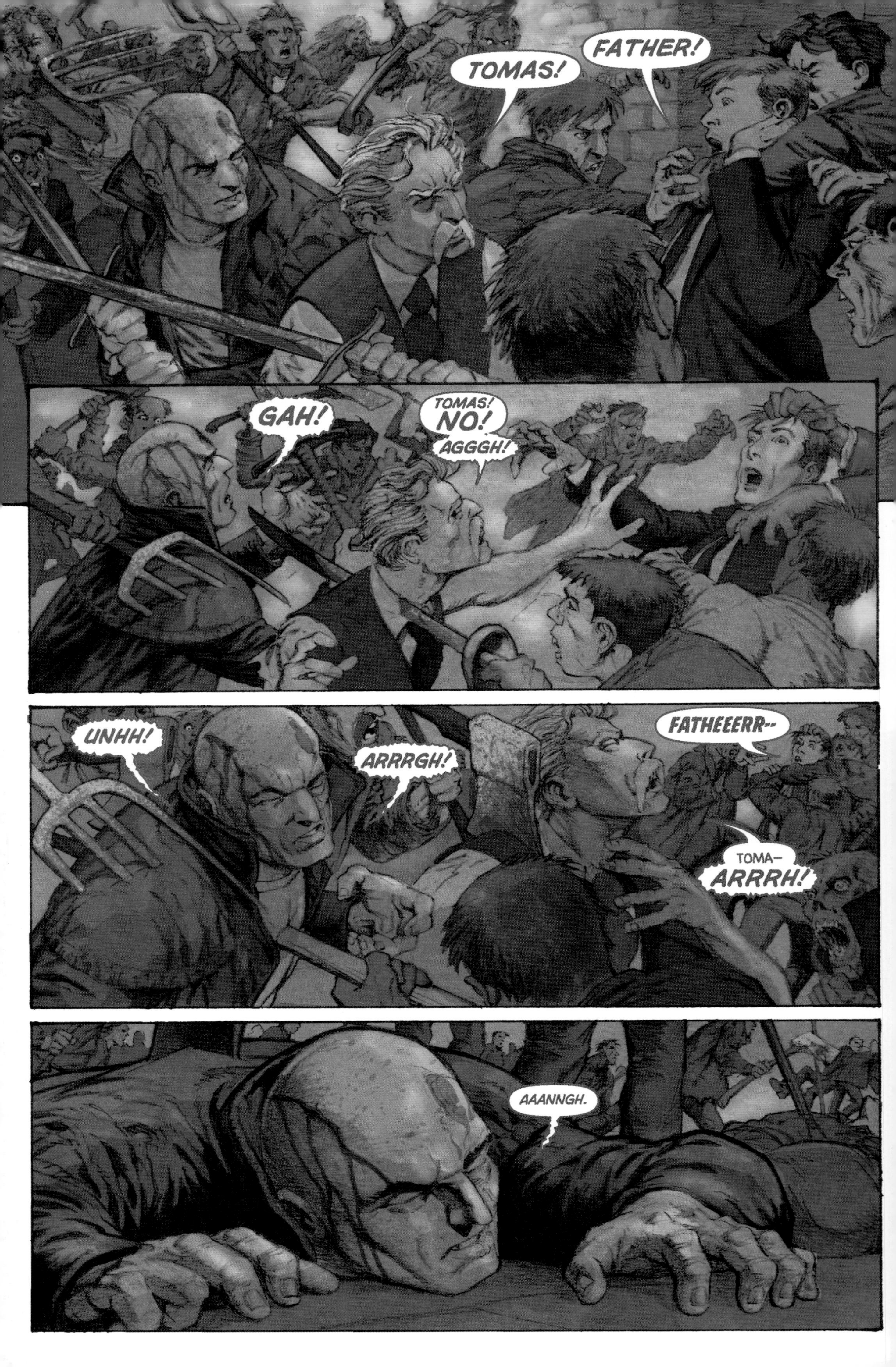
TOMAS!
FATHER!
GAH!
TOMAS! NO!
AGGGH!
UNHH!
ARRRGH!
FATHEEERR--
TOMA-
ARRRH!
AAANNGH.

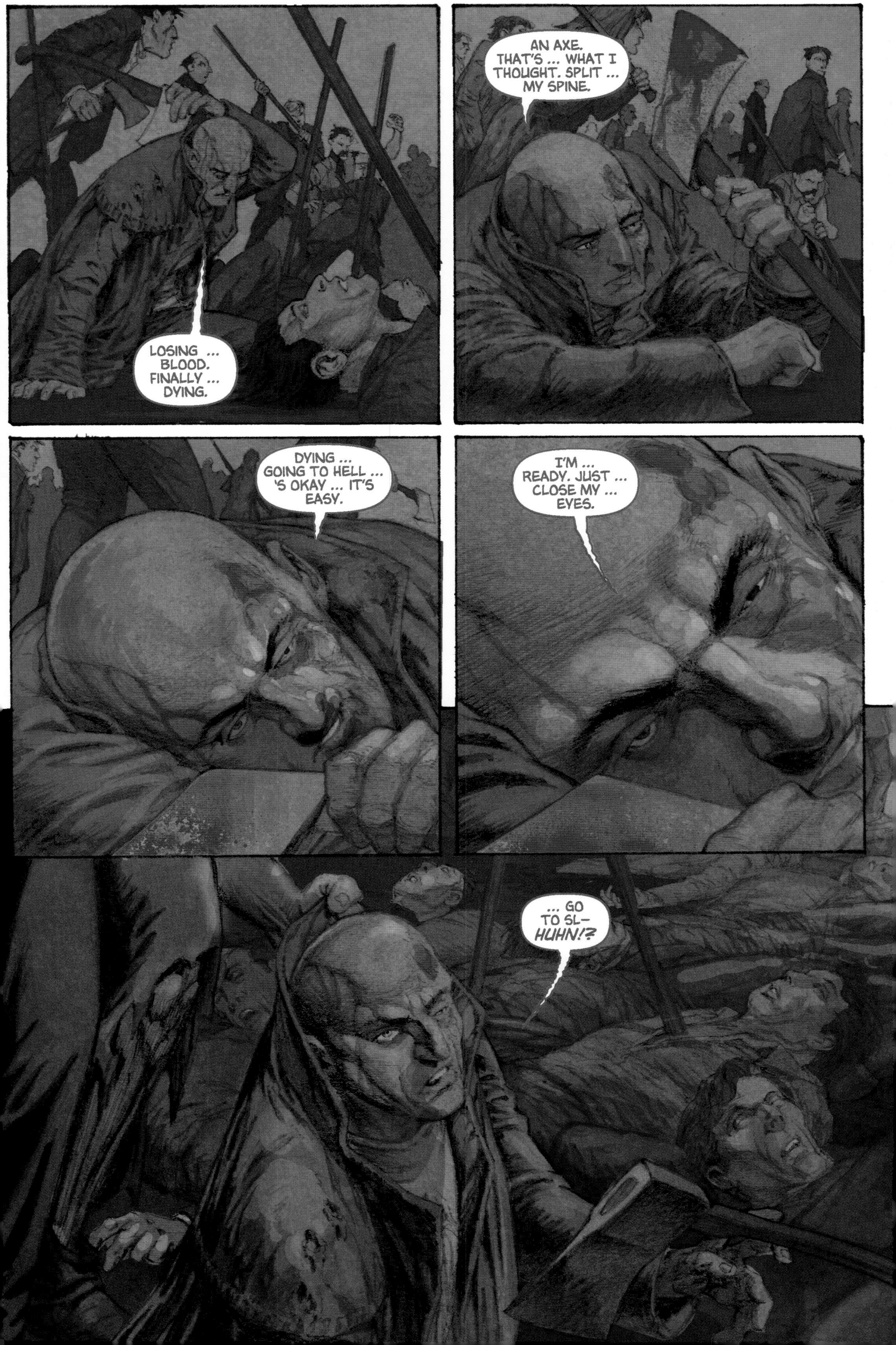
LOSING ... BLOOD. FINALLY ... DYING.
AN AXE. THAT'S ... WHAT I THOUGHT. SPLIT ... MY SPINE.
DYING ... GOING TO HELL ... 'S OKAY ... IT'S EASY.
I'M ... READY. JUST ... CLOSE MY ... EYES.
... GO TO SL— *HUHN!?*

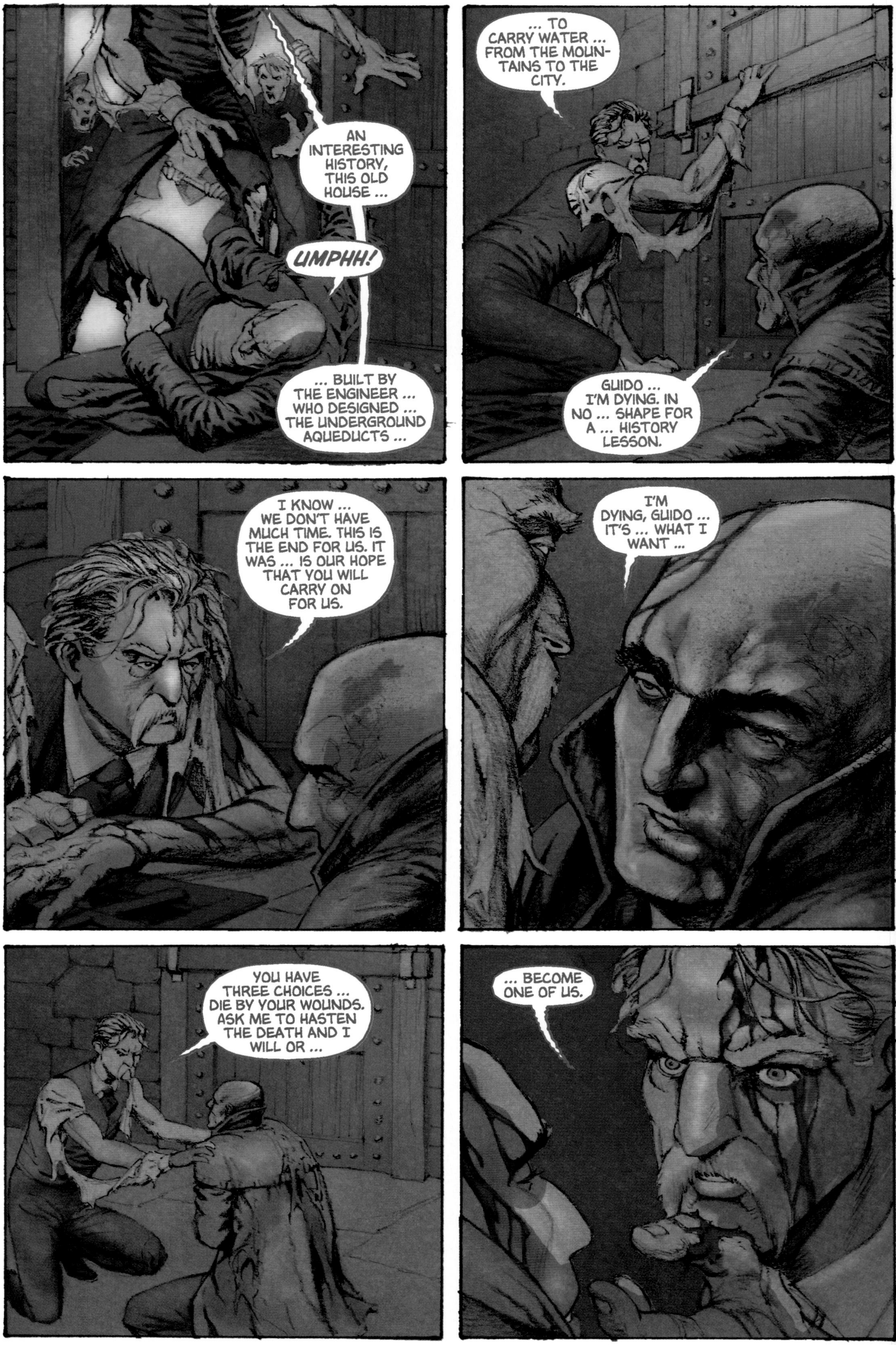
AN INTERESTING HISTORY, THIS OLD HOUSE ...
UMPHH!
... BUILT BY THE ENGINEER ... WHO DESIGNED ... THE UNDERGROUND AQUEDUCTS ...
... TO CARRY WATER ... FROM THE MOUN-TAINS TO THE CITY.
GUIDO ... I'M DYING. IN NO ... SHAPE FOR A ... HISTORY LESSON.
I KNOW ... WE DON'T HAVE MUCH TIME. THIS IS THE END FOR US. IT WAS ... IS OUR HOPE THAT YOU WILL CARRY ON FOR US.
I'M DYING, GUIDO ... IT'S ... WHAT I WANT ...
YOU HAVE THREE CHOICES ... DIE BY YOUR WOUNDS. ASK ME TO HASTEN THE DEATH AND I WILL OR ...
... BECOME ONE OF US.

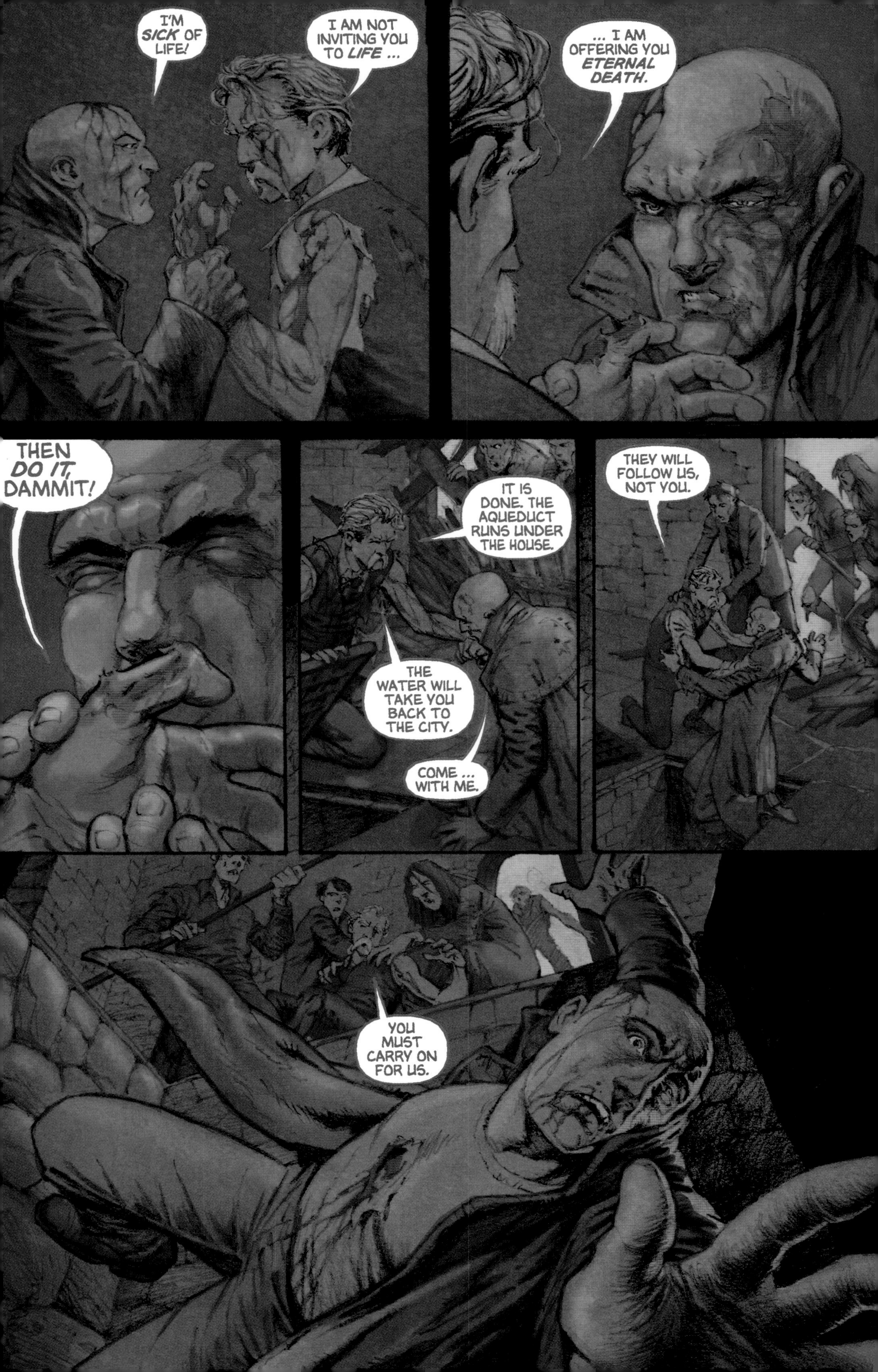
I'M SICK OF LIFE!
I AM NOT INVITING YOU TO LIFE ...
... I AM OFFERING YOU ETERNAL DEATH.
THEN DO IT, DAMMIT!
IT IS DONE. THE AQUEDUCT RUNS UNDER THE HOUSE.
THE WATER WILL TAKE YOU BACK TO THE CITY.
COME ... WITH ME.
THEY WILL FOLLOW US, NOT YOU.
YOU MUST CARRY ON FOR US.

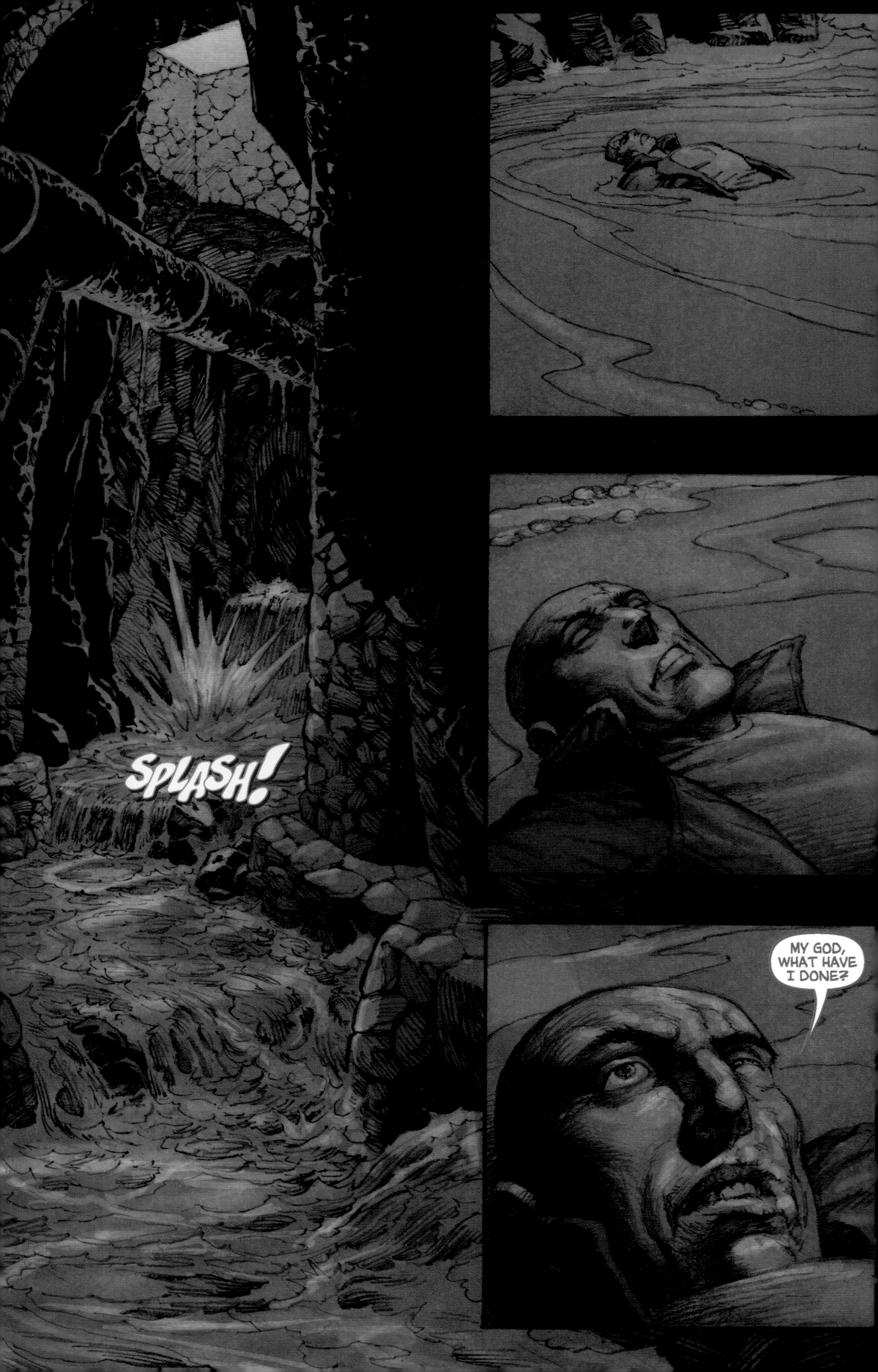
SPLASH!
MY GOD, WHAT HAVE I DONE?

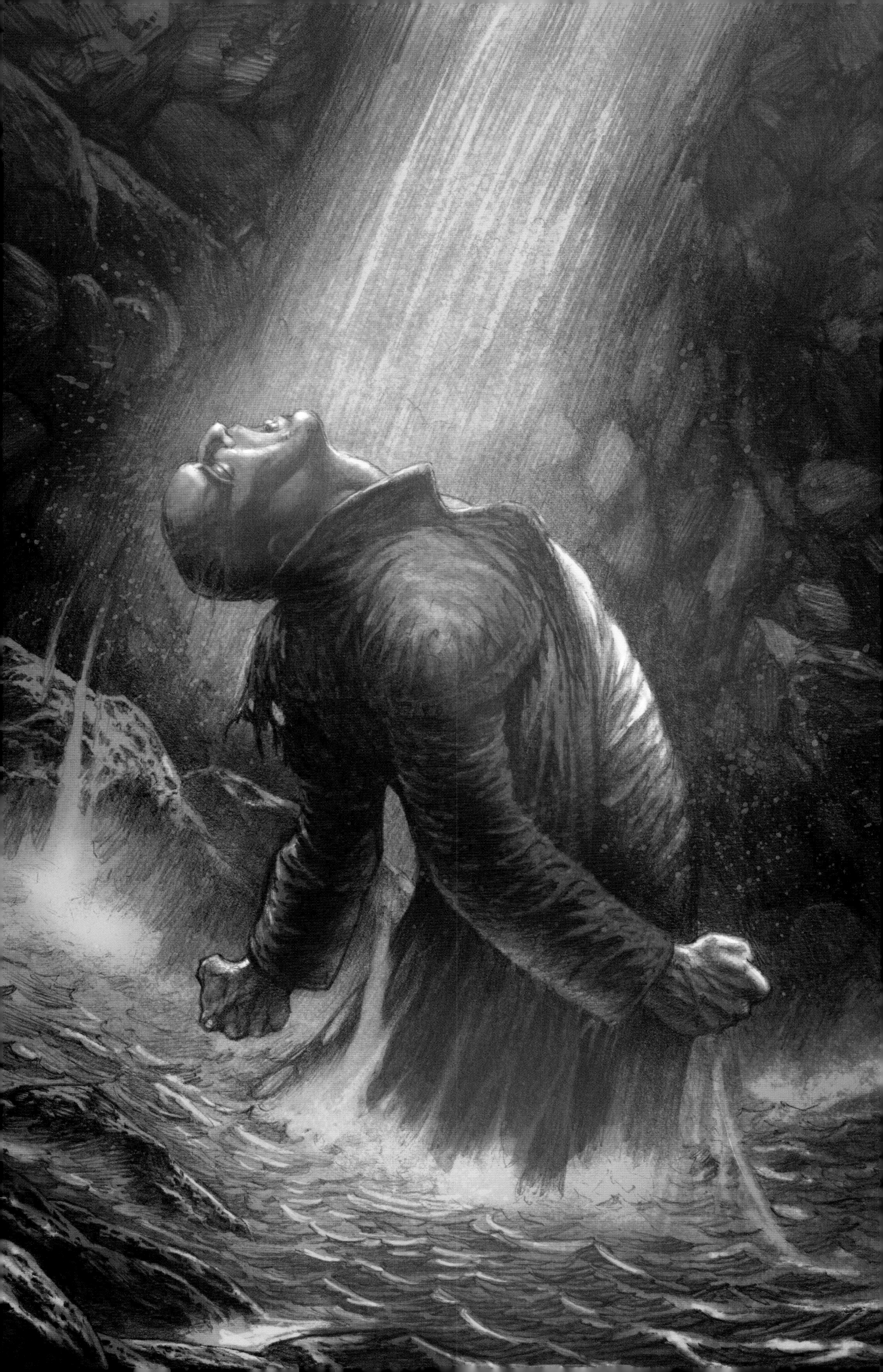

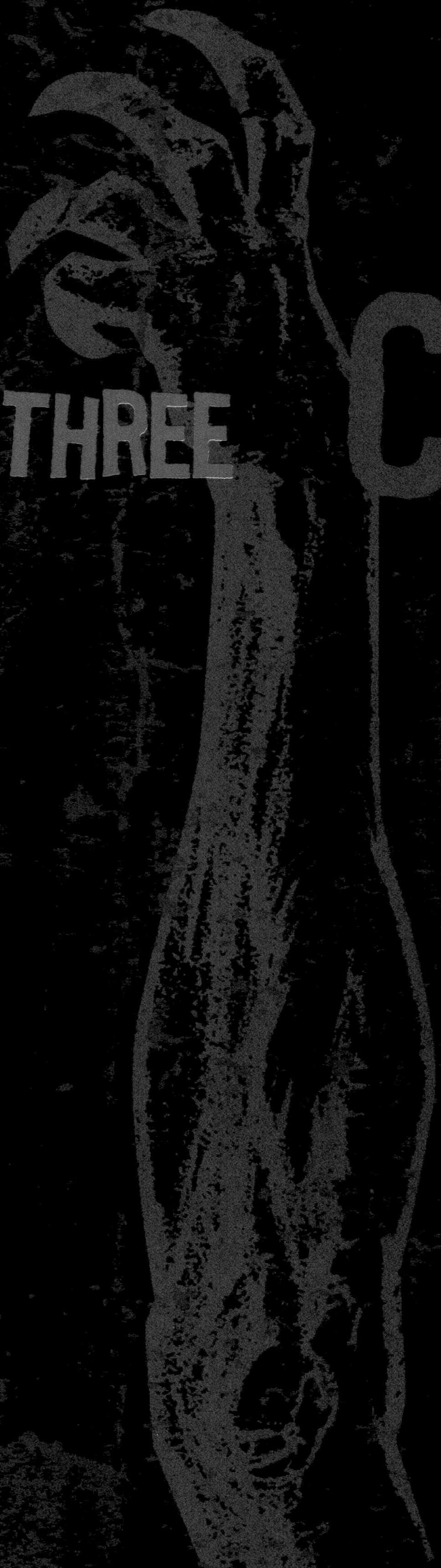

CHAPTER THREE

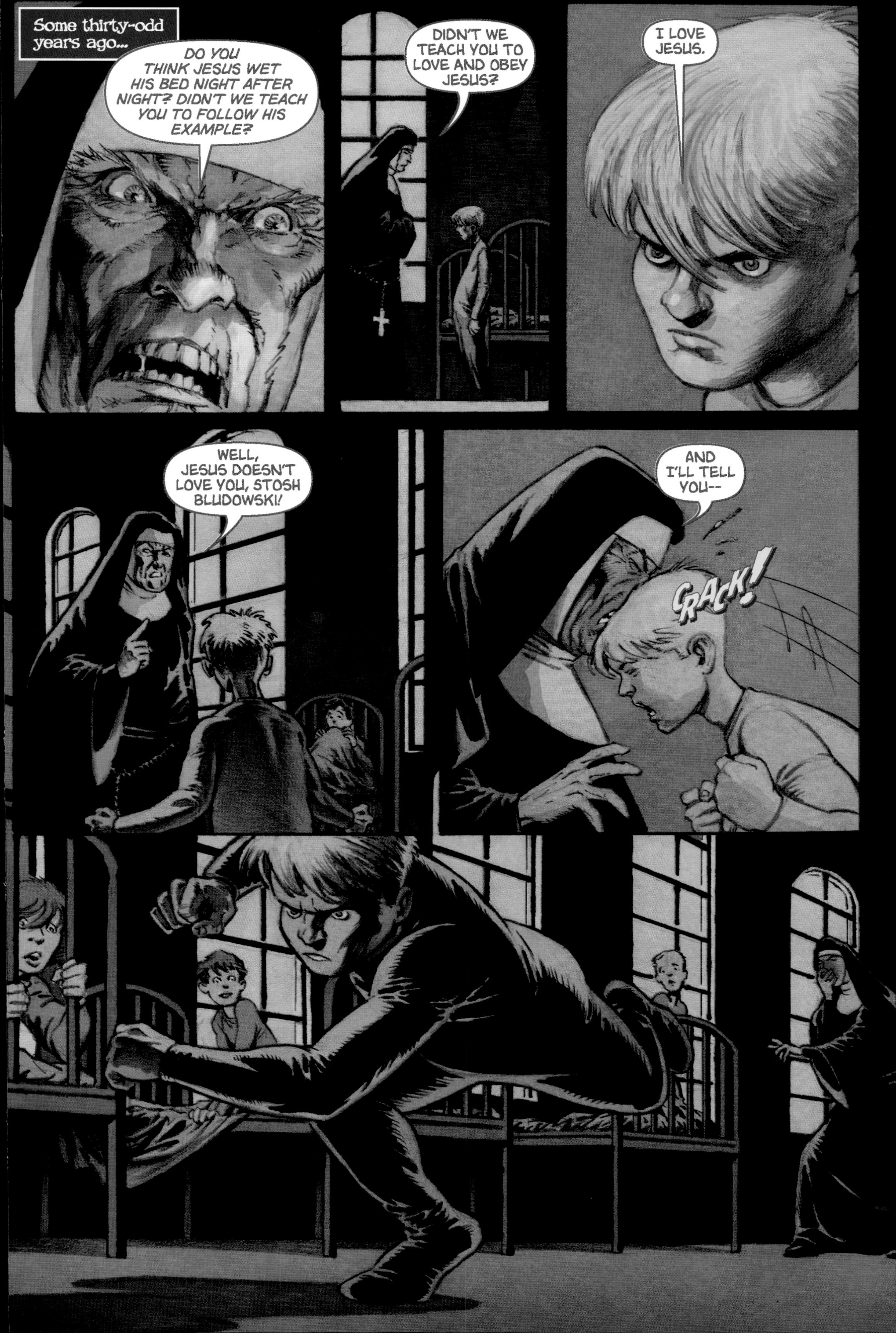

Some thirty-odd years ago...
DO YOU THINK JESUS WET HIS BED NIGHT AFTER NIGHT? DIDN'T WE TEACH YOU TO FOLLOW HIS EXAMPLE?
DIDN'T WE TEACH YOU TO LOVE AND OBEY JESUS?
I LOVE JESUS.
WELL, JESUS DOESN'T LOVE YOU, STOSH BLUDOWSKI!
AND I'LL TELL YOU--
CRACK!

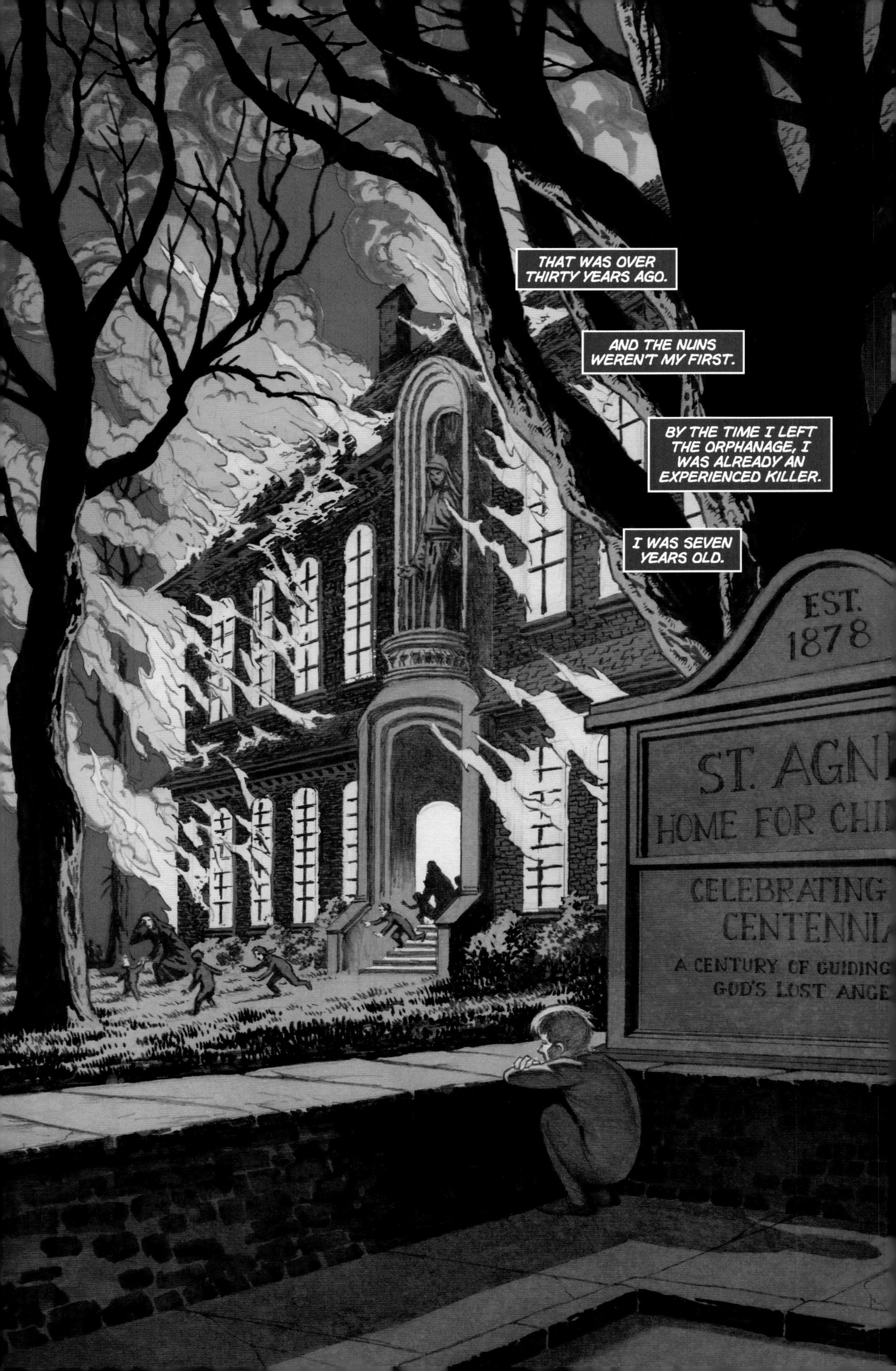
THAT WAS OVER THIRTY YEARS AGO.
AND THE NUNS WEREN'T MY FIRST.
BY THE TIME I LEFT THE ORPHANAGE, I WAS ALREADY AN EXPERIENCED KILLER.
I WAS SEVEN YEARS OLD.
EST. 1878
ST. AGN
HOME FOR CHI
CELEBRATING
CENTENNIA
A CENTURY OF GUIDING
GOD'S LOST ANGE

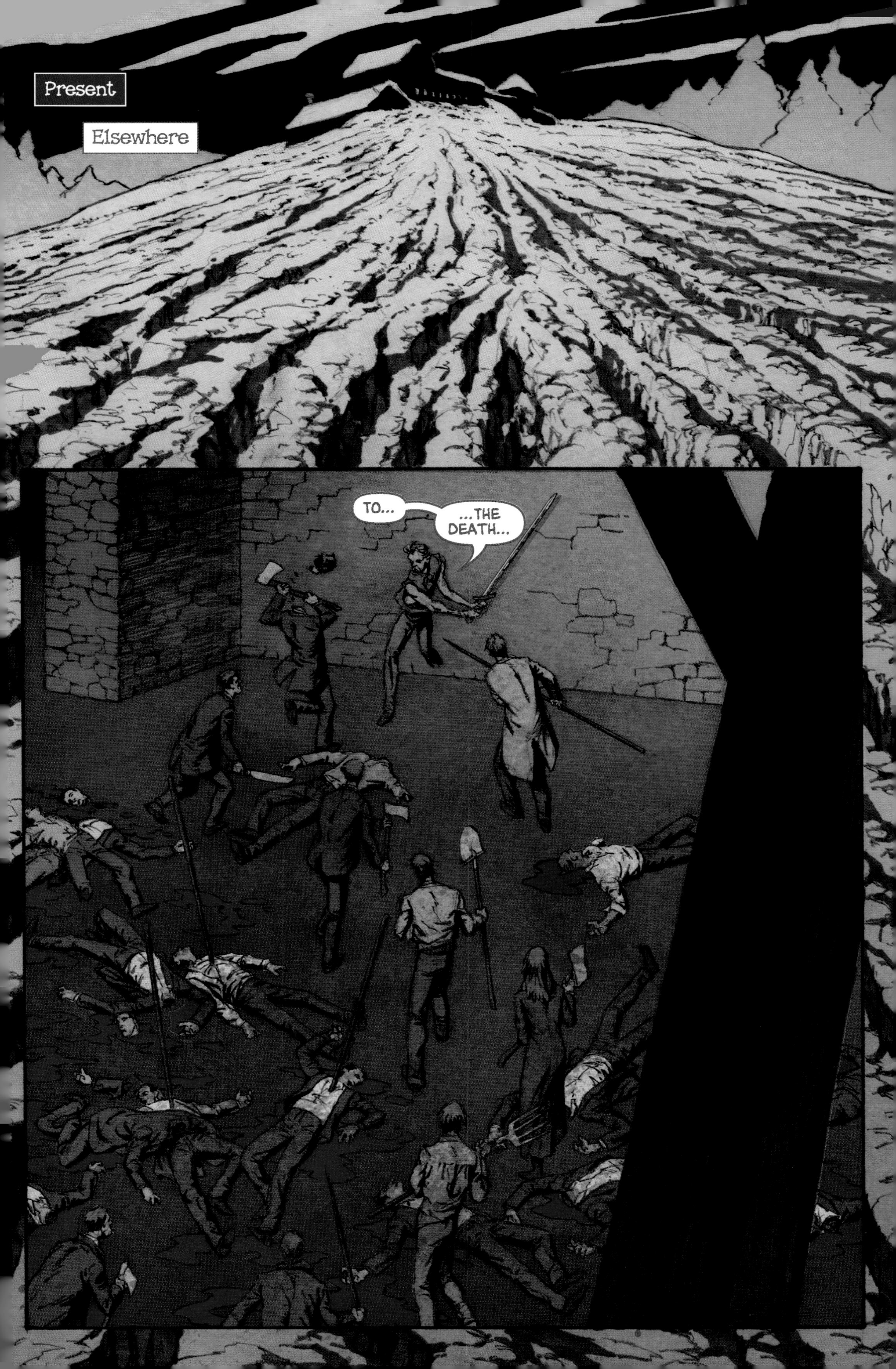
Present
Elsewhere
TO...
...THE DEATH...

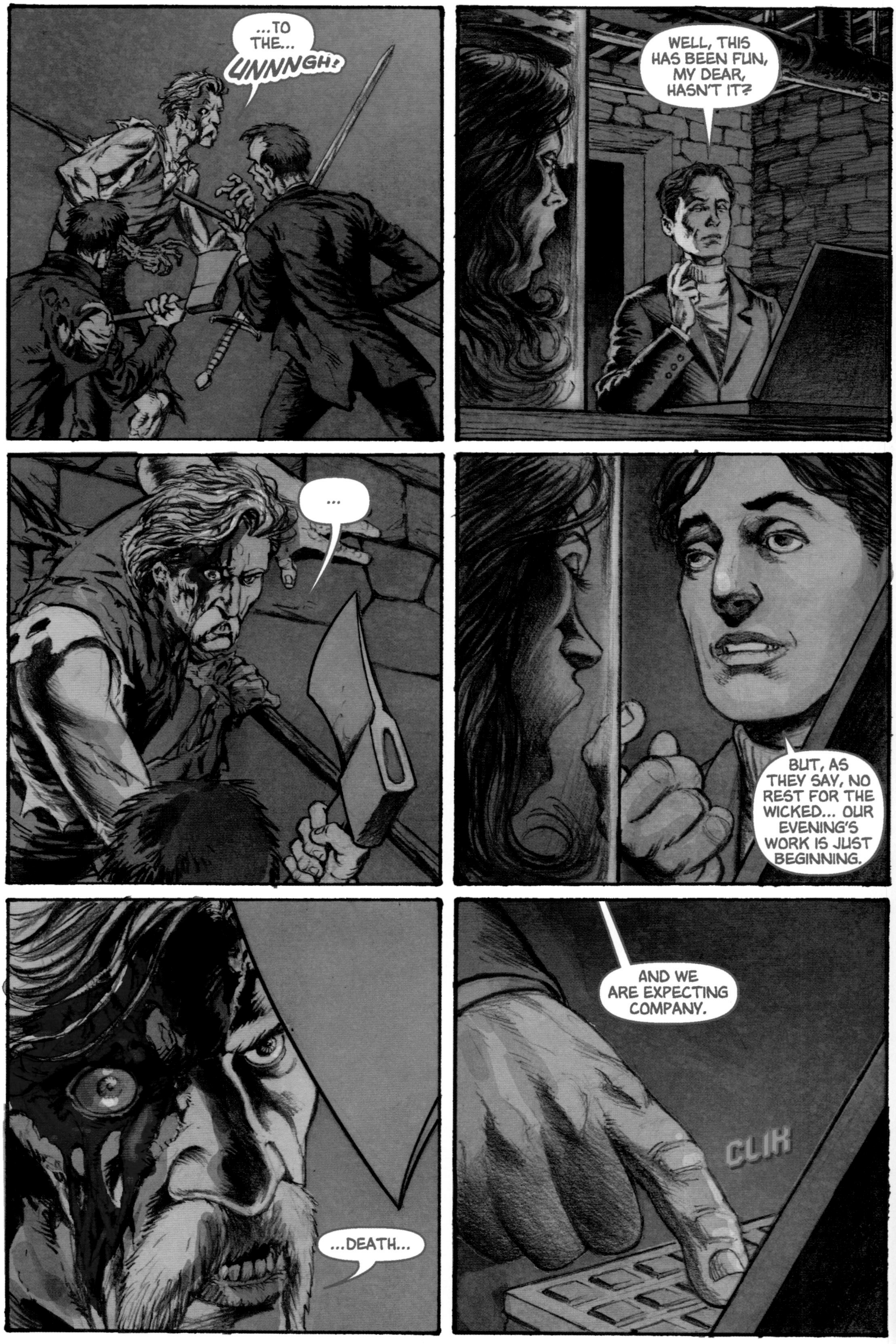
...TO THE... UNNNGH!
WELL, THIS HAS BEEN FUN, MY DEAR, HASN'T IT?
...
BUT, AS THEY SAY, NO REST FOR THE WICKED... OUR EVENING'S WORK IS JUST BEGINNING.
...DEATH...
AND WE ARE EXPECTING COMPANY.
CLIK

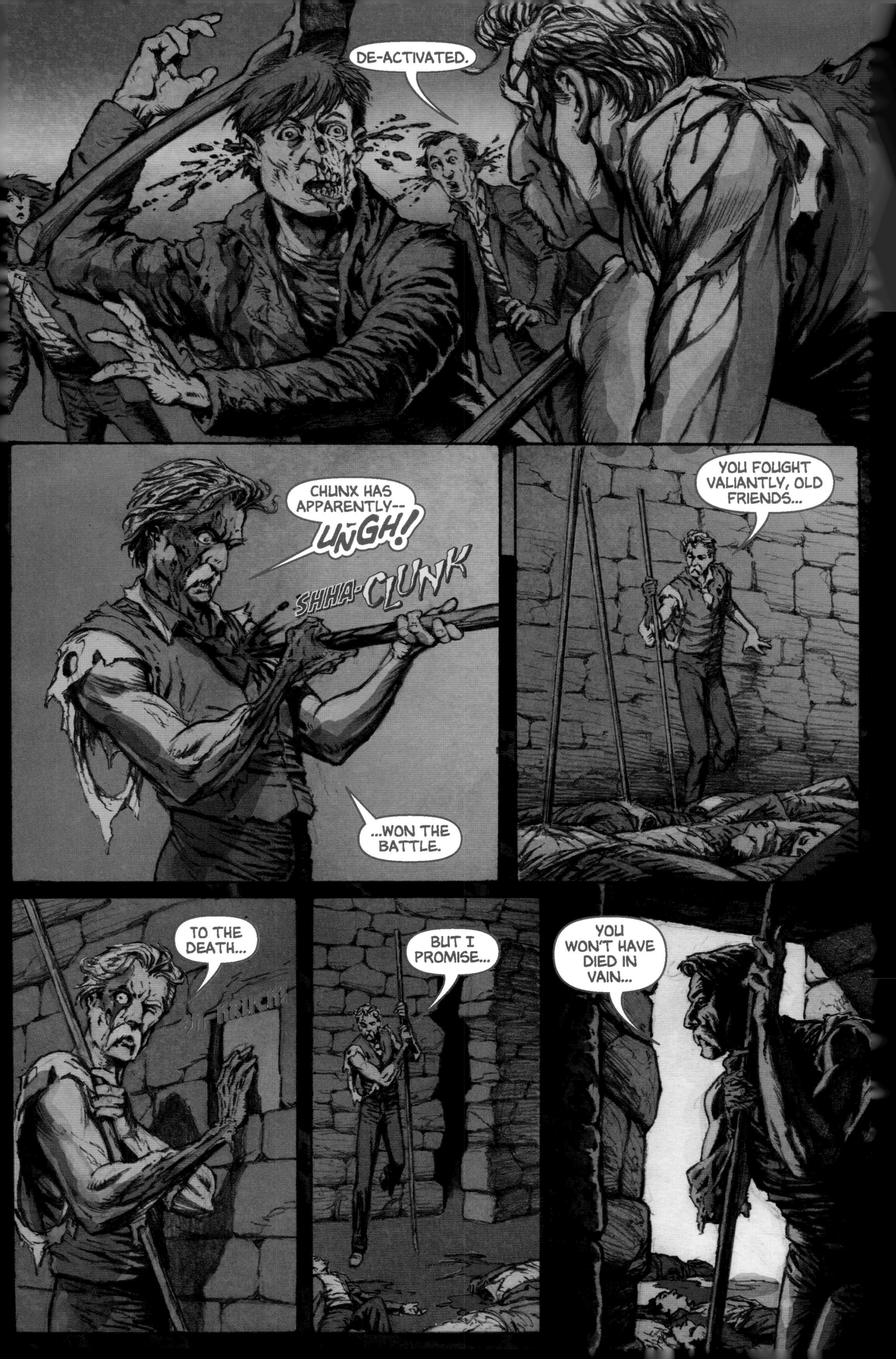
DE-ACTIVATED.
CHUNX HAS APPARENTLY--
UNGH!
SHHA-CLUNK
...WON THE BATTLE.
YOU FOUGHT VALIANTLY, OLD FRIENDS...
TO THE DEATH...
BUT I PROMISE...
YOU WON'T HAVE DIED IN VAIN...

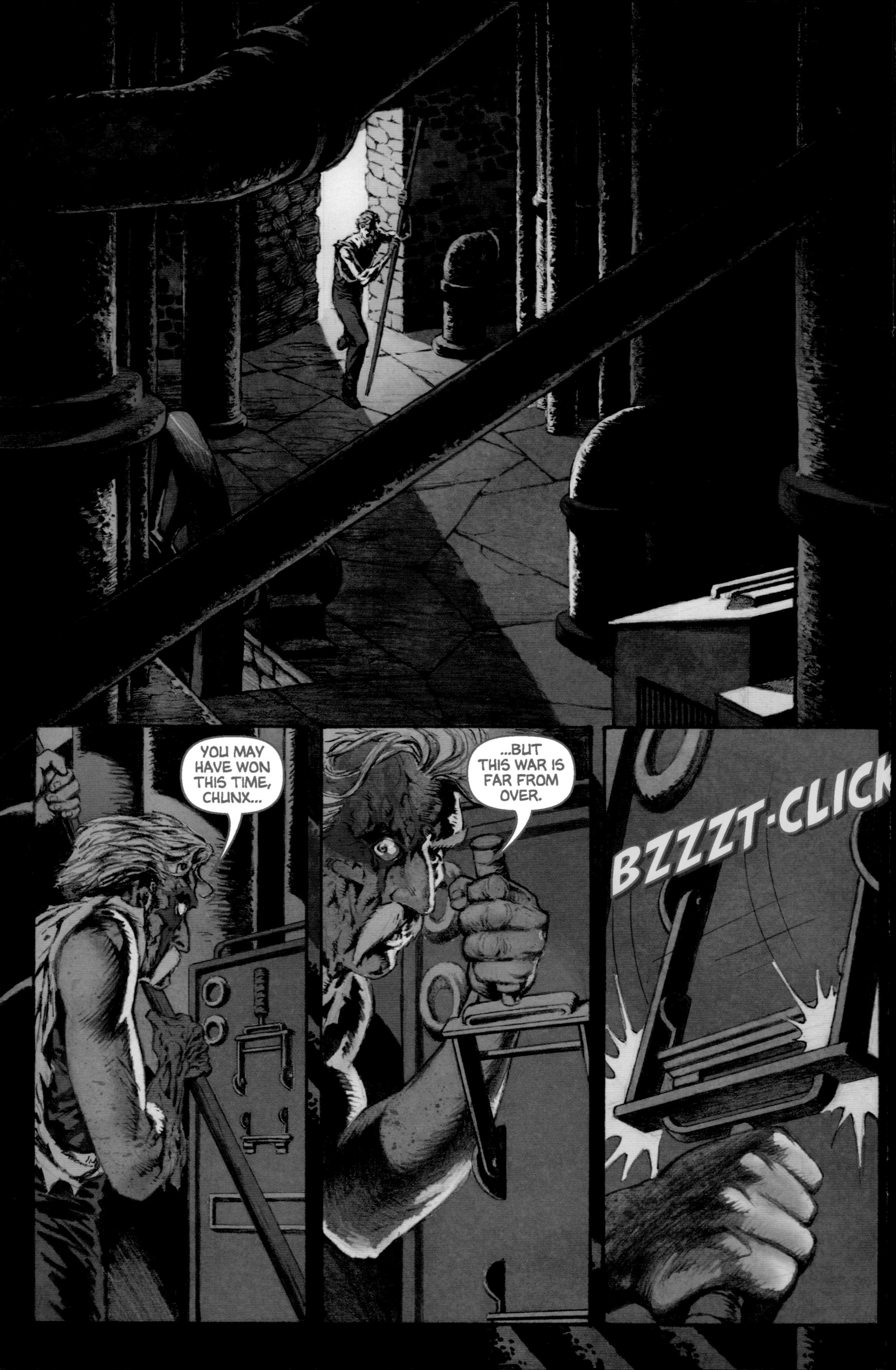
YOU MAY HAVE WON THIS TIME, CHUNX...
...BUT THIS WAR IS FAR FROM OVER.
BZZZT-CLICK

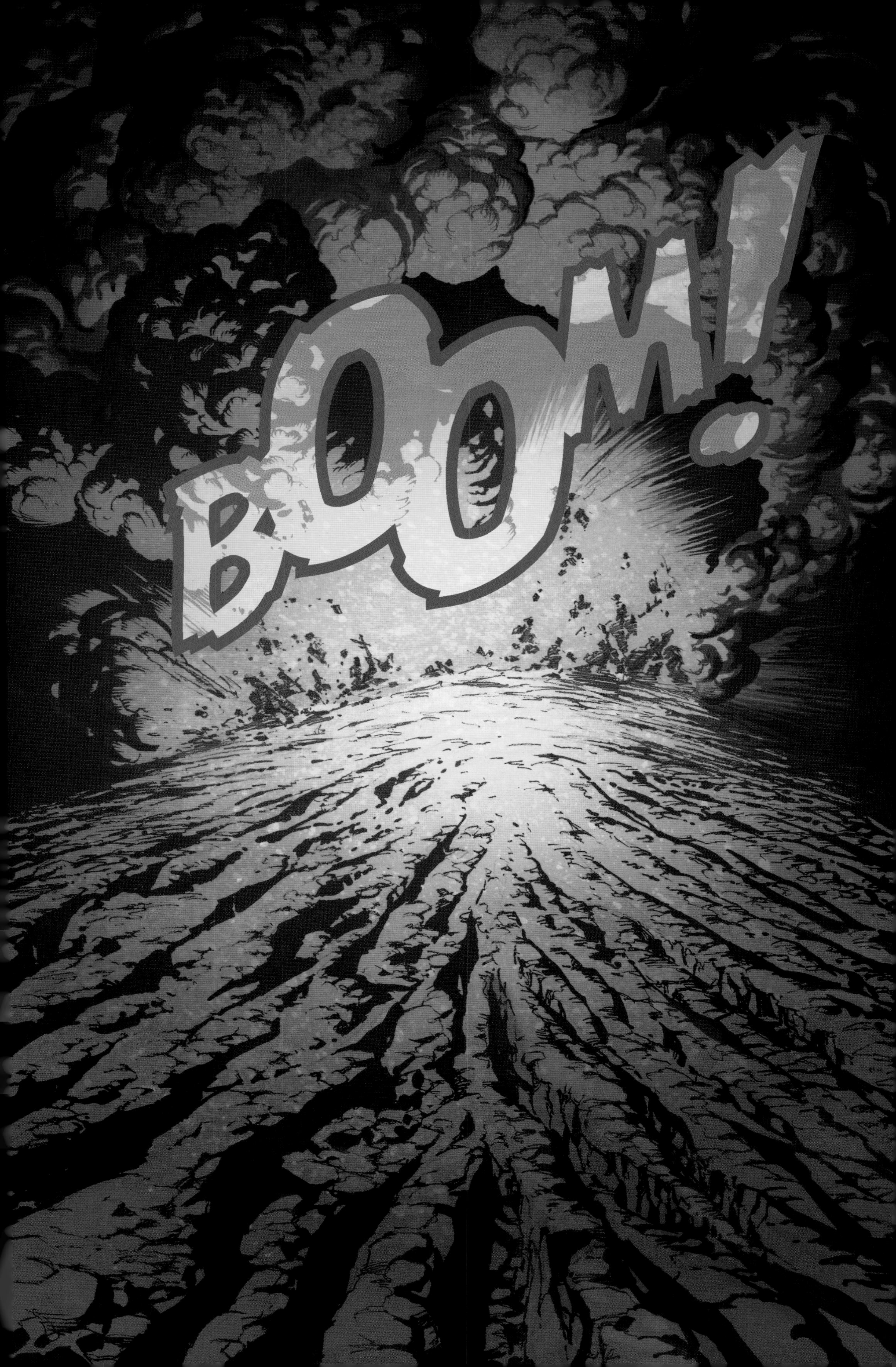
BOOM!

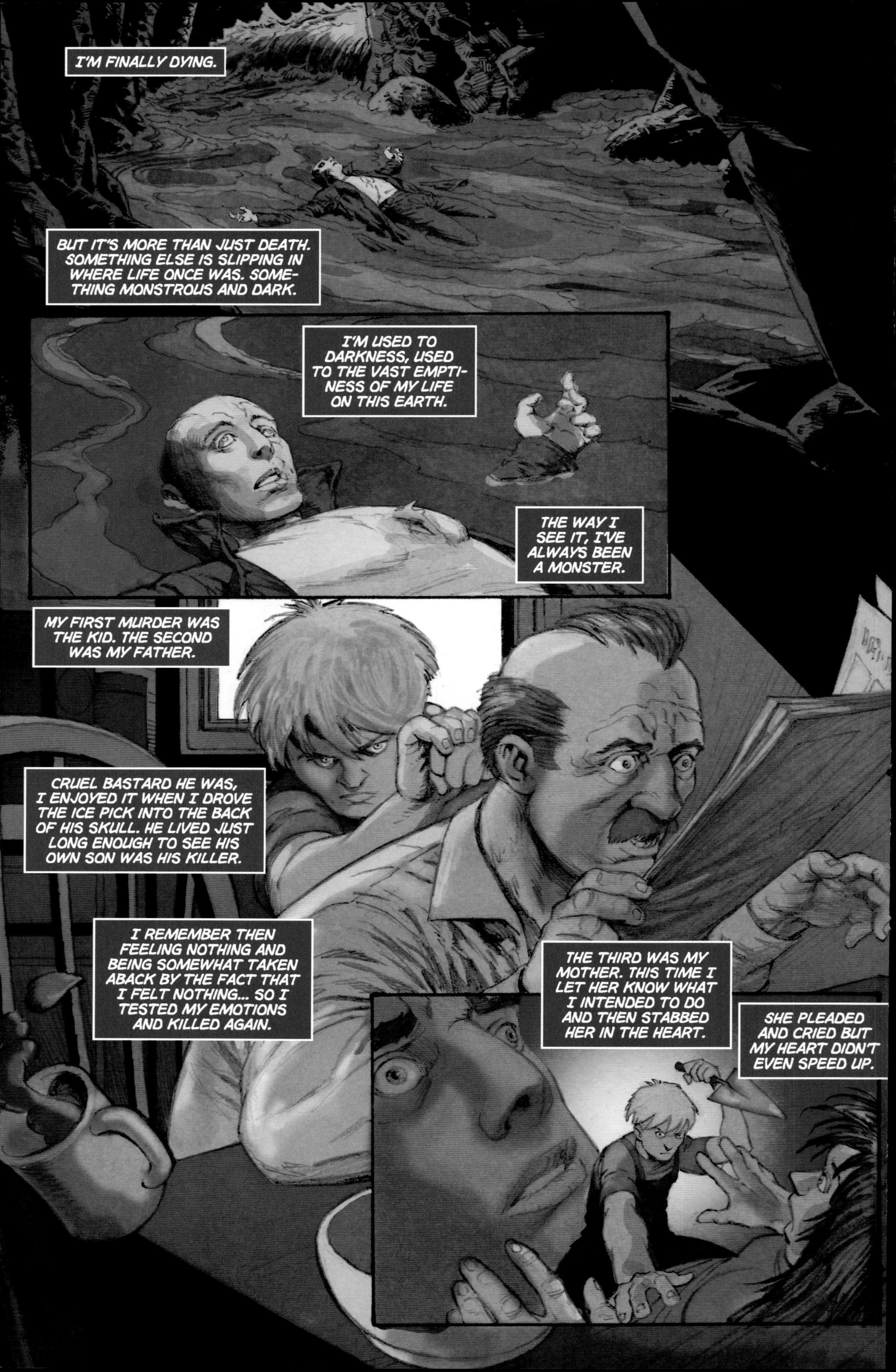
I'M FINALLY DYING.
BUT IT'S MORE THAN JUST DEATH. SOMETHING ELSE IS SLIPPING IN WHERE LIFE ONCE WAS. SOMETHING MONSTROUS AND DARK.
I'M USED TO DARKNESS, USED TO THE VAST EMPTINESS OF MY LIFE ON THIS EARTH.
THE WAY I SEE IT, I'VE ALWAYS BEEN A MONSTER.
MY FIRST MURDER WAS THE KID. THE SECOND WAS MY FATHER.
CRUEL BASTARD HE WAS, I ENJOYED IT WHEN I DROVE THE ICE PICK INTO THE BACK OF HIS SKULL. HE LIVED JUST LONG ENOUGH TO SEE HIS OWN SON WAS HIS KILLER.
I REMEMBER THEN FEELING NOTHING AND BEING SOMEWHAT TAKEN ABACK BY THE FACT THAT I FELT NOTHING... SO I TESTED MY EMOTIONS AND KILLED AGAIN.
THE THIRD WAS MY MOTHER. THIS TIME I LET HER KNOW WHAT I INTENDED TO DO AND THEN STABBED HER IN THE HEART.
SHE PLEADED AND CRIED BUT MY HEART DIDN'T EVEN SPEED UP.

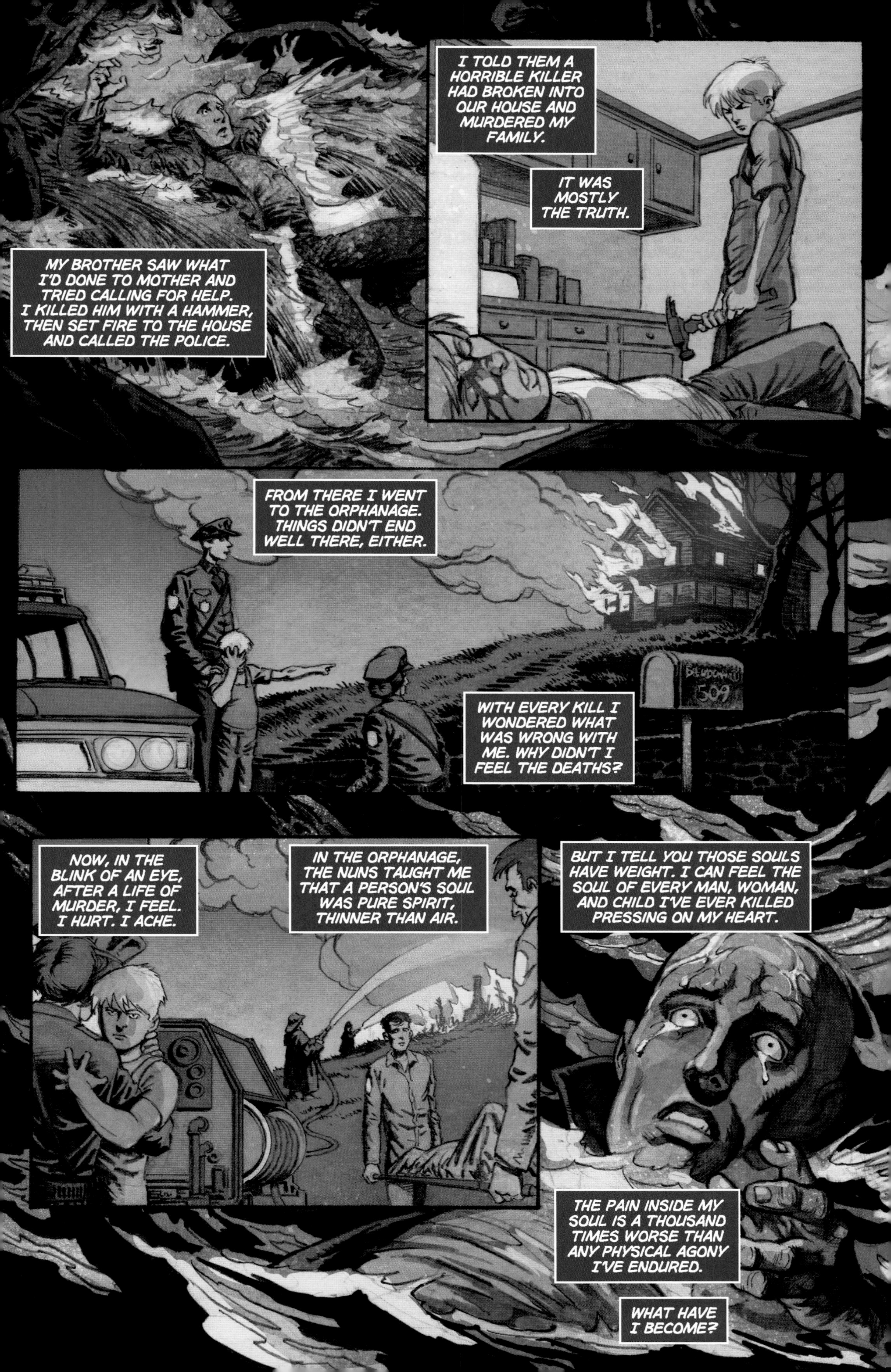

MY BROTHER SAW WHAT I'D DONE TO MOTHER AND TRIED CALLING FOR HELP. I KILLED HIM WITH A HAMMER, THEN SET FIRE TO THE HOUSE AND CALLED THE POLICE.
I TOLD THEM A HORRIBLE KILLER HAD BROKEN INTO OUR HOUSE AND MURDERED MY FAMILY.
IT WAS MOSTLY THE TRUTH.
FROM THERE I WENT TO THE ORPHANAGE. THINGS DIDN'T END WELL THERE, EITHER.
509
WITH EVERY KILL I WONDERED WHAT WAS WRONG WITH ME. WHY DIDN'T I FEEL THE DEATHS?
NOW, IN THE BLINK OF AN EYE, AFTER A LIFE OF MURDER, I FEEL. I HURT. I ACHE.
IN THE ORPHANAGE, THE NUNS TAUGHT ME THAT A PERSON'S SOUL WAS PURE SPIRIT, THINNER THAN AIR.
BUT I TELL YOU THOSE SOULS HAVE WEIGHT. I CAN FEEL THE SOUL OF EVERY MAN, WOMAN, AND CHILD I'VE EVER KILLED PRESSING ON MY HEART.
THE PAIN INSIDE MY SOUL IS A THOUSAND TIMES WORSE THAN ANY PHYSICAL AGONY I'VE ENDURED.
WHAT HAVE I BECOME?

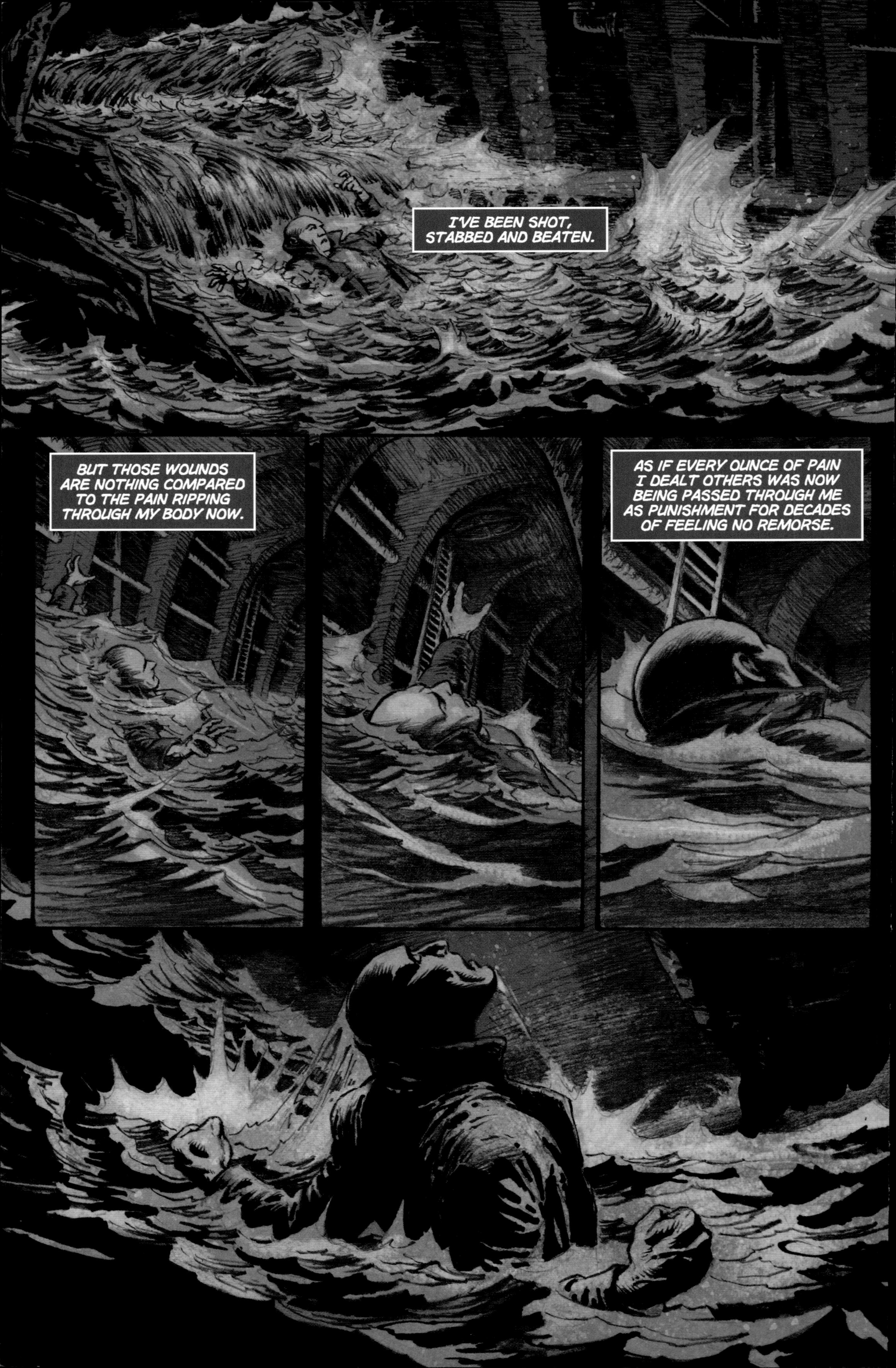
I'VE BEEN SHOT, STABBED AND BEATEN.
BUT THOSE WOUNDS ARE NOTHING COMPARED TO THE PAIN RIPPING THROUGH MY BODY NOW.
AS IF EVERY OUNCE OF PAIN I DEALT OTHERS WAS NOW BEING PASSED THROUGH ME AS PUNISHMENT FOR DECADES OF FEELING NO REMORSE.

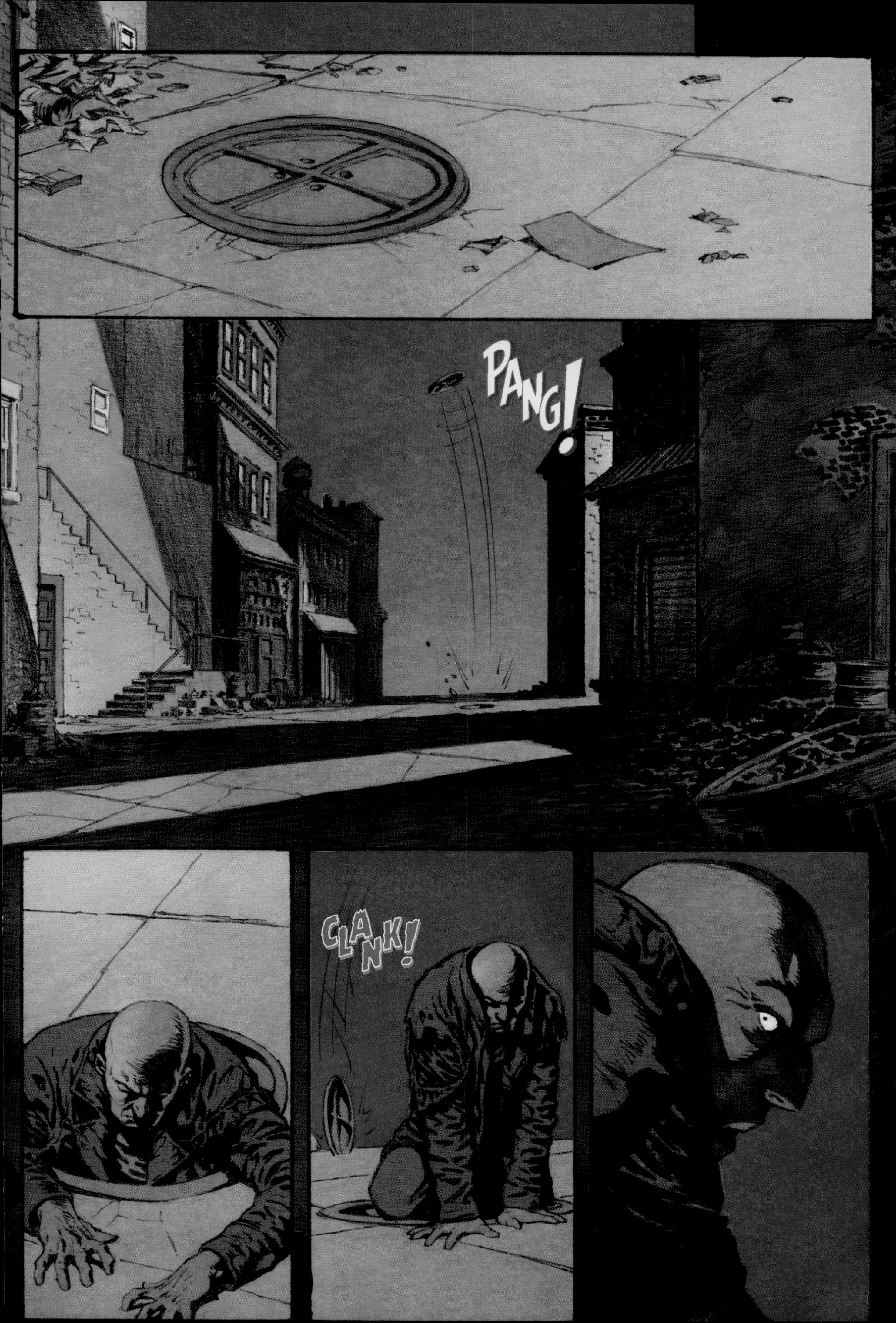
PANG!
CLANK!

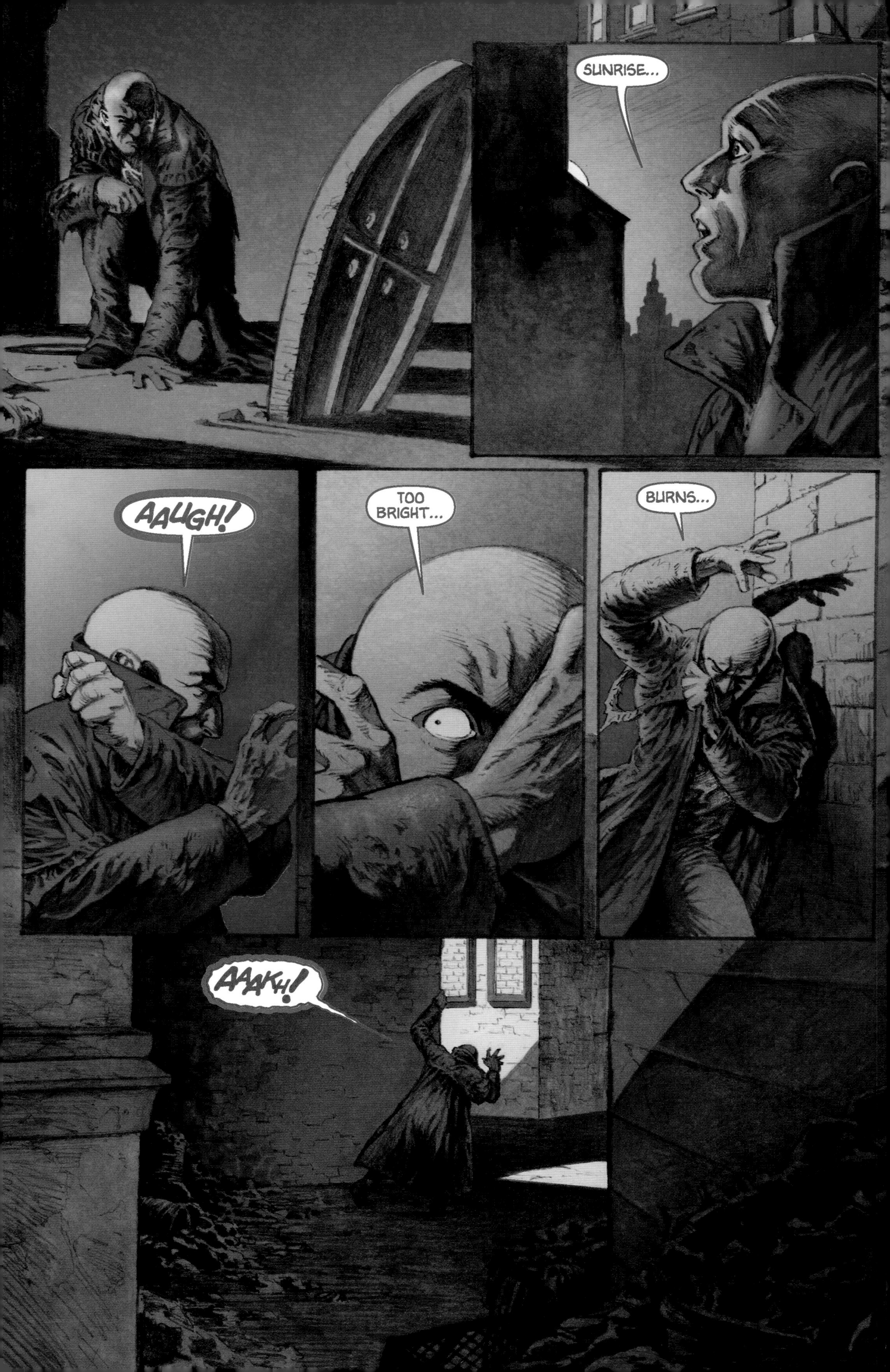
SUNRISE...
AAUGH!
TOO BRIGHT...
BURNS...
AAAKH!

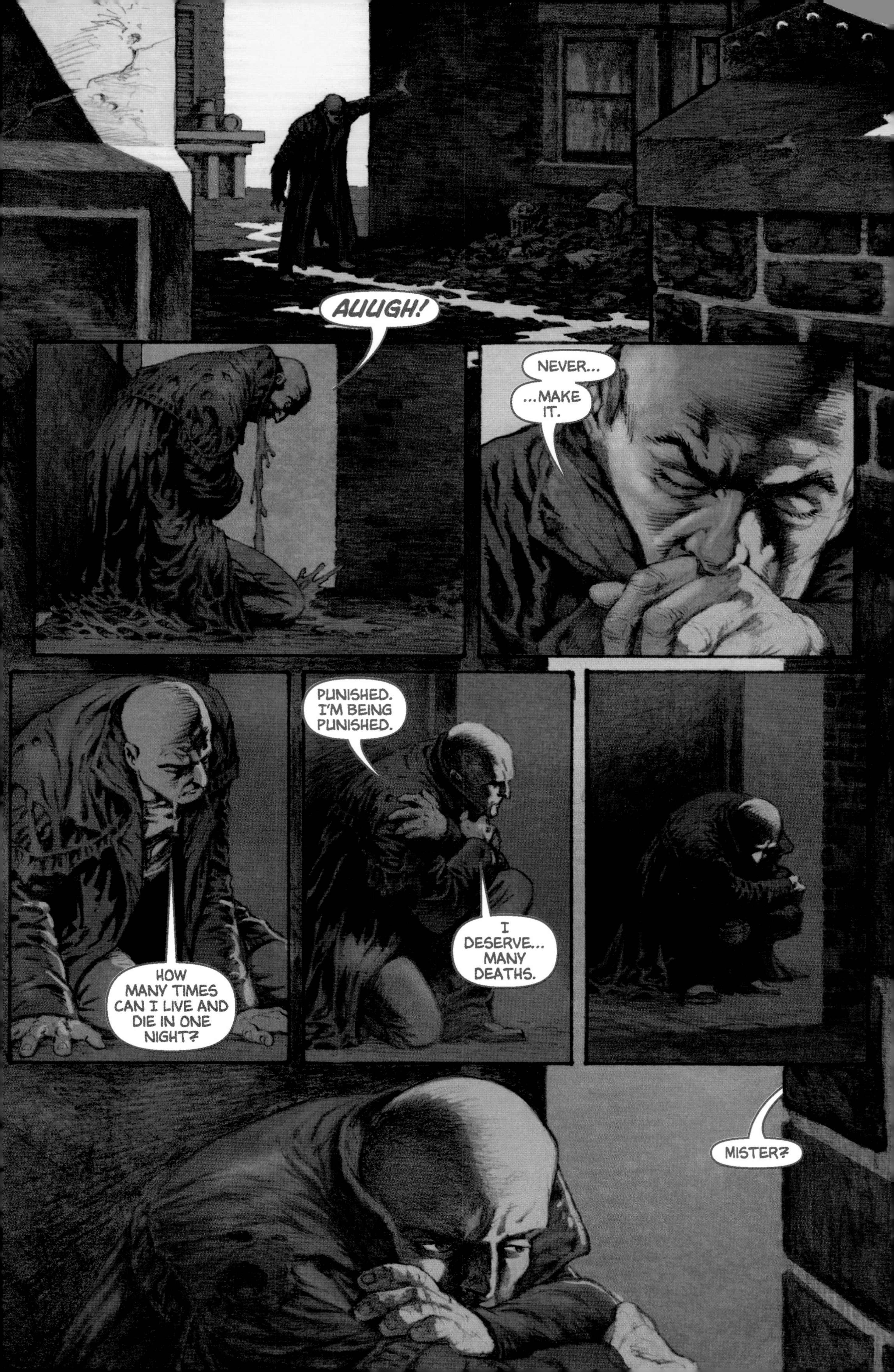
AUUGH!
NEVER...
...MAKE IT.
HOW MANY TIMES CAN I LIVE AND DIE IN ONE NIGHT?
PUNISHED. I'M BEING PUNISHED.
I DESERVE... MANY DEATHS.
MISTER?

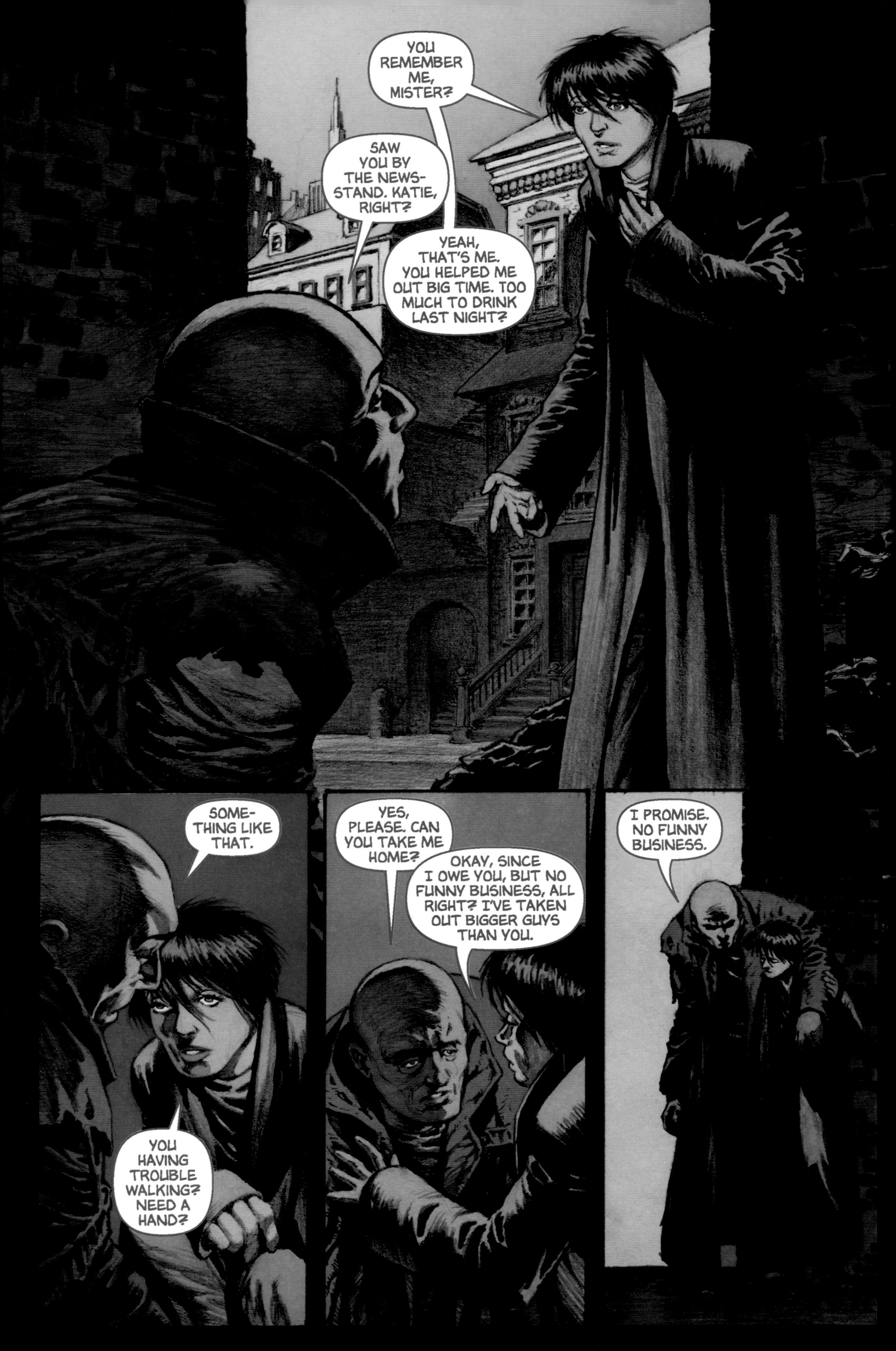
YOU REMEMBER ME, MISTER?
SAW YOU BY THE NEWS-STAND. KATIE, RIGHT?
YEAH, THAT'S ME. YOU HELPED ME OUT BIG TIME. TOO MUCH TO DRINK LAST NIGHT?
SOME-THING LIKE THAT.
YOU HAVING TROUBLE WALKING? NEED A HAND?
YES, PLEASE. CAN YOU TAKE ME HOME?
OKAY, SINCE I OWE YOU, BUT NO FUNNY BUSINESS, ALL RIGHT? I'VE TAKEN OUT BIGGER GUYS THAN YOU.
I PROMISE. NO FUNNY BUSINESS.

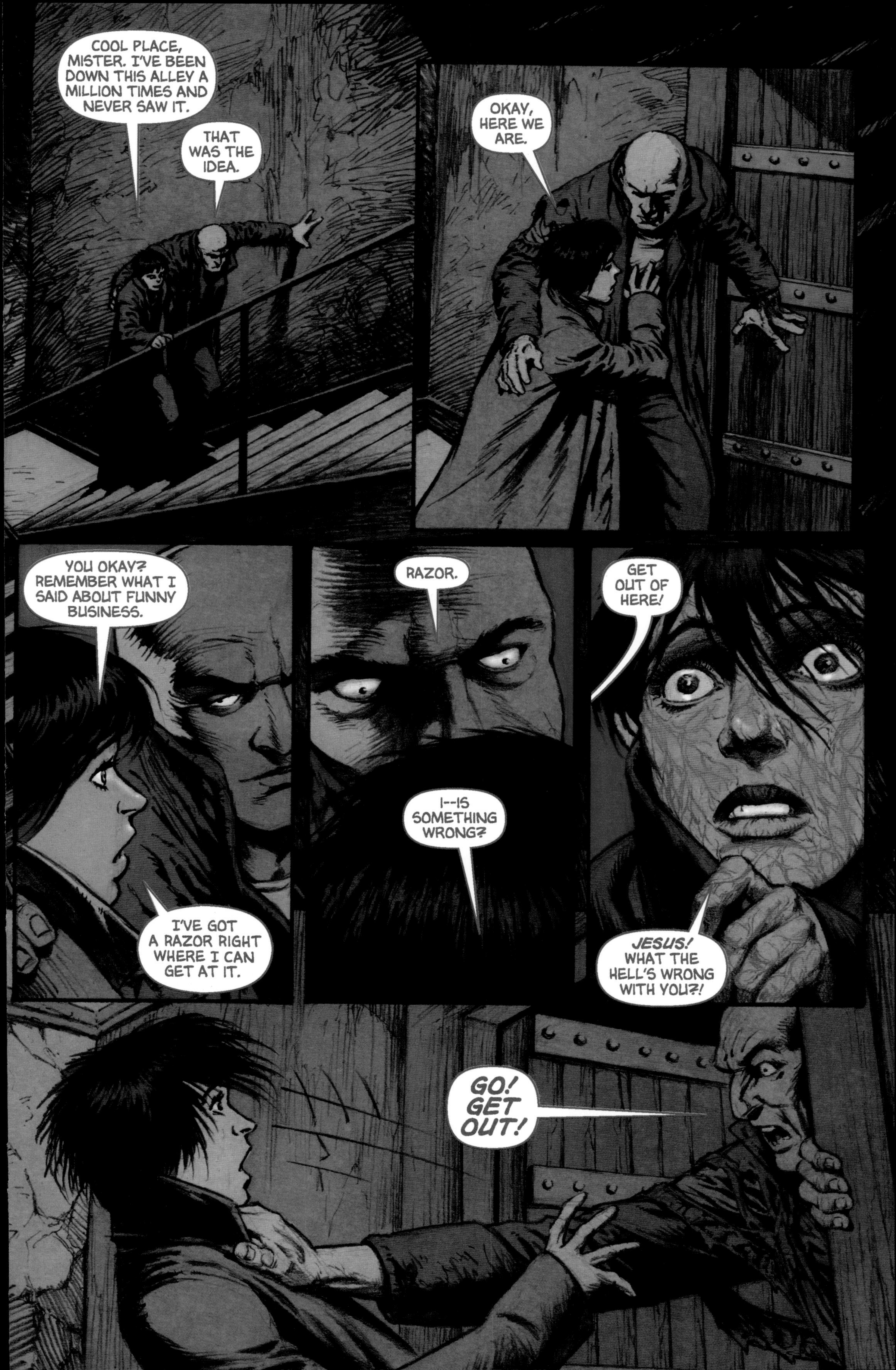
COOL PLACE, MISTER. I'VE BEEN DOWN THIS ALLEY A MILLION TIMES AND NEVER SAW IT.
THAT WAS THE IDEA.
OKAY, HERE WE ARE.
YOU OKAY? REMEMBER WHAT I SAID ABOUT FUNNY BUSINESS.
I'VE GOT A RAZOR RIGHT WHERE I CAN GET AT IT.
RAZOR.
I--IS SOMETHING WRONG?
GET OUT OF HERE!
JESUS! WHAT THE HELL'S WRONG WITH YOU?!
GO! GET OUT!

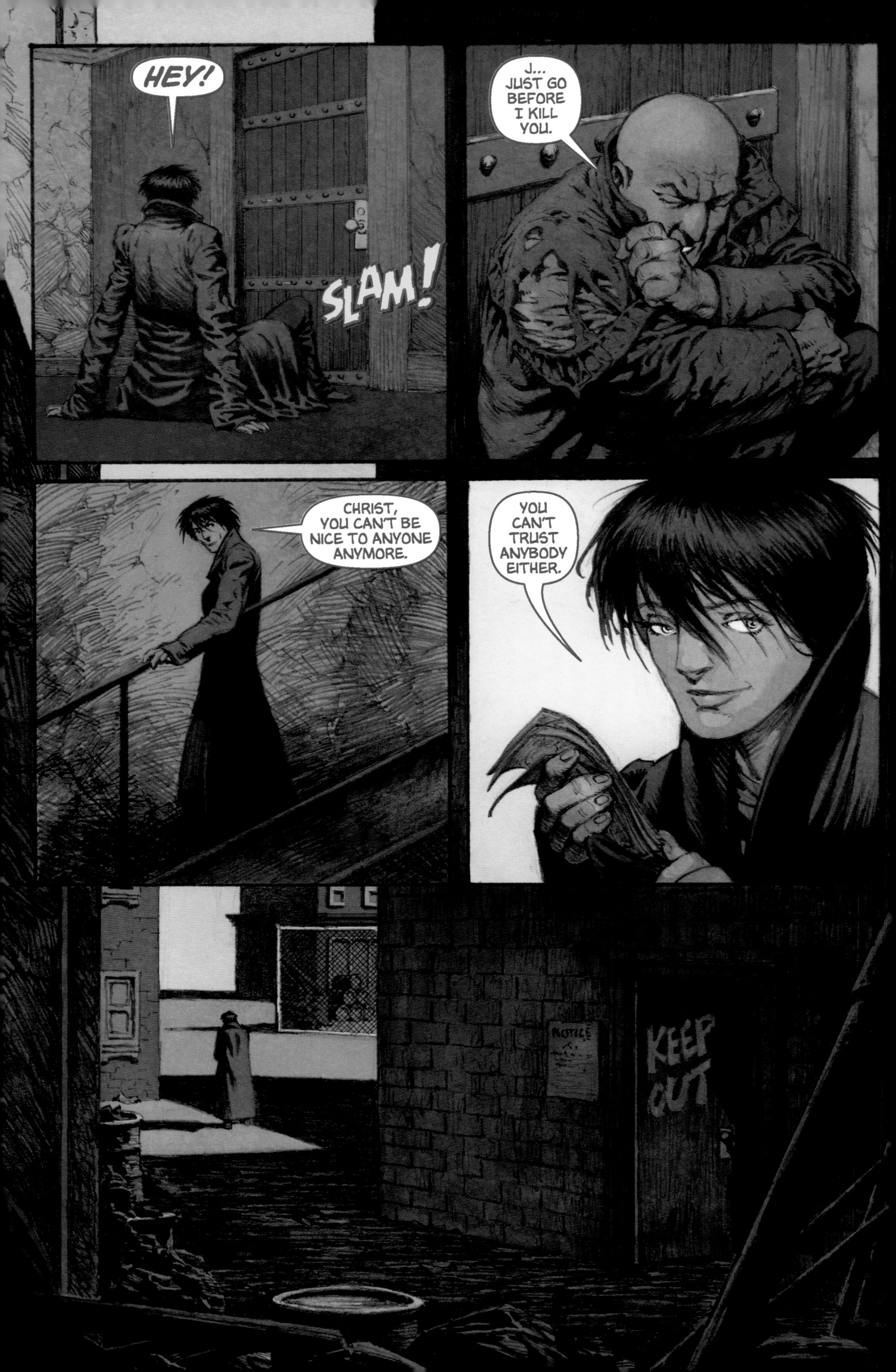
HEY!
SLAM!
J... JUST GO BEFORE I KILL YOU.
CHRIST, YOU CAN'T BE NICE TO ANYONE ANYMORE.
YOU CAN'T TRUST ANYBODY EITHER.
KEEP OUT

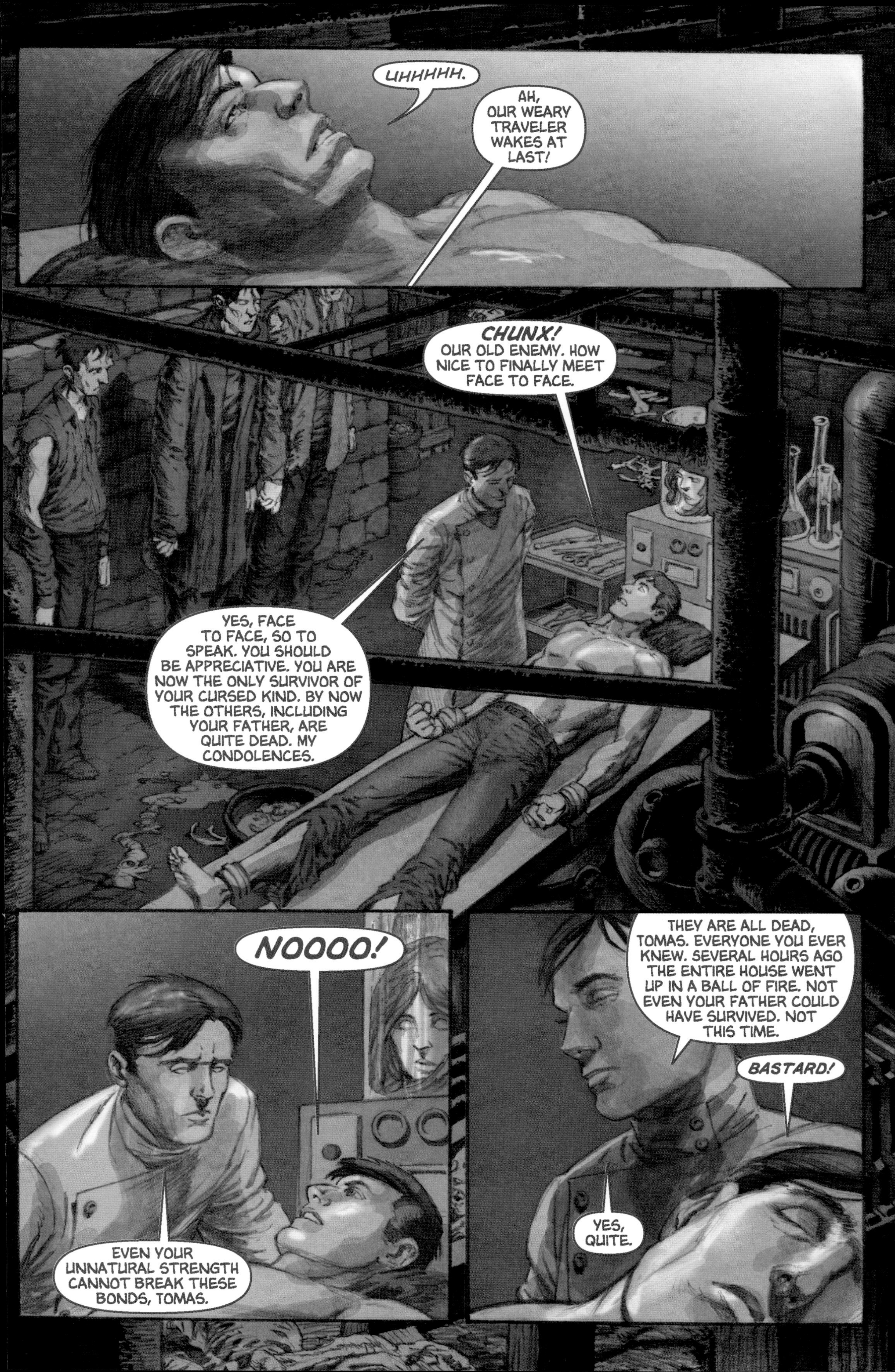
UHHHHH.
AH, OUR WEARY TRAVELER WAKES AT LAST!
CHUNX! OUR OLD ENEMY. HOW NICE TO FINALLY MEET FACE TO FACE.
YES, FACE TO FACE, SO TO SPEAK. YOU SHOULD BE APPRECIATIVE. YOU ARE NOW THE ONLY SURVIVOR OF YOUR CURSED KIND. BY NOW THE OTHERS, INCLUDING YOUR FATHER, ARE QUITE DEAD. MY CONDOLENCES.
NOOOO!
EVEN YOUR UNNATURAL STRENGTH CANNOT BREAK THESE BONDS, TOMAS.
THEY ARE ALL DEAD, TOMAS. EVERYONE YOU EVER KNEW. SEVERAL HOURS AGO THE ENTIRE HOUSE WENT UP IN A BALL OF FIRE. NOT EVEN YOUR FATHER COULD HAVE SURVIVED. NOT THIS TIME.
BASTARD!
YES, QUITE.

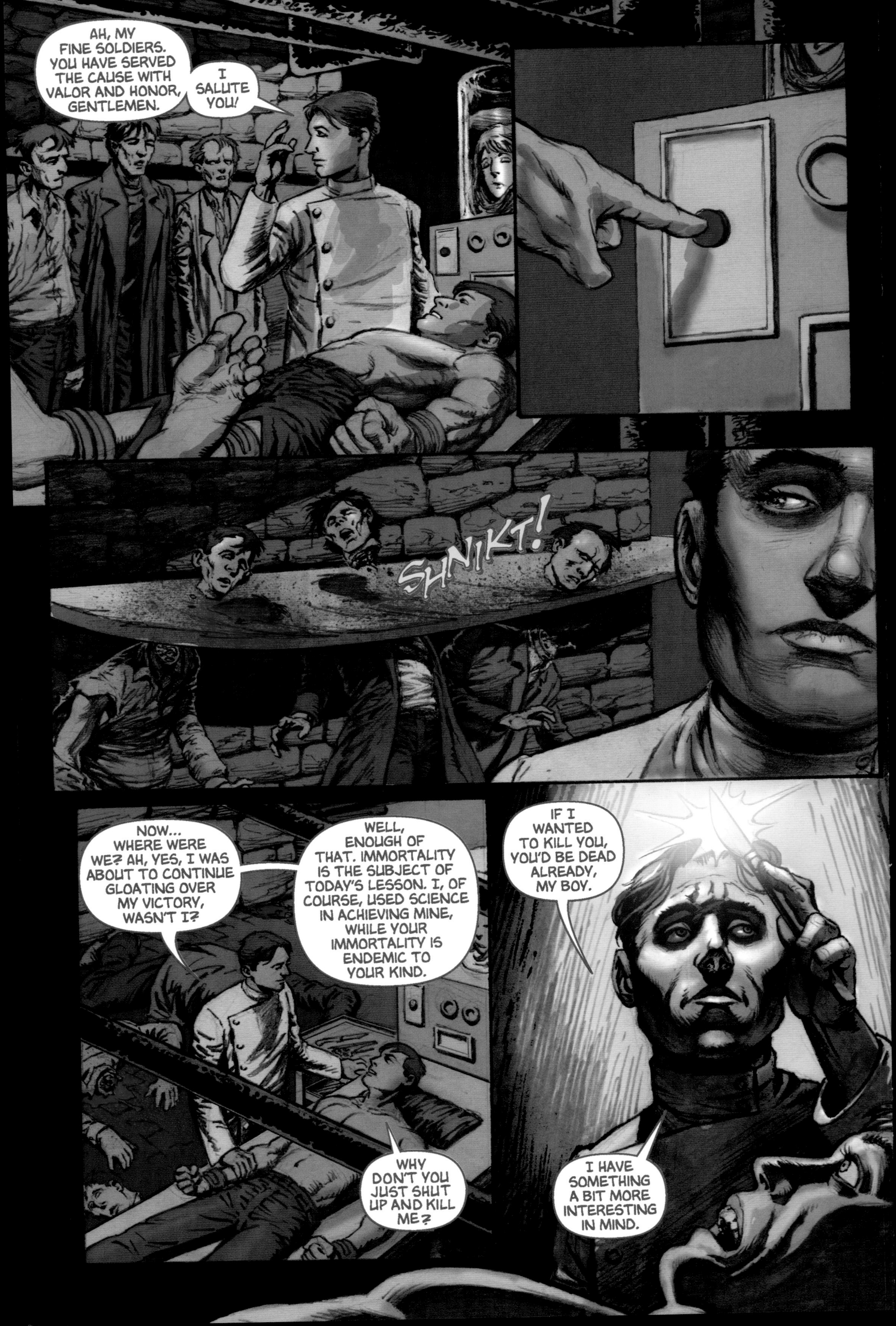
AH, MY FINE SOLDIERS. YOU HAVE SERVED THE CAUSE WITH VALOR AND HONOR, GENTLEMEN.
I SALUTE YOU!
SHNIKT!
NOW... WHERE WERE WE? AH, YES, I WAS ABOUT TO CONTINUE GLOATING OVER MY VICTORY, WASN'T I?
WELL, ENOUGH OF THAT. IMMORTALITY IS THE SUBJECT OF TODAY'S LESSON. I, OF COURSE, USED SCIENCE IN ACHIEVING MINE, WHILE YOUR IMMORTALITY IS ENDEMIC TO YOUR KIND.
WHY DON'T YOU JUST SHUT UP AND KILL ME?
IF I WANTED TO KILL YOU, YOU'D BE DEAD ALREADY, MY BOY.
I HAVE SOMETHING A BIT MORE INTERESTING IN MIND.

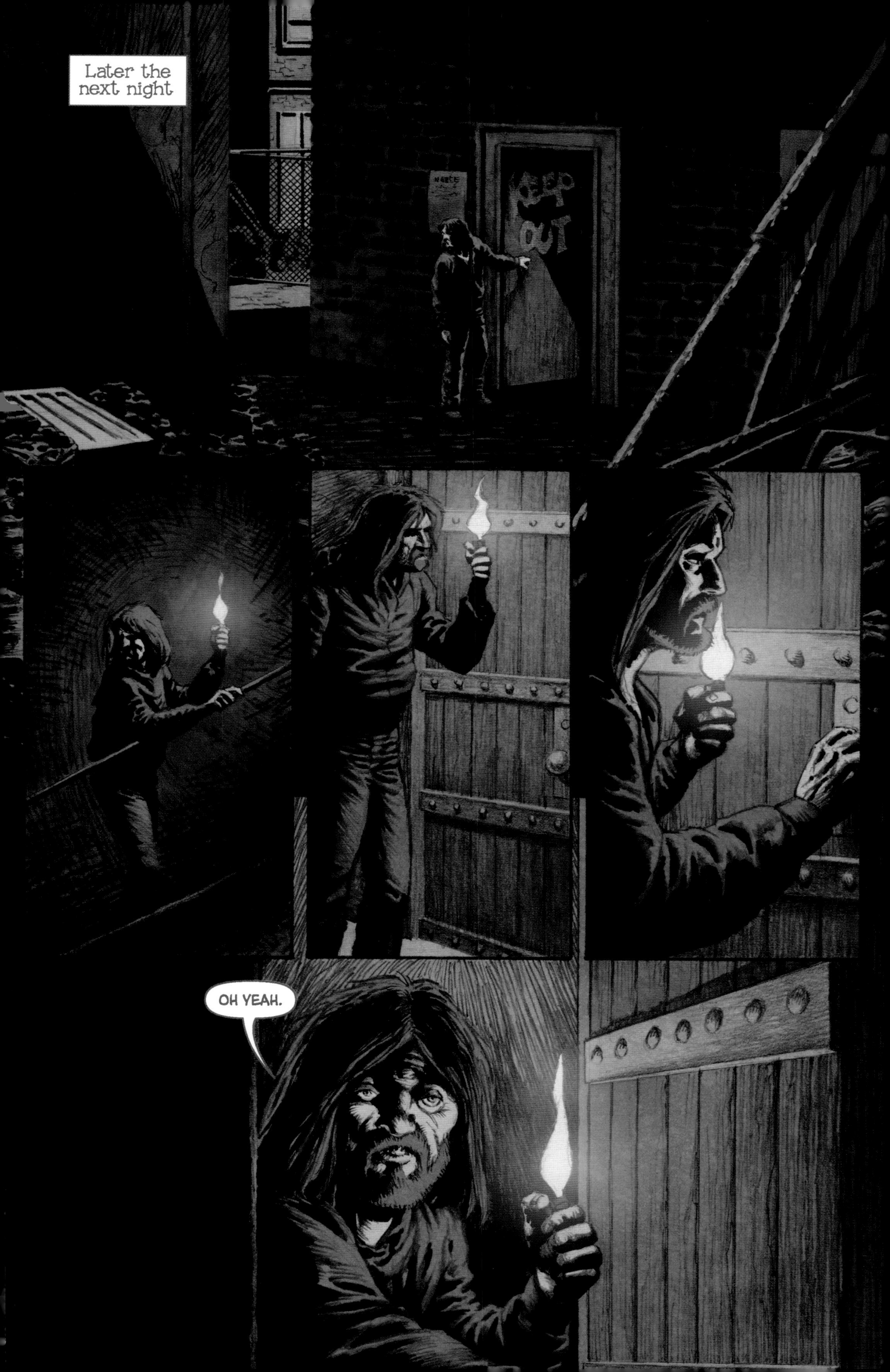
Later the next night
KEEP OUT
OH YEAH.

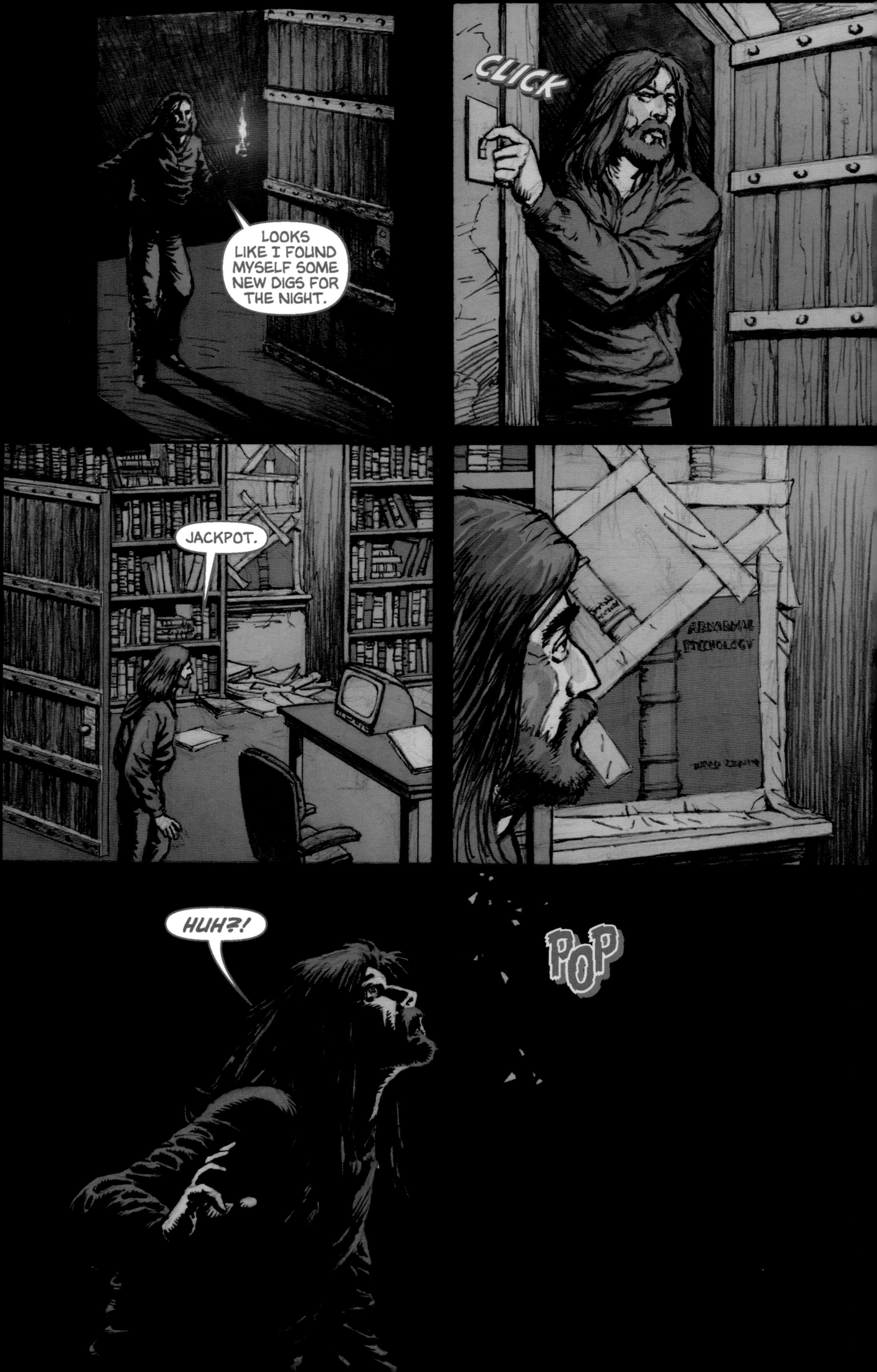
LOOKS LIKE I FOUND MYSELF SOME NEW DIGS FOR THE NIGHT.
CLICK
JACKPOT.
ABNORMAL PSYCHOLOGY
HUH?!
POP

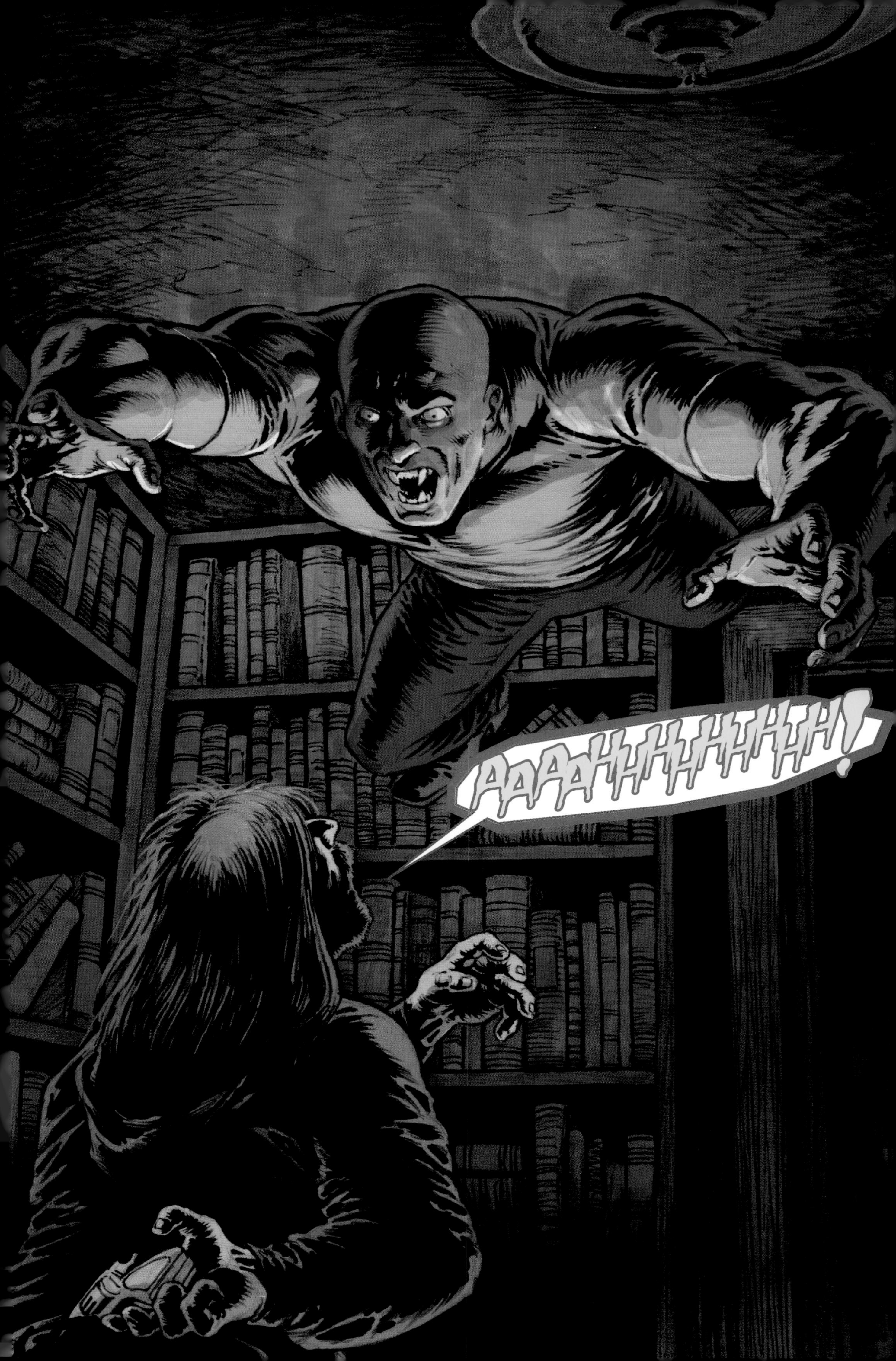
AAAAHHHHHHHHHH!

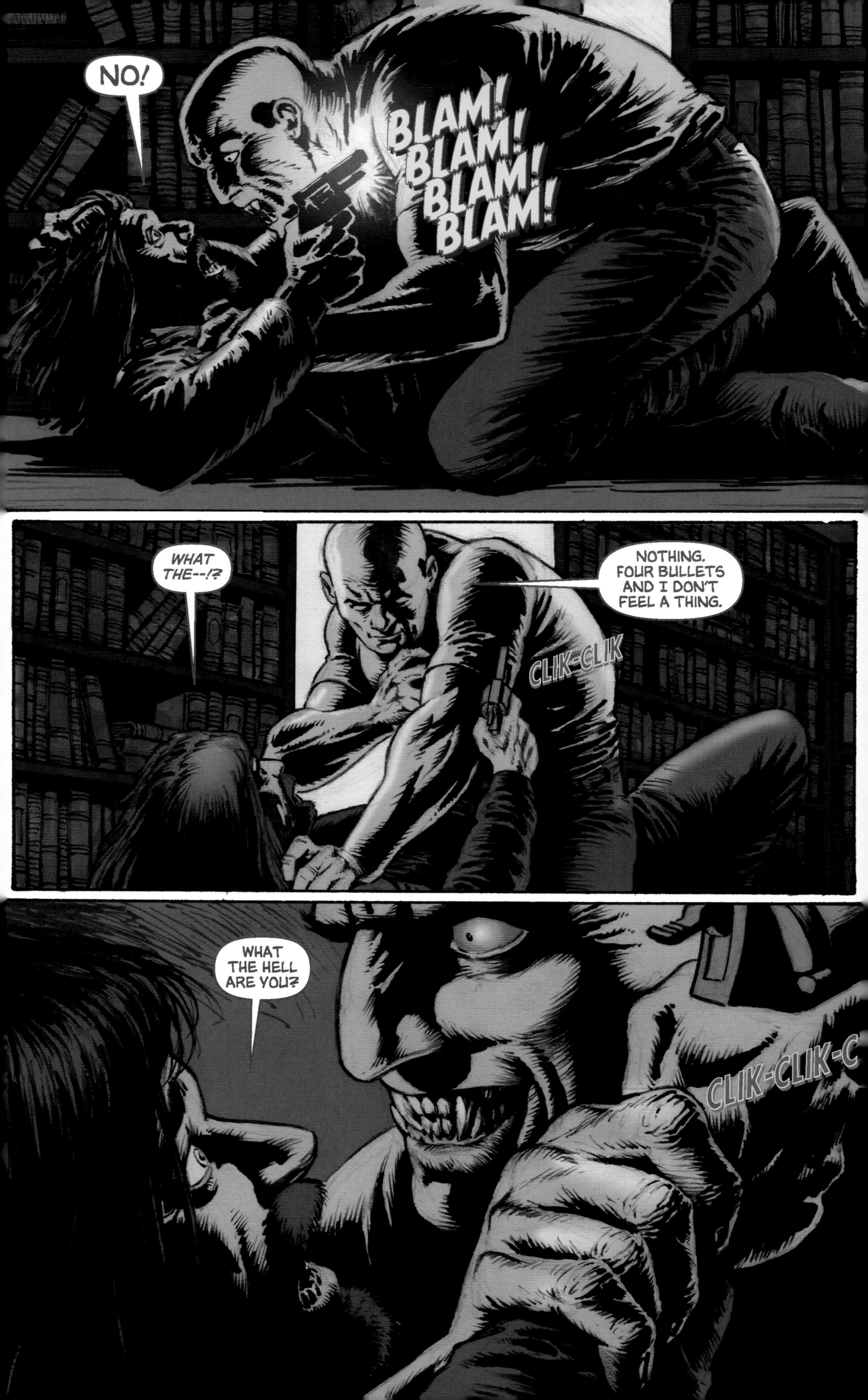
NO!
BLAM! BLAM! BLAM! BLAM!
WHAT THE--!?
NOTHING. FOUR BULLETS AND I DON'T FEEL A THING.
CLIK-CLIK
WHAT THE HELL ARE YOU?
CLIK-CLIK-C

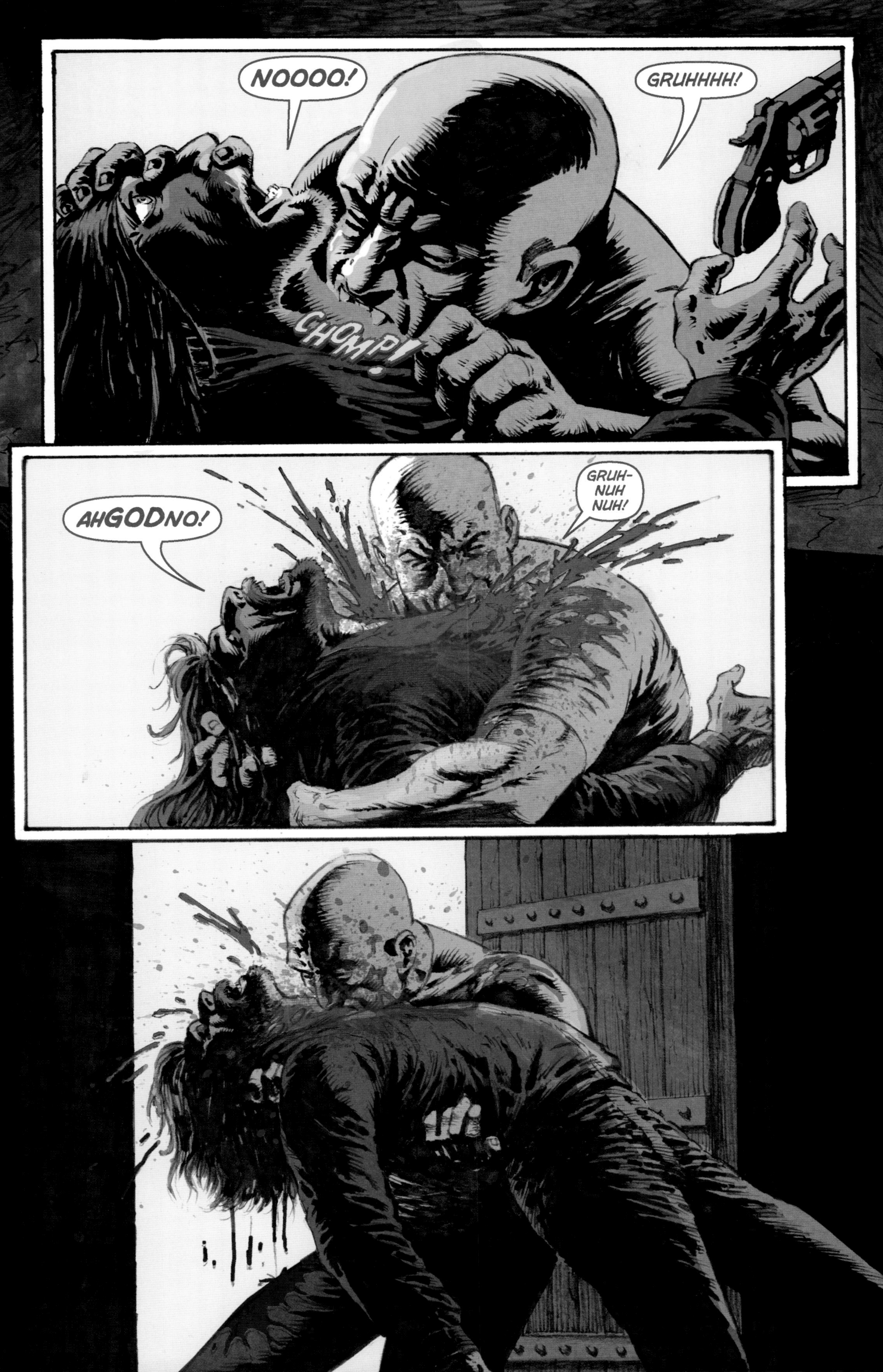
NOOOO!
GRUHHHH!
CHOMP!
AHGODNO!
GRUH-NUH NUH!

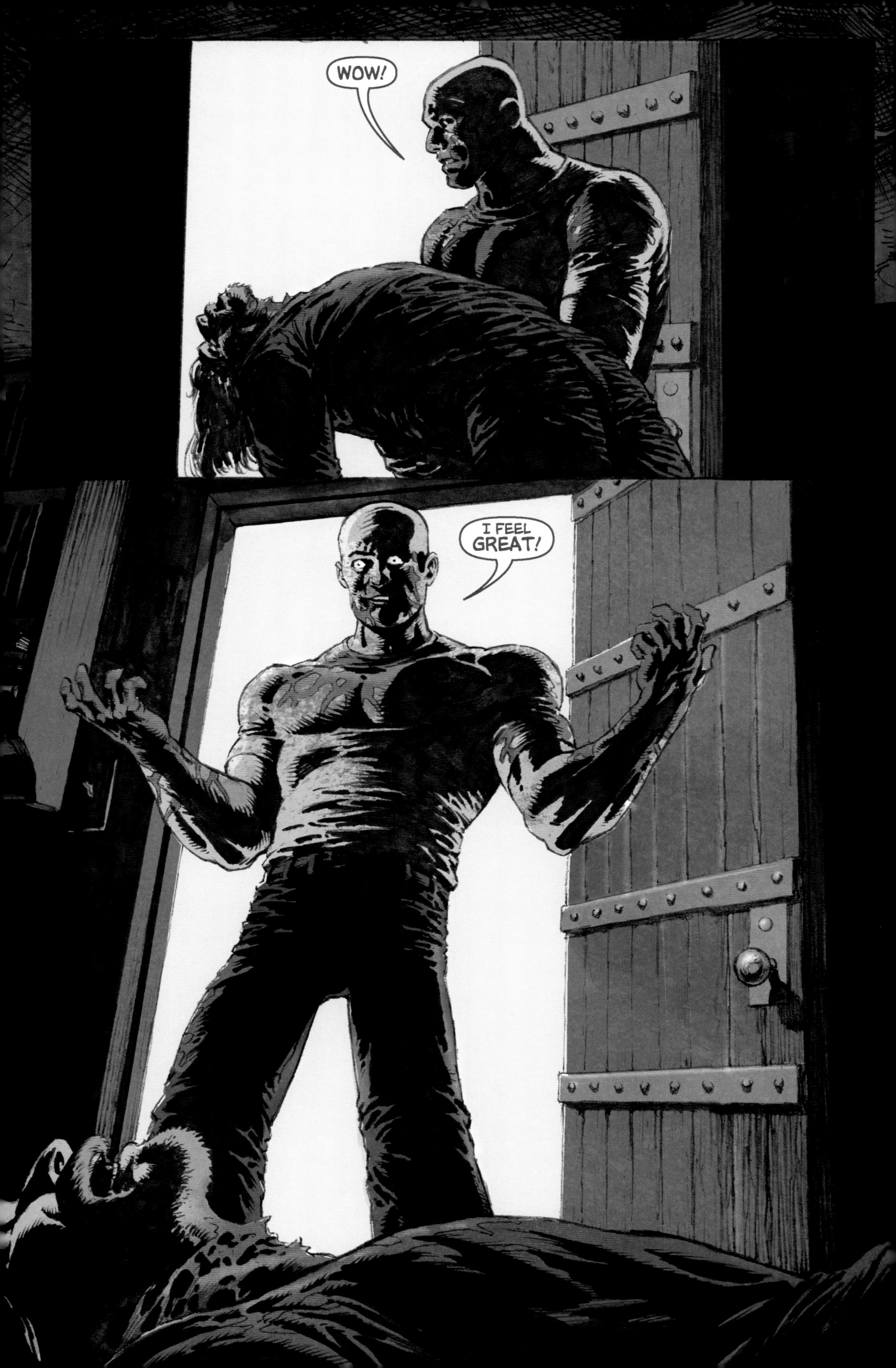
WOW!
I FEEL GREAT!

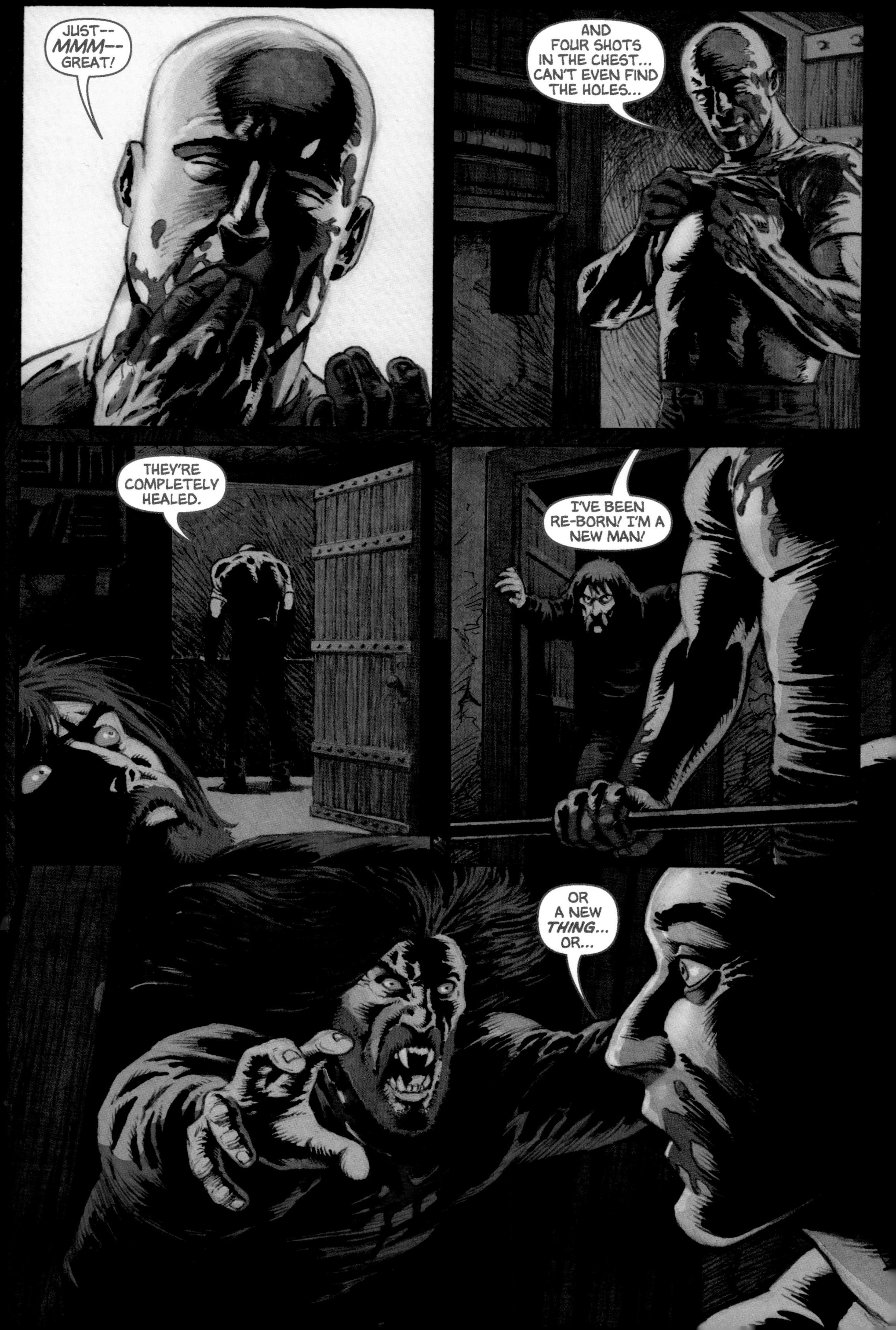
JUST--
MMM--
GREAT!
AND FOUR SHOTS IN THE CHEST... CAN'T EVEN FIND THE HOLES...
THEY'RE COMPLETELY HEALED.
I'VE BEEN RE-BORN! I'M A NEW MAN!
OR A NEW *THING*... OR...

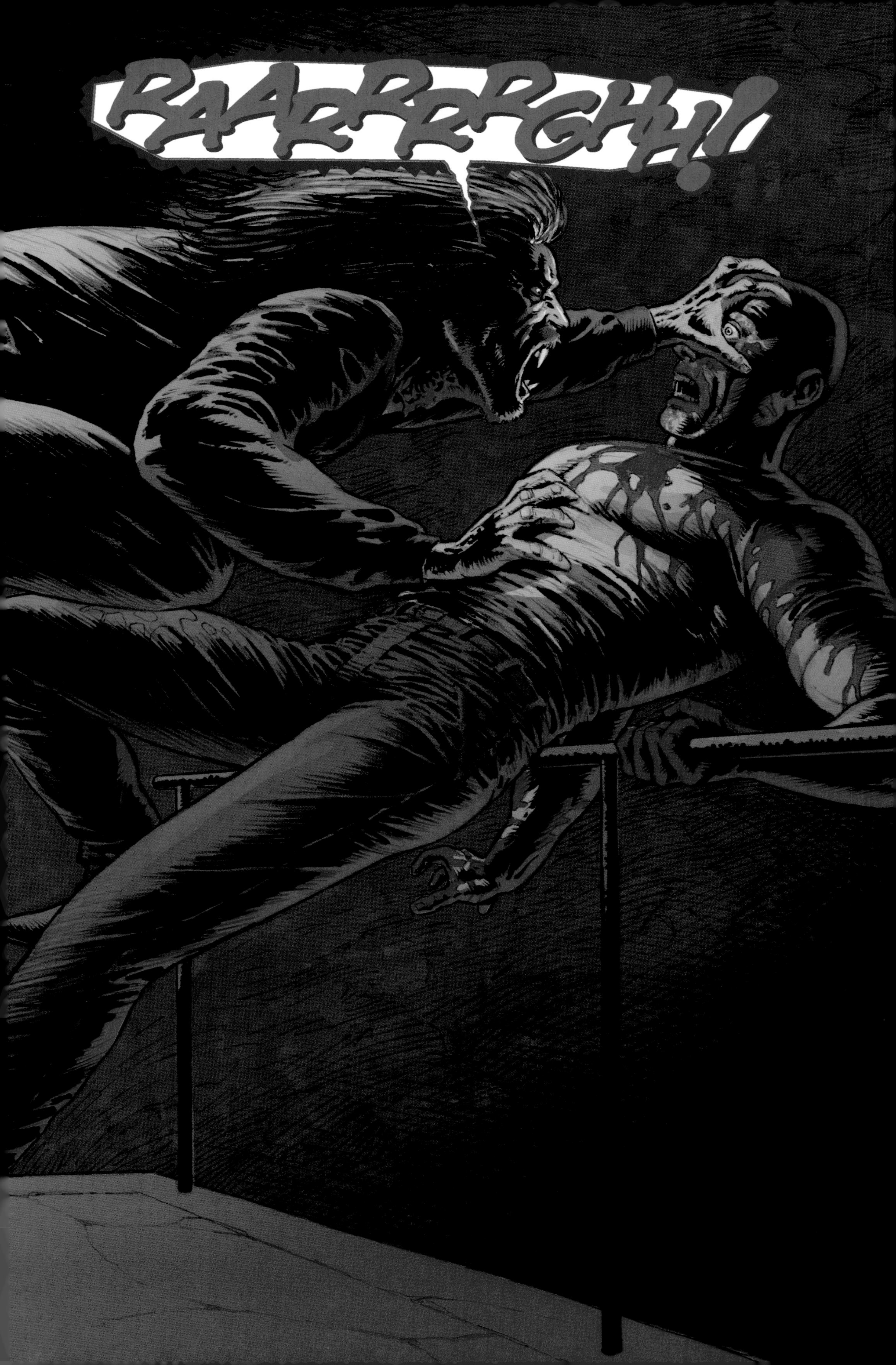
BAARRRRGHH!!

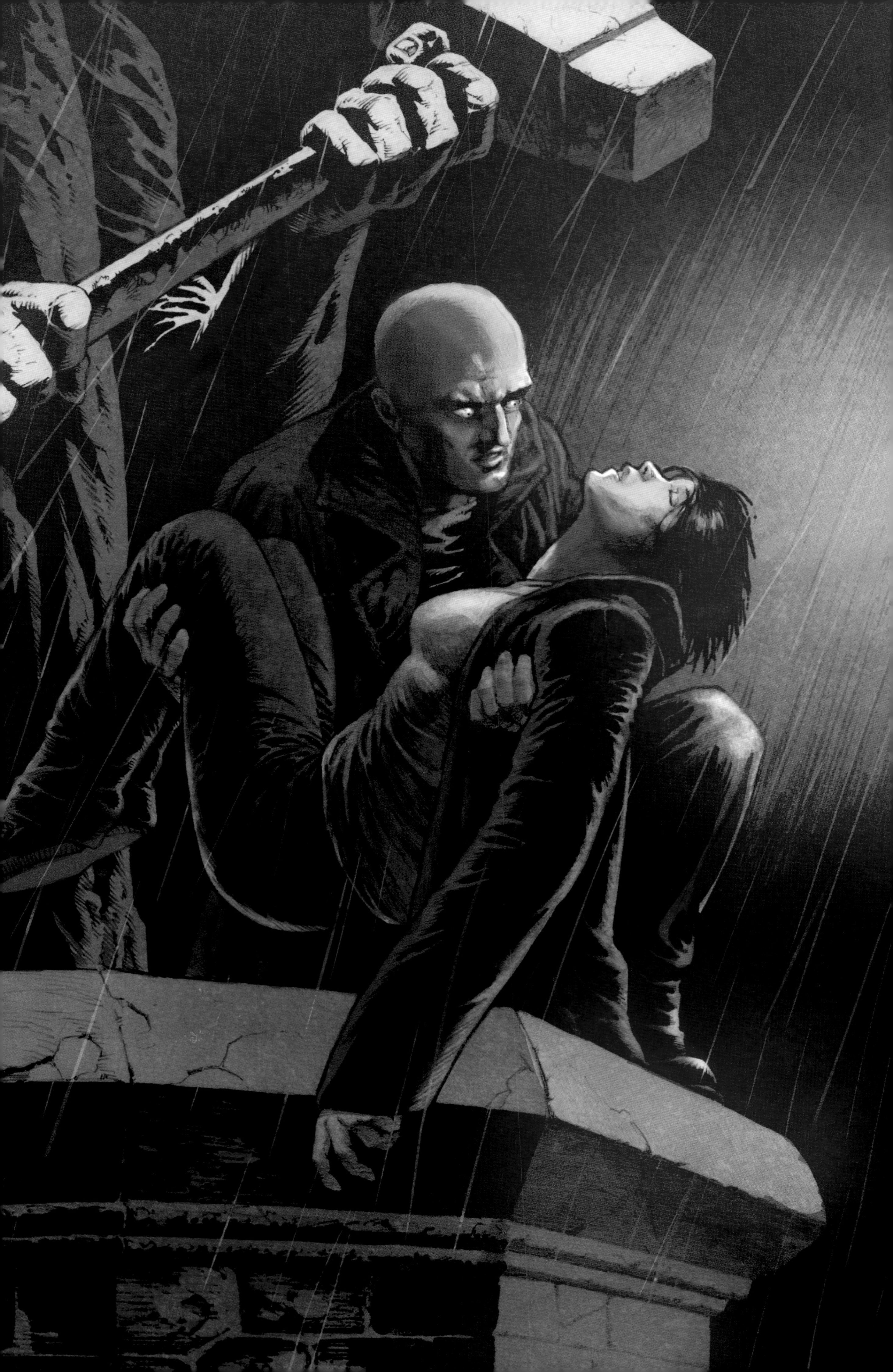

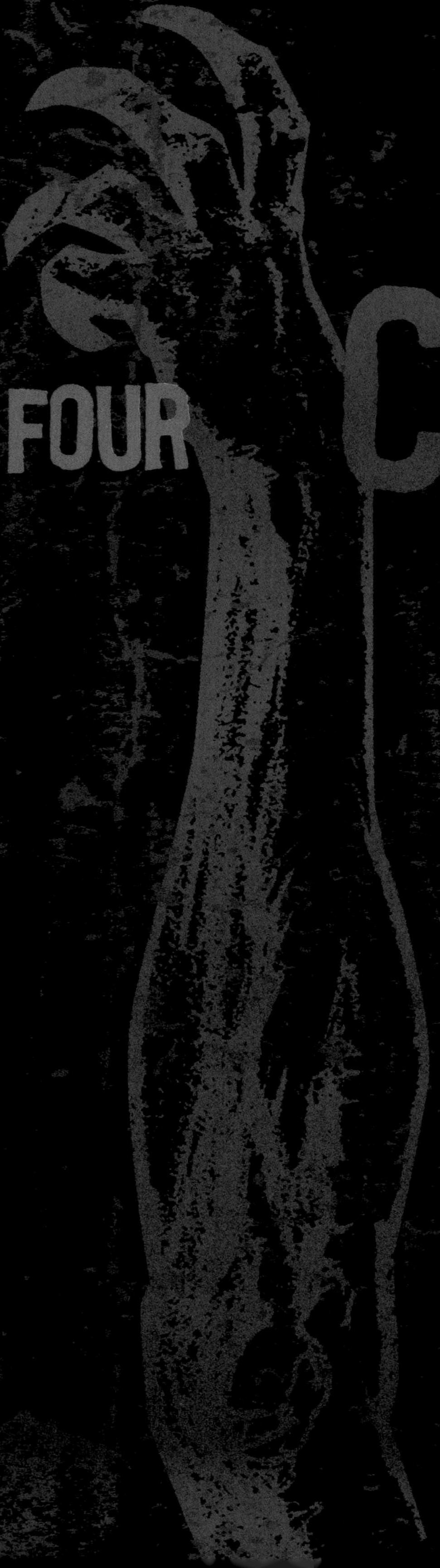

CHAPTER FOUR

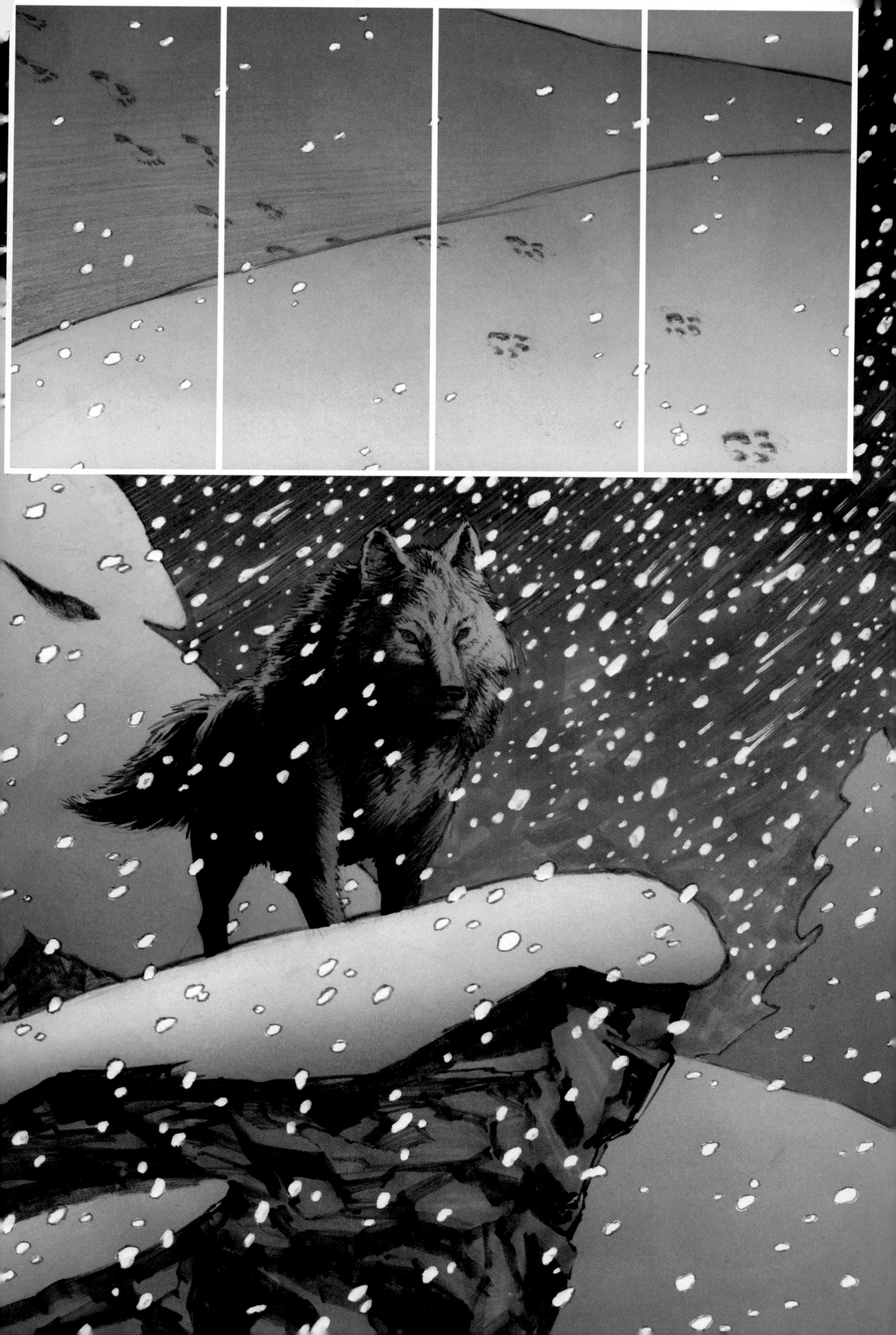

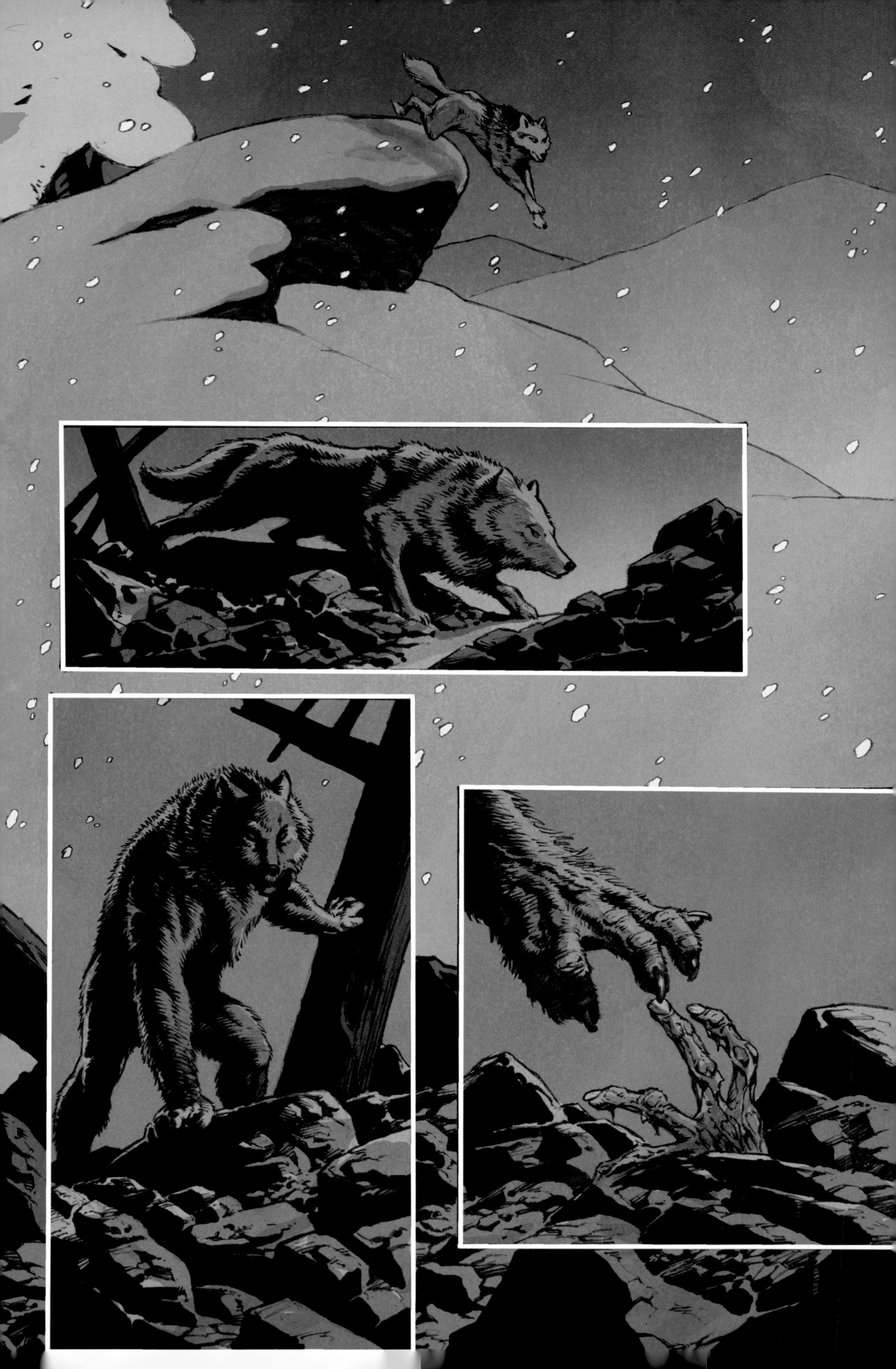

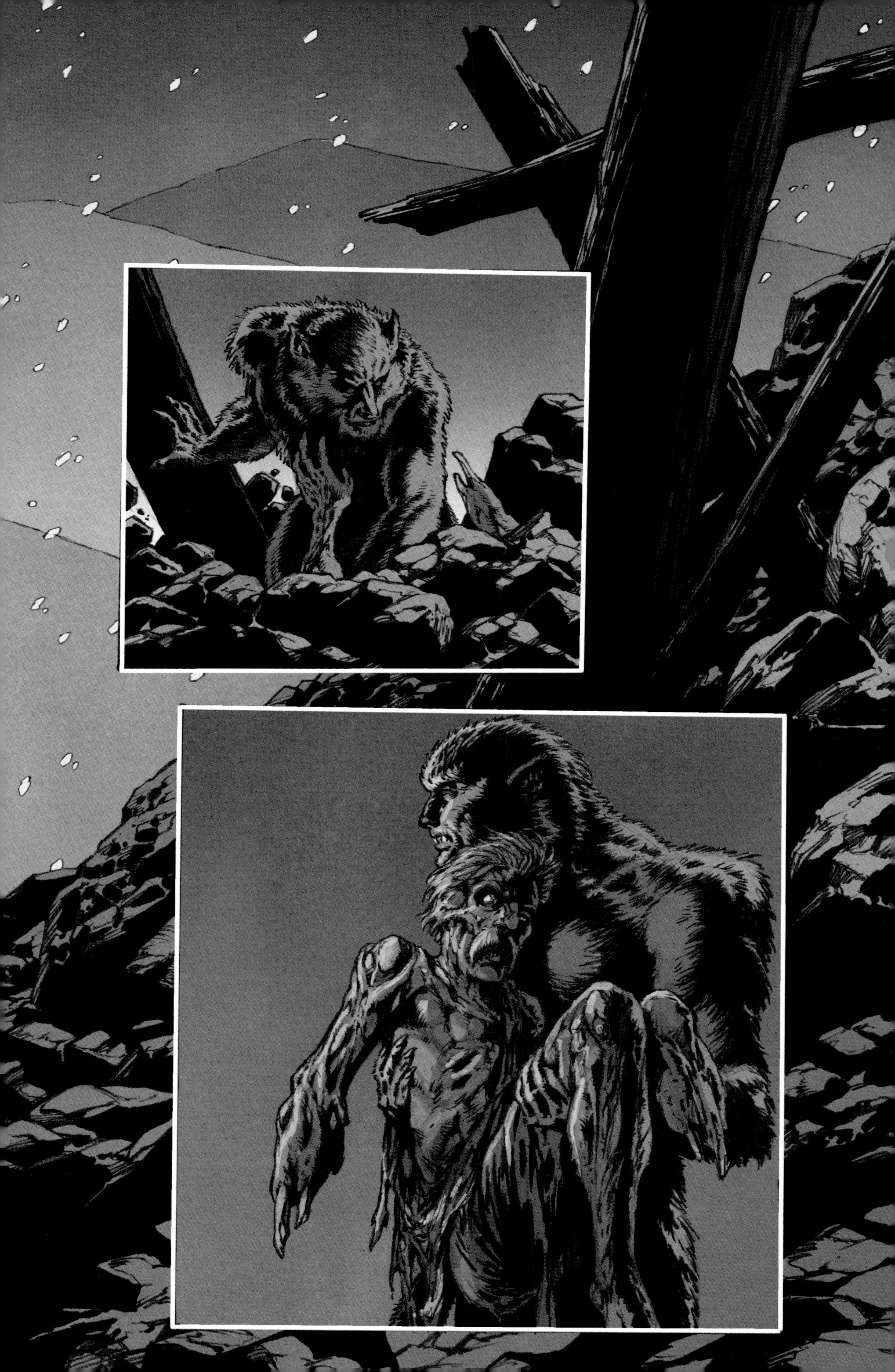

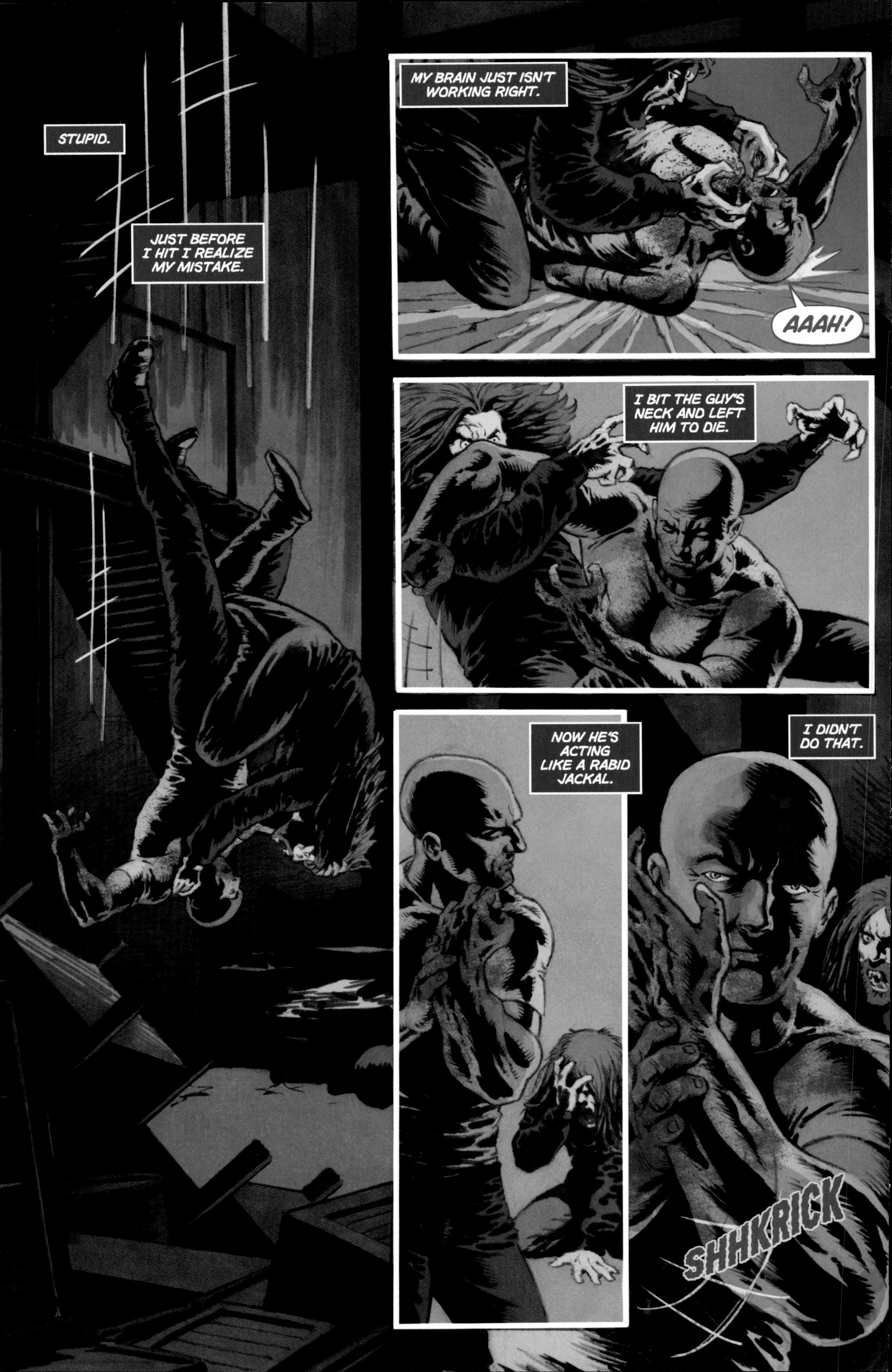

STUPID.
JUST BEFORE I HIT I REALIZE MY MISTAKE.
MY BRAIN JUST ISN'T WORKING RIGHT.
AAAH!
I BIT THE GUY'S NECK AND LEFT HIM TO DIE.
NOW HE'S ACTING LIKE A RABID JACKAL.
I DIDN'T DO THAT.
SHHKRICK

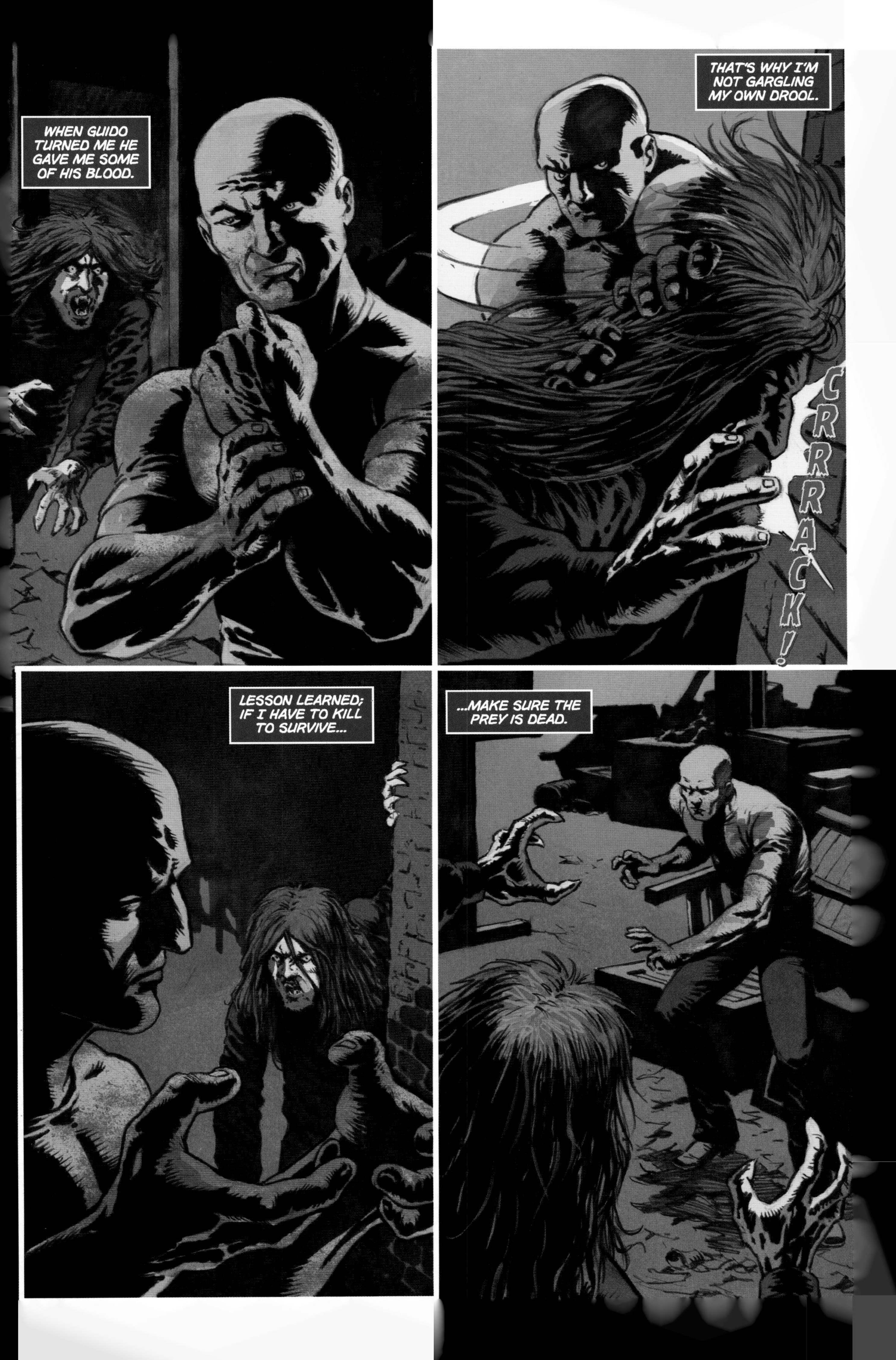
WHEN GUIDO TURNED ME HE GAVE ME SOME OF HIS BLOOD.
THAT'S WHY I'M NOT GARGLING MY OWN DROOL.
CRRRACK!
LESSON LEARNED; IF I HAVE TO KILL TO SURVIVE...
...MAKE SURE THE PREY IS DEAD.

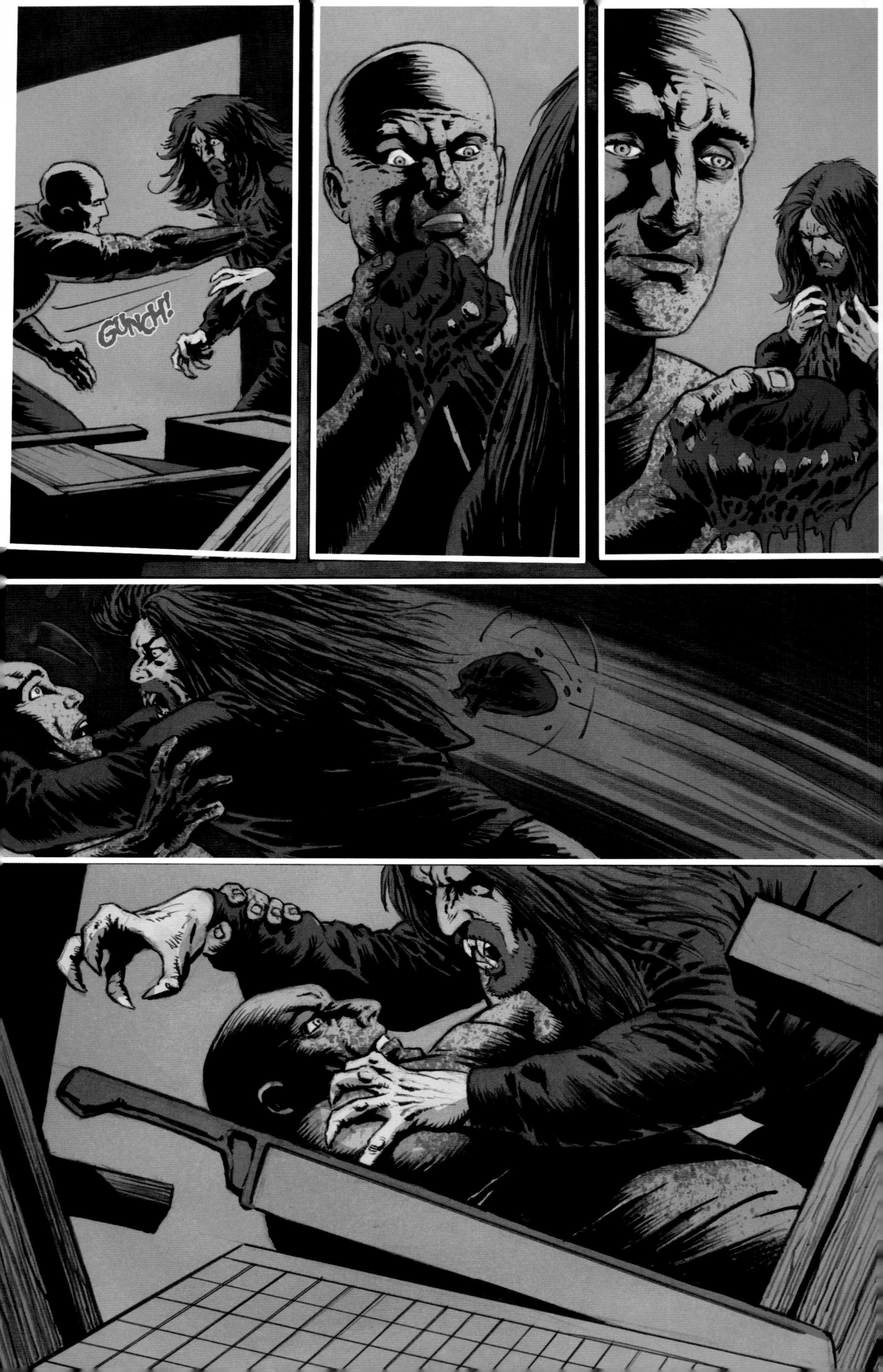
GUNCH!

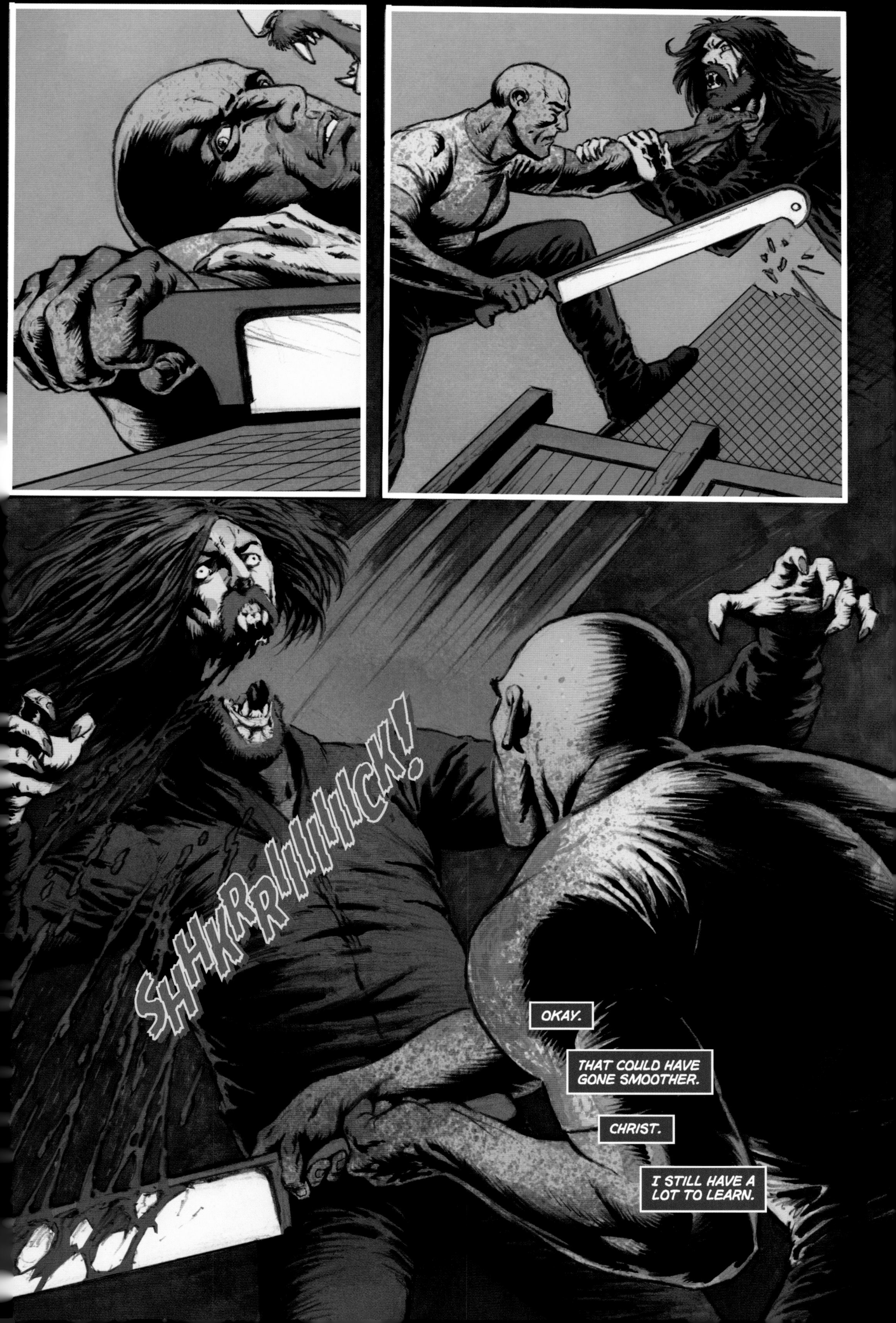
SHKRRIIIIIIICK!
OKAY.
THAT COULD HAVE GONE SMOOTHER.
CHRIST.
I STILL HAVE A LOT TO LEARN.

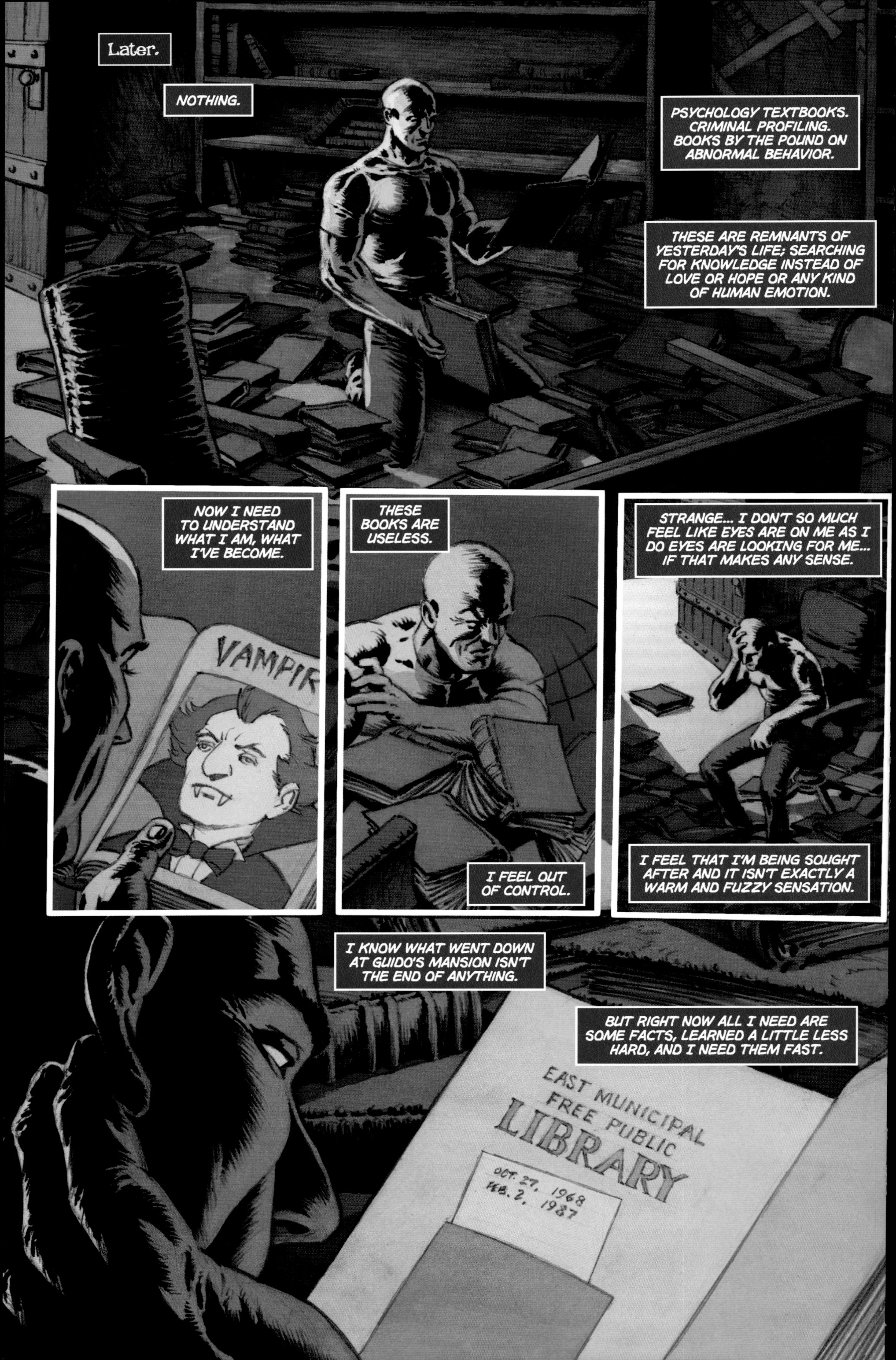
Later.
NOTHING.
PSYCHOLOGY TEXTBOOKS. CRIMINAL PROFILING. BOOKS BY THE POUND ON ABNORMAL BEHAVIOR.
THESE ARE REMNANTS OF YESTERDAY'S LIFE; SEARCHING FOR KNOWLEDGE INSTEAD OF LOVE OR HOPE OR ANY KIND OF HUMAN EMOTION.
NOW I NEED TO UNDERSTAND WHAT I AM, WHAT I'VE BECOME.
VAMPIR
THESE BOOKS ARE USELESS.
I FEEL OUT OF CONTROL.
STRANGE... I DON'T SO MUCH FEEL LIKE EYES ARE ON ME AS I DO EYES ARE LOOKING FOR ME... IF THAT MAKES ANY SENSE.
I FEEL THAT I'M BEING SOUGHT AFTER AND IT ISN'T EXACTLY A WARM AND FUZZY SENSATION.
I KNOW WHAT WENT DOWN AT GUIDO'S MANSION ISN'T THE END OF ANYTHING.
BUT RIGHT NOW ALL I NEED ARE SOME FACTS, LEARNED A LITTLE LESS HARD, AND I NEED THEM FAST.
EAST MUNICIPAL FREE PUBLIC LIBRARY
OCT. 27, 1968
FEB. 2, 1987

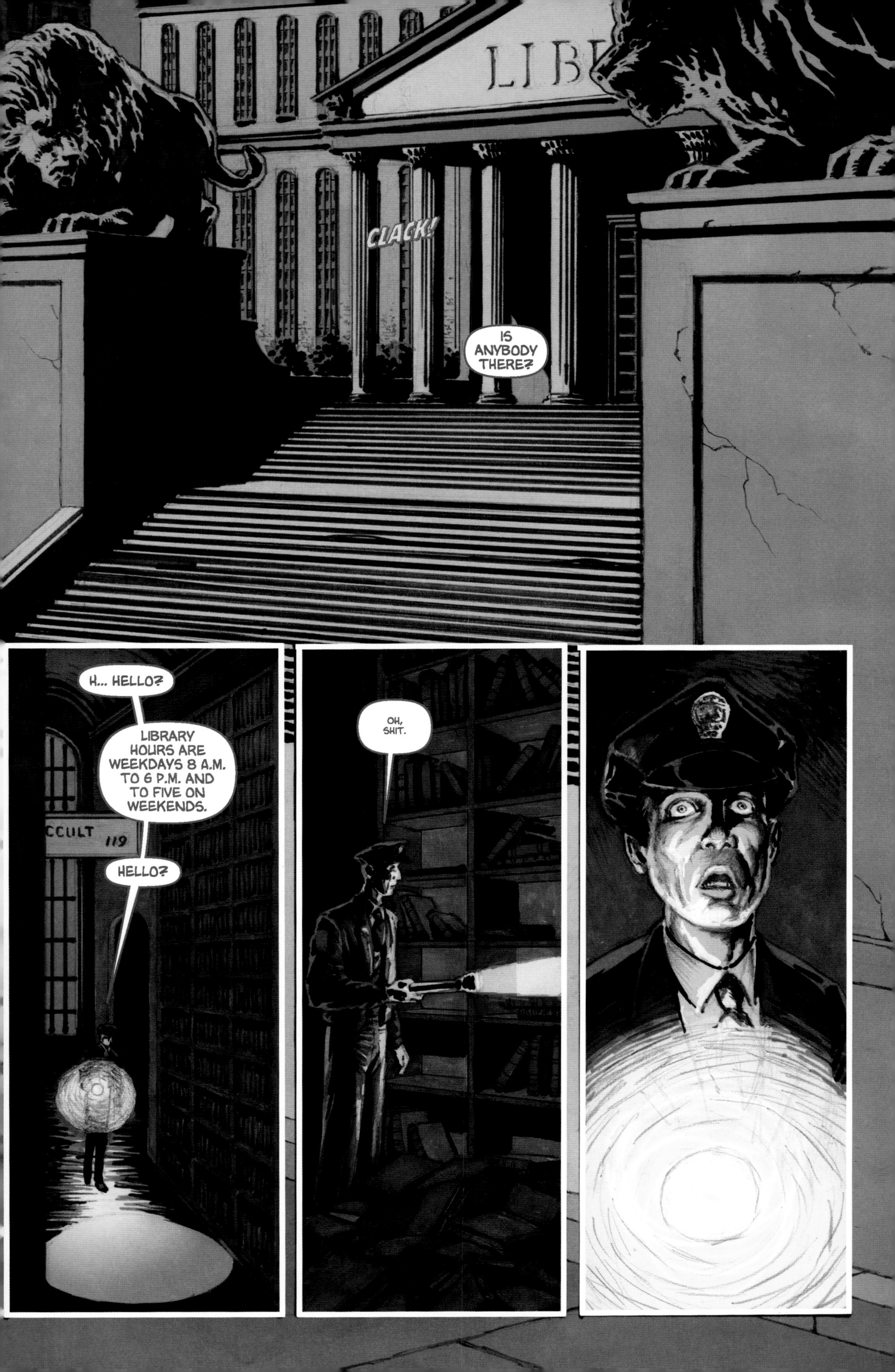
LIB
CLACK!
IS ANYBODY THERE?
H... HELLO?
LIBRARY HOURS ARE WEEKDAYS 8 A.M. TO 6 P.M. AND TO FIVE ON WEEKENDS.
CCULT 119
HELLO?
OH, SHIT.

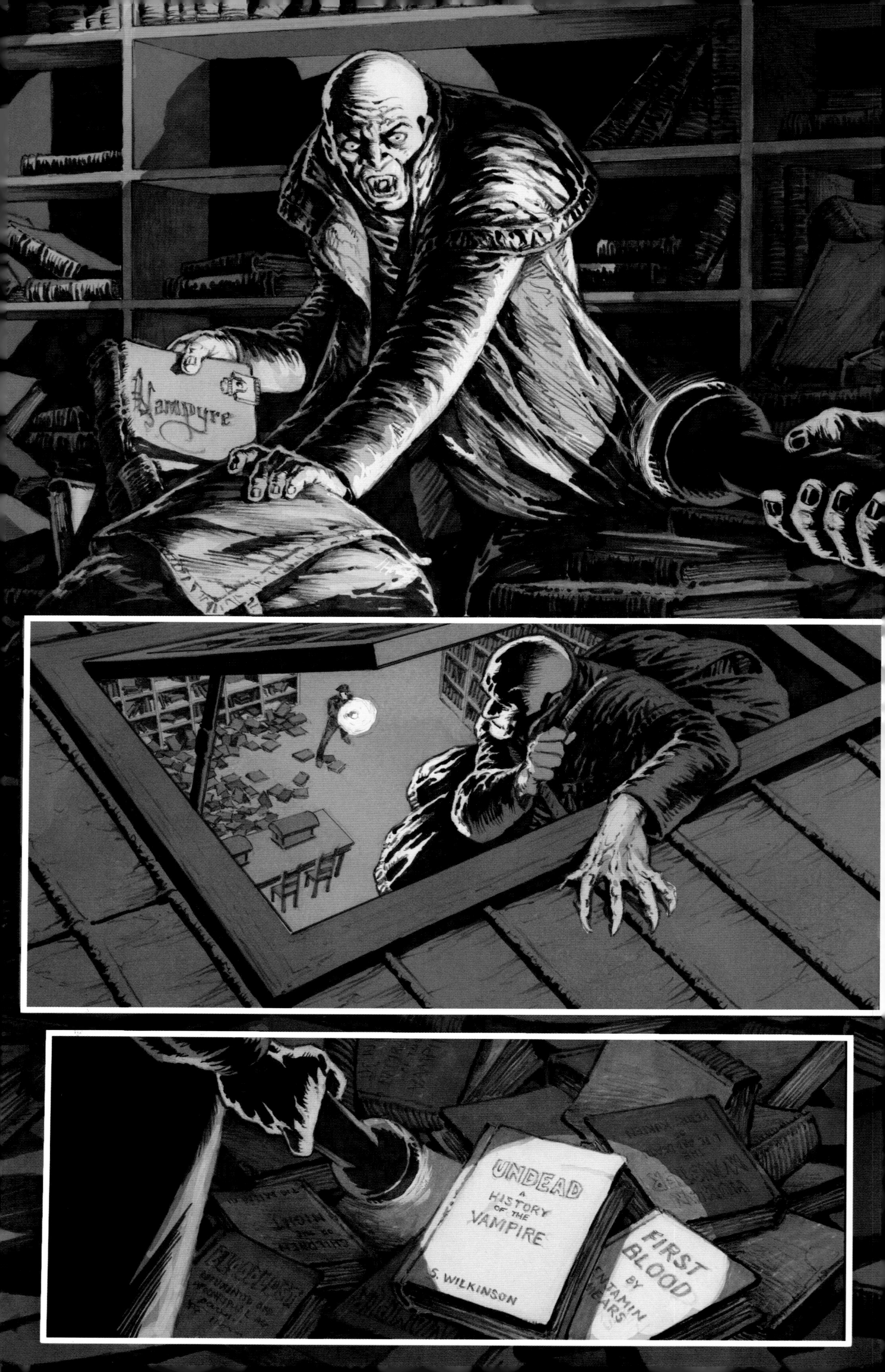
Vampyre
UNDEAD
A HISTORY OF THE VAMPIRE
S. WILKINSON
FIRST BLOOD
BY

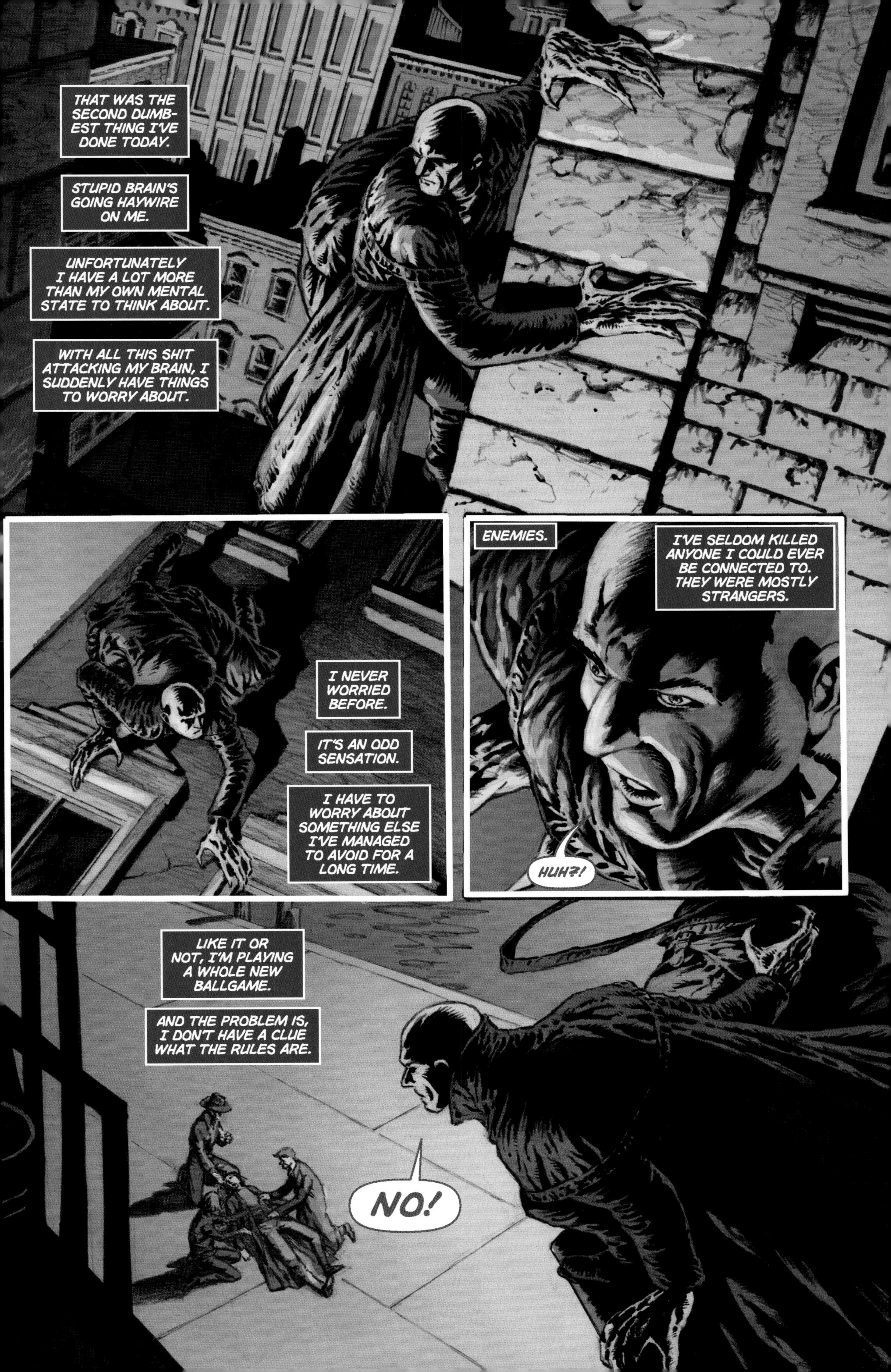
THAT WAS THE SECOND DUMB-EST THING I'VE DONE TODAY.
STUPID BRAIN'S GOING HAYWIRE ON ME.
UNFORTUNATELY I HAVE A LOT MORE THAN MY OWN MENTAL STATE TO THINK ABOUT.
WITH ALL THIS SHIT ATTACKING MY BRAIN, I SUDDENLY HAVE THINGS TO WORRY ABOUT.
I NEVER WORRIED BEFORE.
IT'S AN ODD SENSATION.
I HAVE TO WORRY ABOUT SOMETHING ELSE I'VE MANAGED TO AVOID FOR A LONG TIME.
ENEMIES.
I'VE SELDOM KILLED ANYONE I COULD EVER BE CONNECTED TO. THEY WERE MOSTLY STRANGERS.
HUH?!
LIKE IT OR NOT, I'M PLAYING A WHOLE NEW BALLGAME.
AND THE PROBLEM IS, I DON'T HAVE A CLUE WHAT THE RULES ARE.
NO!

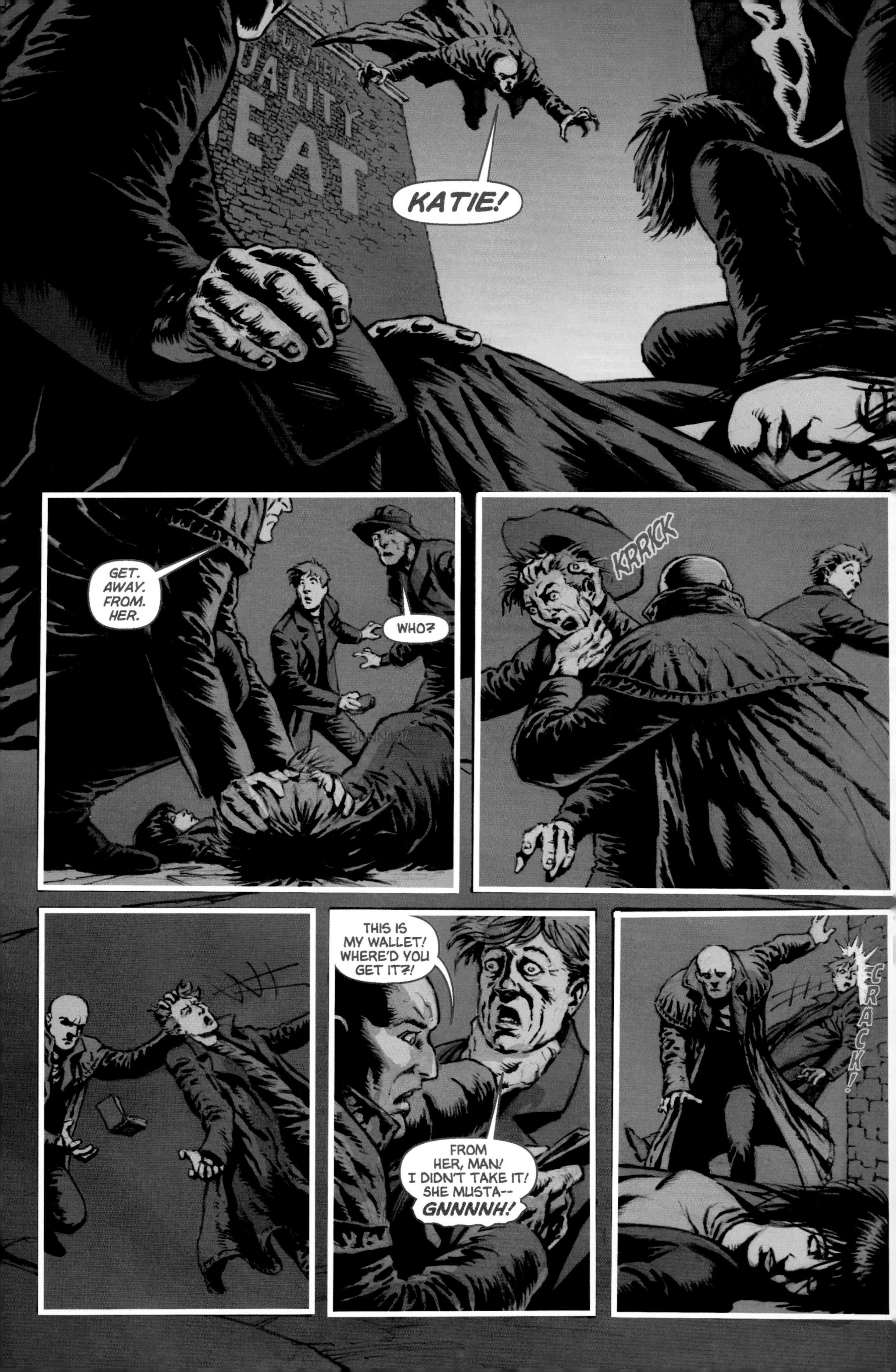
KATIE!
GET. AWAY. FROM. HER.
WHO?
KRRICK
THIS IS MY WALLET! WHERE'D YOU GET IT?!
FROM HER, MAN! I DIDN'T TAKE IT! SHE MUSTA-- GNNNNH!
CRACK!

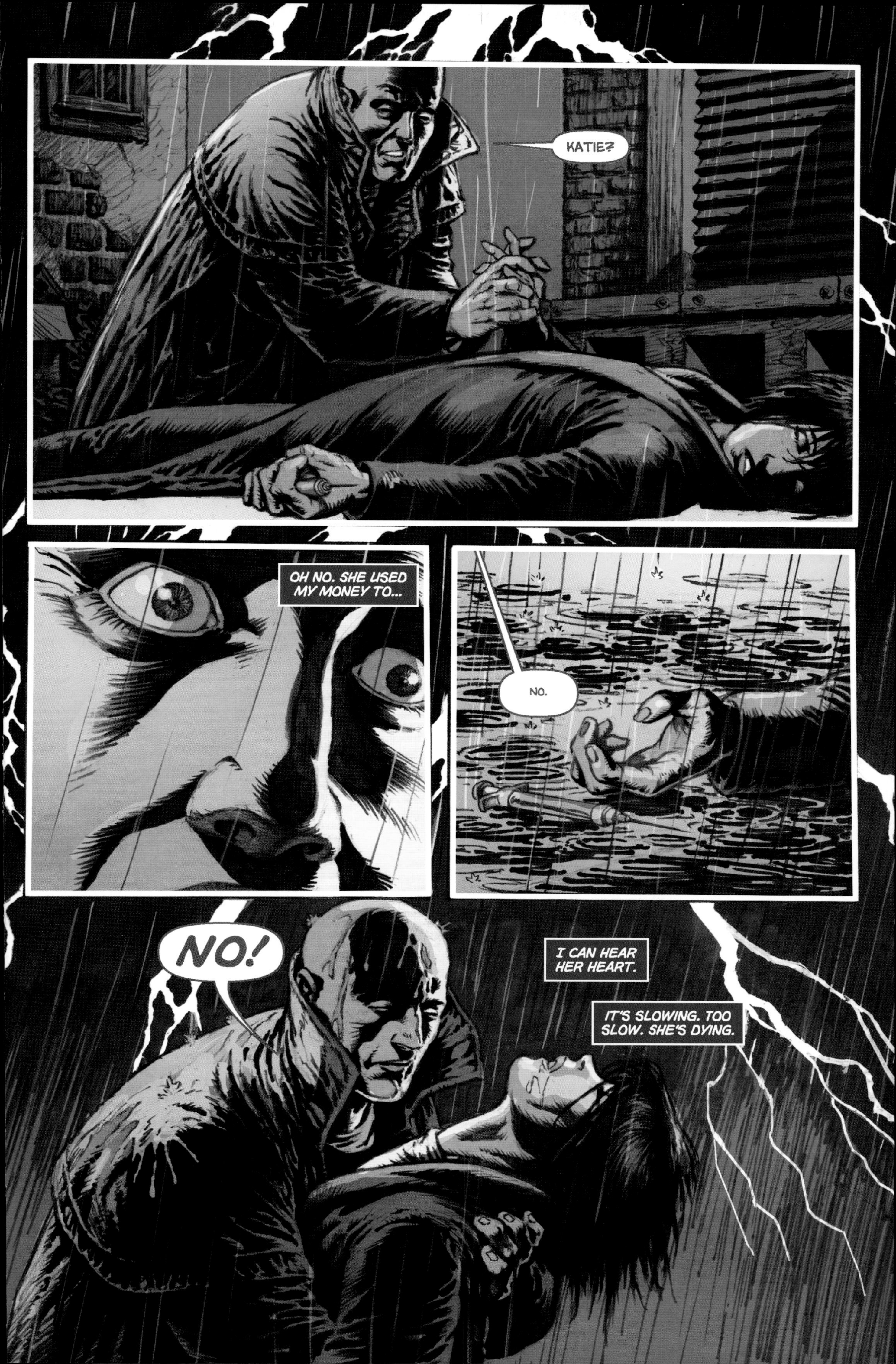
KATIE?
OH NO. SHE USED MY MONEY TO...
NO.
NO!
I CAN HEAR HER HEART.
IT'S SLOWING. TOO SLOW. SHE'S DYING.

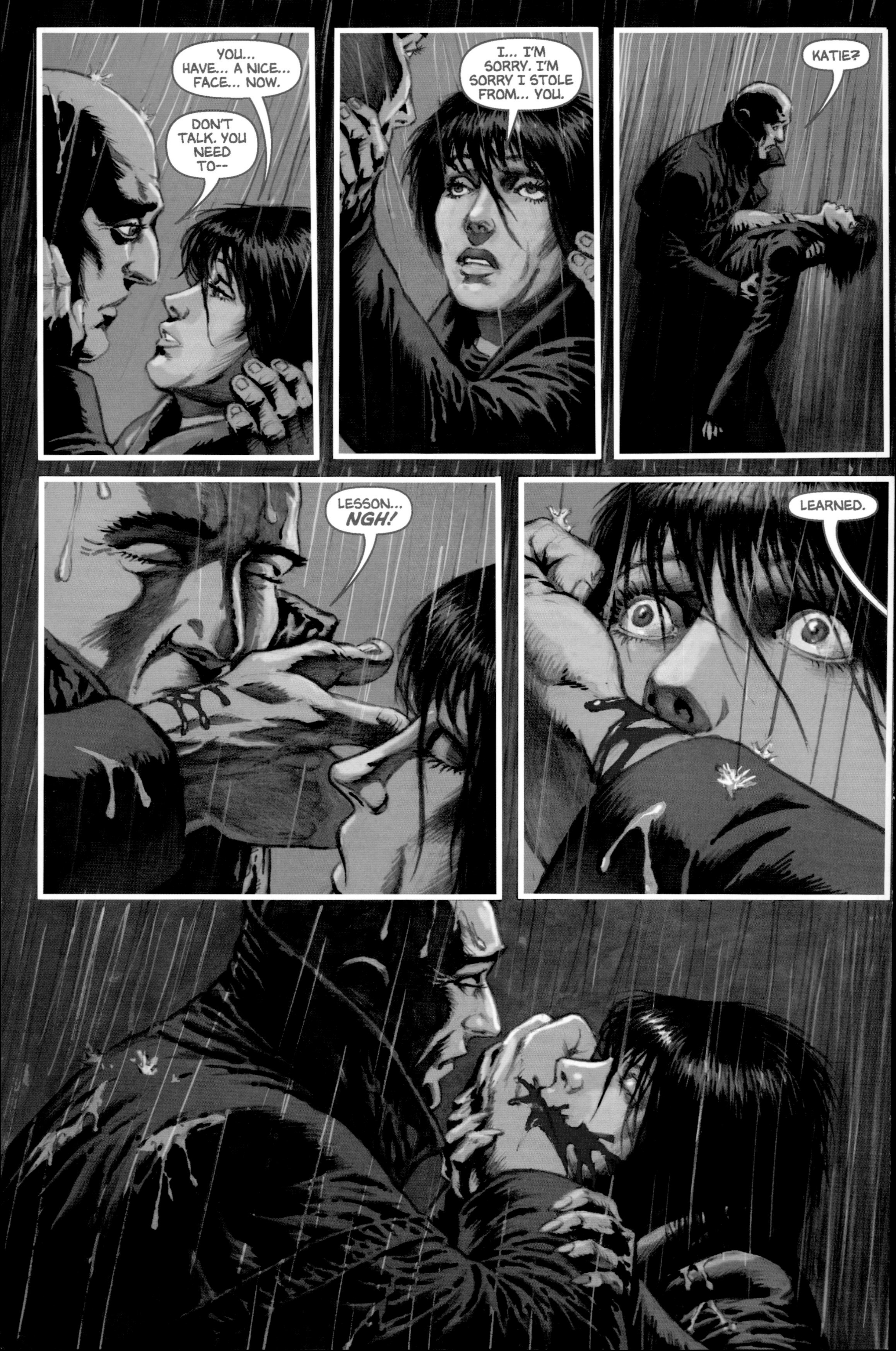
YOU... HAVE... A NICE... FACE... NOW.
DON'T TALK. YOU NEED TO--
I... I'M SORRY. I'M SORRY I STOLE FROM... YOU.
KATIE?
LESSON... **NGH!**
LEARNED.

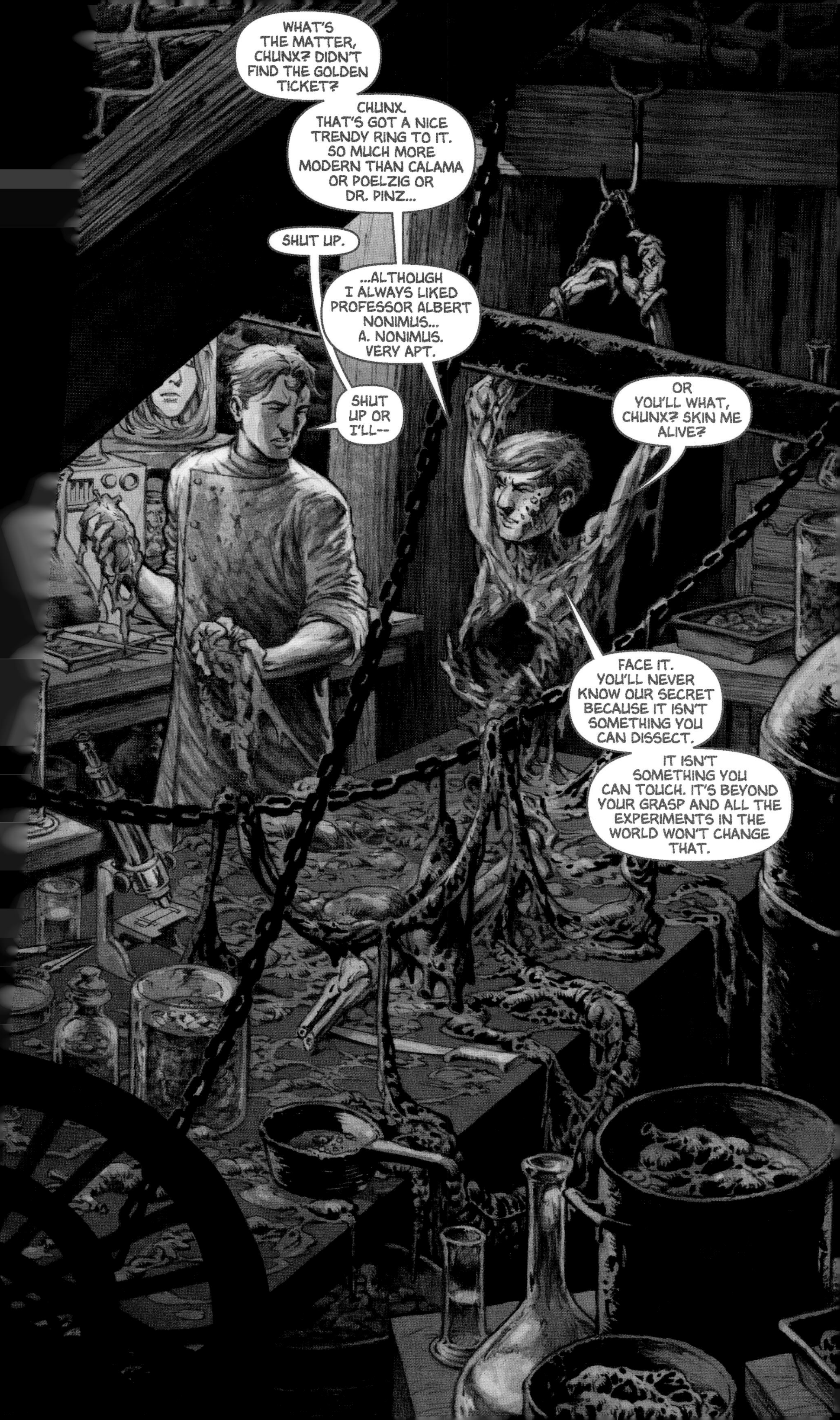
WHAT'S THE MATTER, CHUNX? DIDN'T FIND THE GOLDEN TICKET?
CHUNX. THAT'S GOT A NICE TRENDY RING TO IT. SO MUCH MORE MODERN THAN CALAMA OR POELZIG OR DR. PINZ...
SHUT UP.
...ALTHOUGH I ALWAYS LIKED PROFESSOR ALBERT NONIMUS... A. NONIMUS. VERY APT.
SHUT UP OR I'LL--
OR YOU'LL WHAT, CHUNX? SKIN ME ALIVE?
FACE IT. YOU'LL NEVER KNOW OUR SECRET BECAUSE IT ISN'T SOMETHING YOU CAN DISSECT.
IT ISN'T SOMETHING YOU CAN TOUCH. IT'S BEYOND YOUR GRASP AND ALL THE EXPERIMENTS IN THE WORLD WON'T CHANGE THAT.

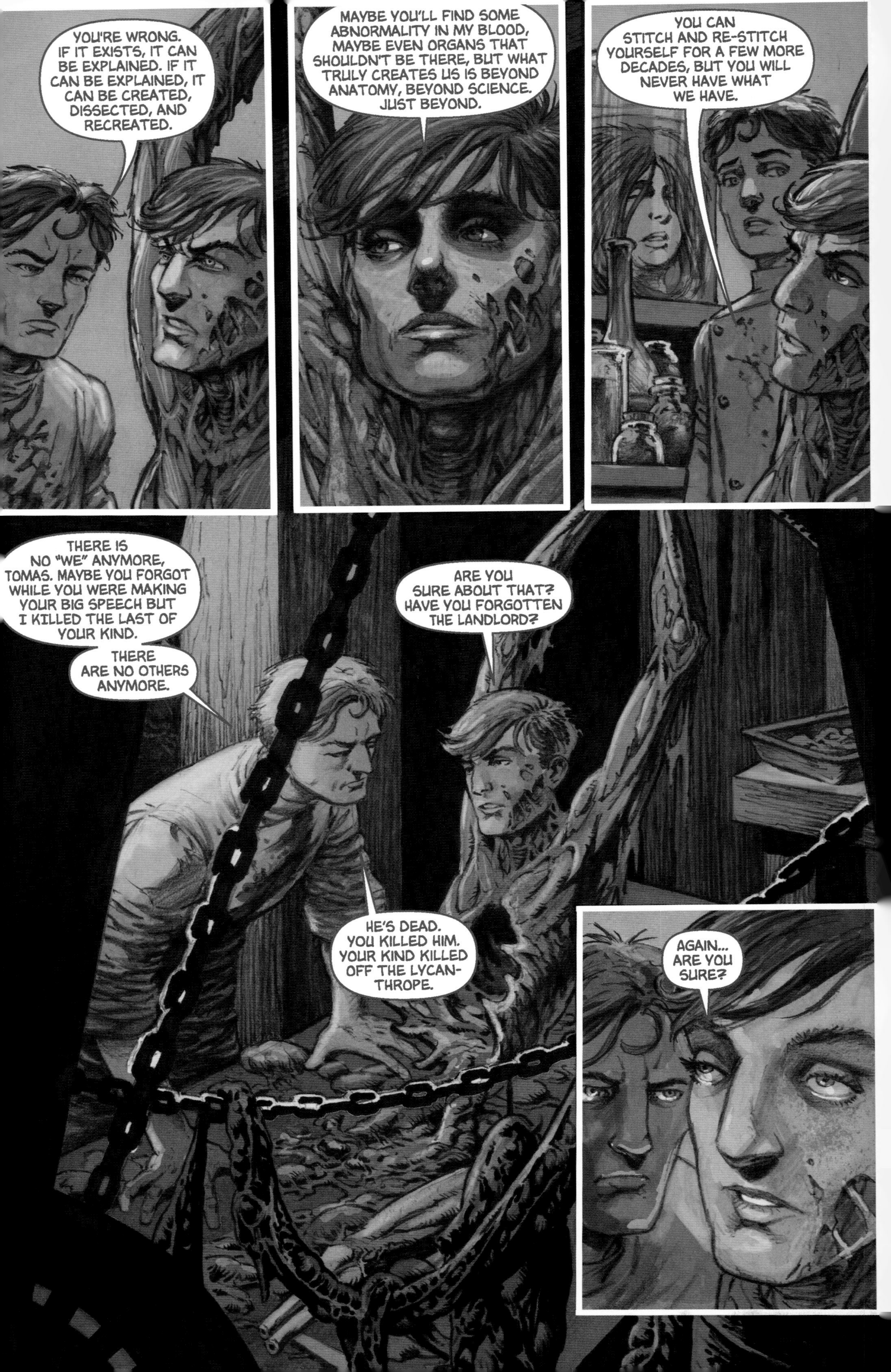
YOU'RE WRONG. IF IT EXISTS, IT CAN BE EXPLAINED. IF IT CAN BE EXPLAINED, IT CAN BE CREATED, DISSECTED, AND RECREATED.
MAYBE YOU'LL FIND SOME ABNORMALITY IN MY BLOOD, MAYBE EVEN ORGANS THAT SHOULDN'T BE THERE, BUT WHAT TRULY CREATES US IS BEYOND ANATOMY, BEYOND SCIENCE. JUST BEYOND.
YOU CAN STITCH AND RE-STITCH YOURSELF FOR A FEW MORE DECADES, BUT YOU WILL NEVER HAVE WHAT WE HAVE.
THERE IS NO "WE" ANYMORE, TOMAS. MAYBE YOU FORGOT WHILE YOU WERE MAKING YOUR BIG SPEECH BUT I KILLED THE LAST OF YOUR KIND.
THERE ARE NO OTHERS ANYMORE.
ARE YOU SURE ABOUT THAT? HAVE YOU FORGOTTEN THE LANDLORD?
HE'S DEAD. YOU KILLED HIM. YOUR KIND KILLED OFF THE LYCAN-THROPE.
AGAIN... ARE YOU SURE?

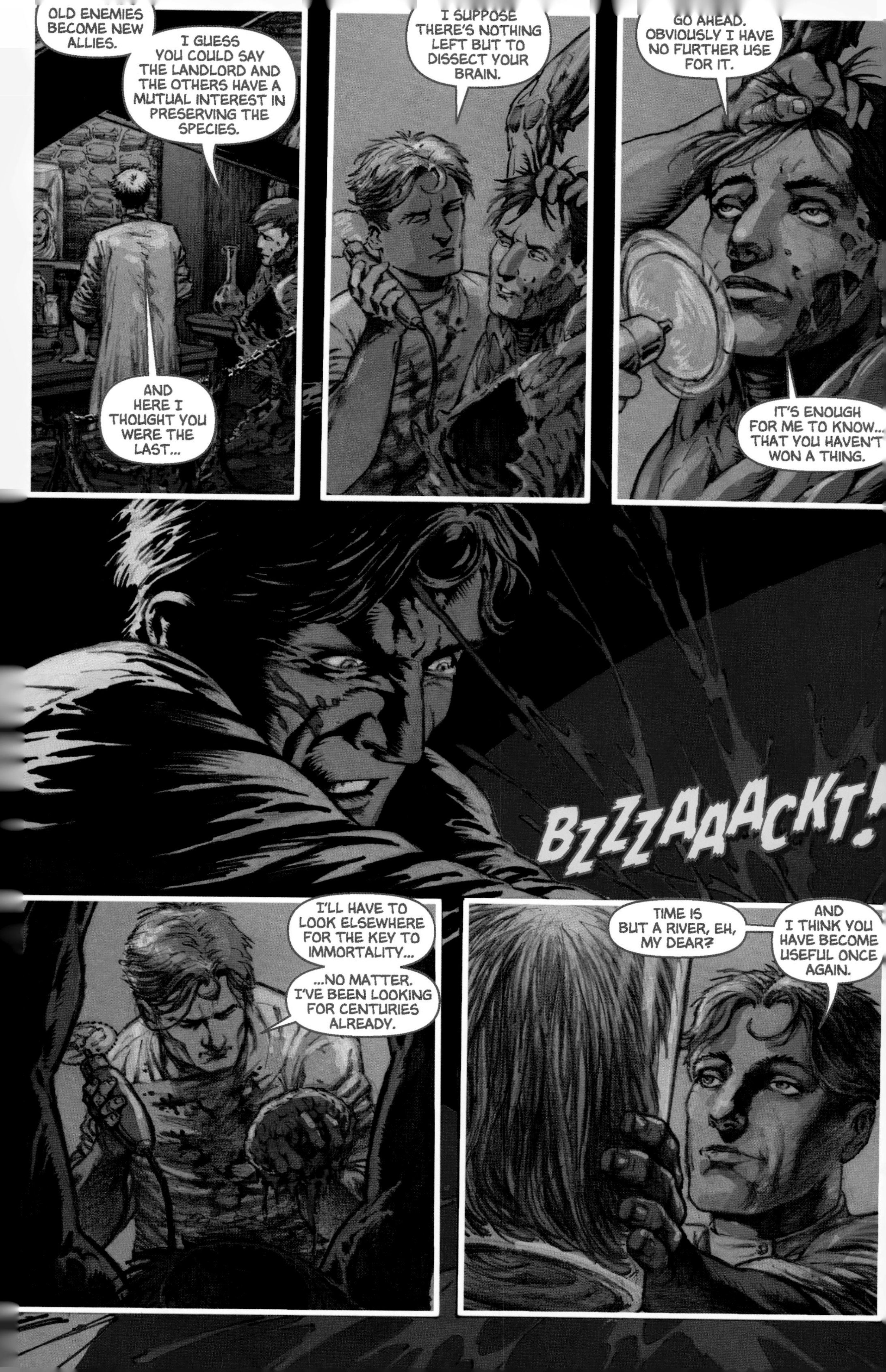
OLD ENEMIES BECOME NEW ALLIES.
I GUESS YOU COULD SAY THE LANDLORD AND THE OTHERS HAVE A MUTUAL INTEREST IN PRESERVING THE SPECIES.
AND HERE I THOUGHT YOU WERE THE LAST...
I SUPPOSE THERE'S NOTHING LEFT BUT TO DISSECT YOUR BRAIN.
GO AHEAD. OBVIOUSLY I HAVE NO FURTHER USE FOR IT.
IT'S ENOUGH FOR ME TO KNOW... THAT YOU HAVEN'T WON A THING.
BZZZAAACKT!
I'LL HAVE TO LOOK ELSEWHERE FOR THE KEY TO IMMORTALITY...
...NO MATTER. I'VE BEEN LOOKING FOR CENTURIES ALREADY.
TIME IS BUT A RIVER, EH, MY DEAR?
AND I THINK YOU HAVE BECOME USEFUL ONCE AGAIN.

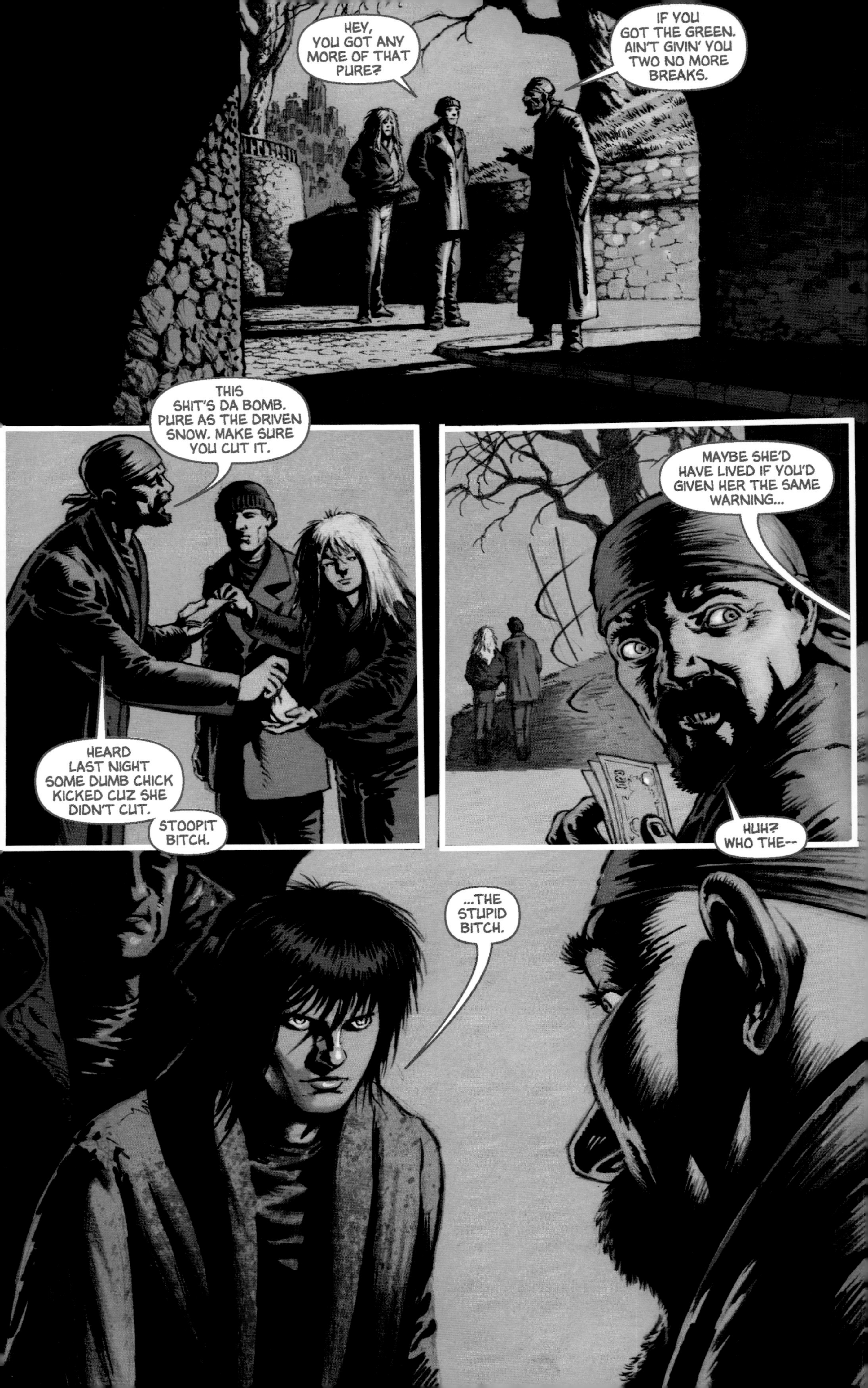
HEY, YOU GOT ANY MORE OF THAT PURE?
IF YOU GOT THE GREEN. AIN'T GIVIN' YOU TWO NO MORE BREAKS.
THIS SHIT'S DA BOMB. PURE AS THE DRIVEN SNOW. MAKE SURE YOU CUT IT.
HEARD LAST NIGHT SOME DUMB CHICK KICKED CUZ SHE DIDN'T CUT.
STOOPIT BITCH.
MAYBE SHE'D HAVE LIVED IF YOU'D GIVEN HER THE SAME WARNING...
HUH? WHO THE--
...THE STUPID BITCH.

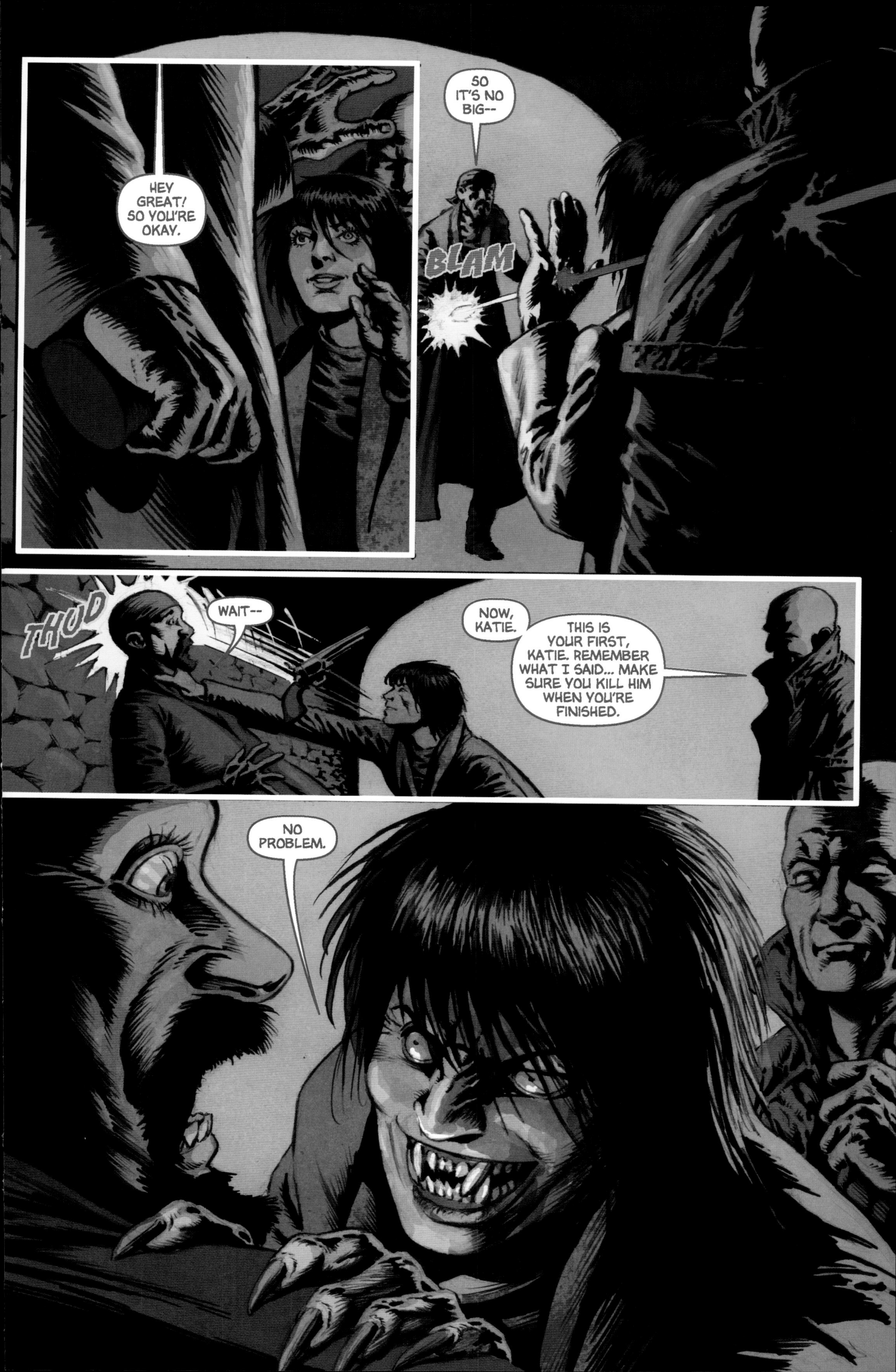
HEY GREAT! SO YOU'RE OKAY.
SO IT'S NO BIG--
BLAM
THUD
WAIT--
NOW, KATIE.
THIS IS YOUR FIRST, KATIE. REMEMBER WHAT I SAID... MAKE SURE YOU KILL HIM WHEN YOU'RE FINISHED.
NO PROBLEM.

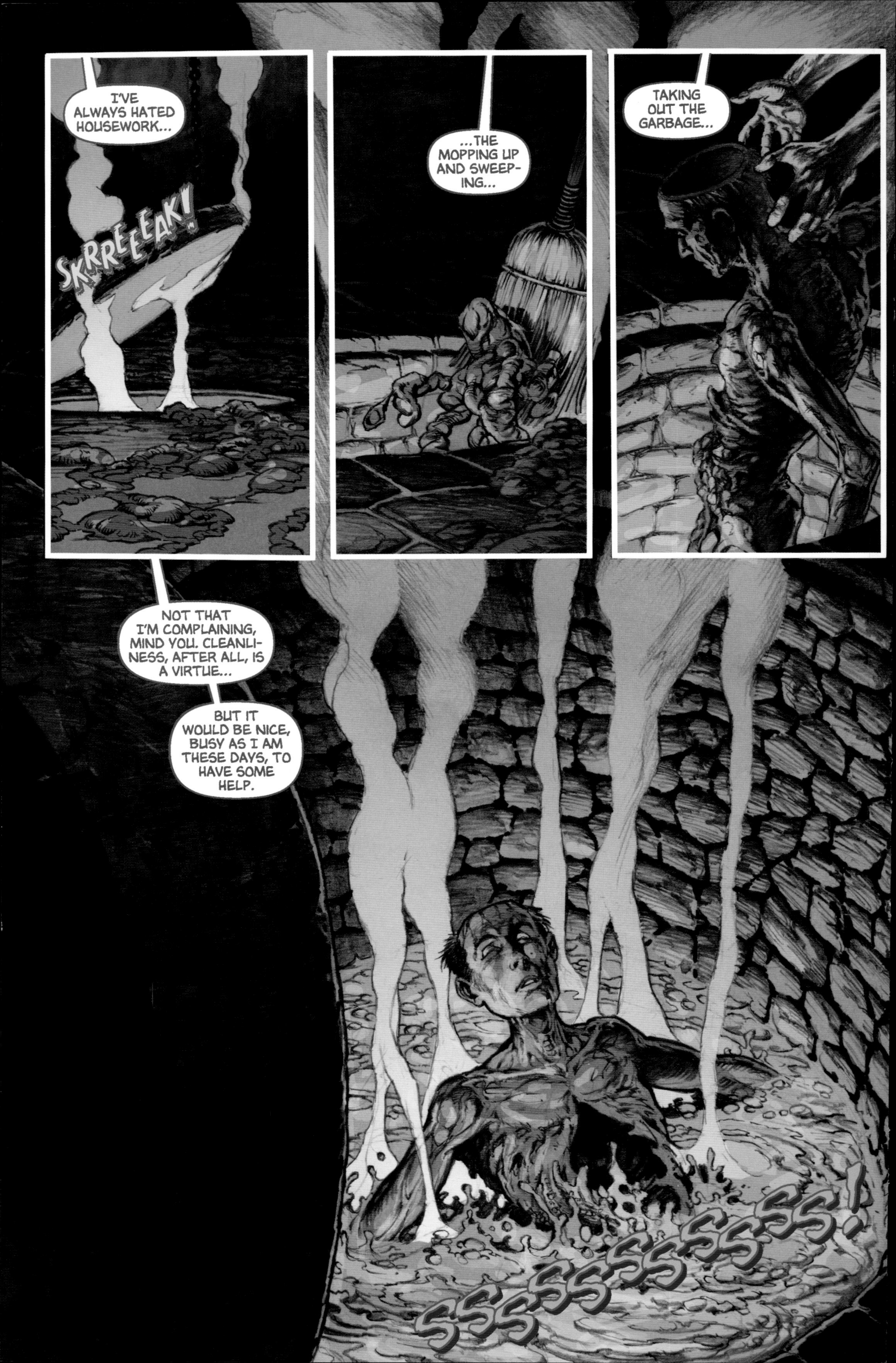
I'VE ALWAYS HATED HOUSEWORK...
SKRREEEAK!
...THE MOPPING UP AND SWEEP-ING...
TAKING OUT THE GARBAGE...
NOT THAT I'M COMPLAINING, MIND YOU. CLEANLI-NESS, AFTER ALL, IS A VIRTUE...
BUT IT WOULD BE NICE, BUSY AS I AM THESE DAYS, TO HAVE SOME HELP.
SSSSSSSSSSSS!

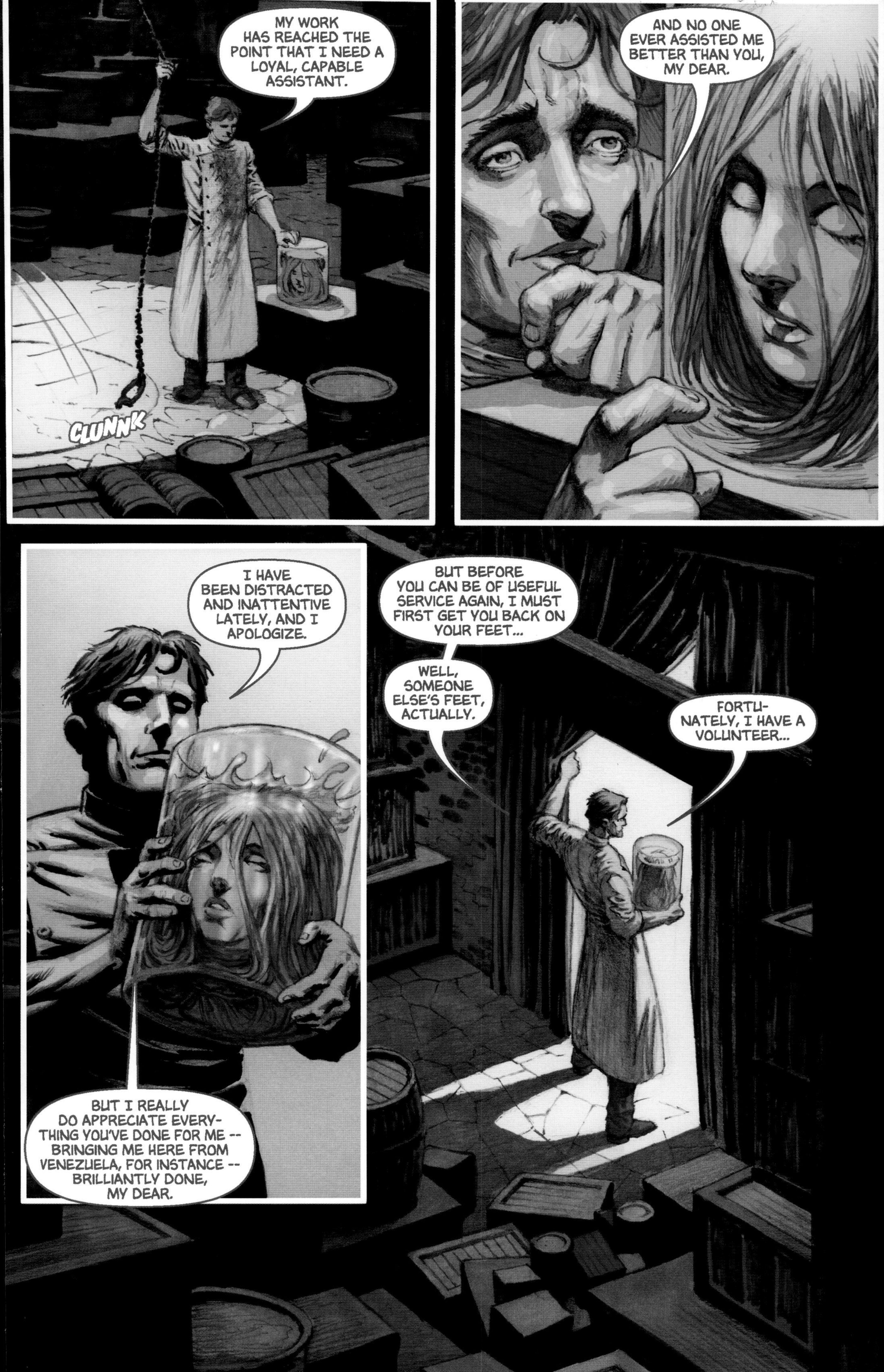
MY WORK HAS REACHED THE POINT THAT I NEED A LOYAL, CAPABLE ASSISTANT.
CLUNNK
AND NO ONE EVER ASSISTED ME BETTER THAN YOU, MY DEAR.
I HAVE BEEN DISTRACTED AND INATTENTIVE LATELY, AND I APOLOGIZE.
BUT I REALLY DO APPRECIATE EVERY-THING YOU'VE DONE FOR ME -- BRINGING ME HERE FROM VENEZUELA, FOR INSTANCE -- BRILLIANTLY DONE, MY DEAR.
BUT BEFORE YOU CAN BE OF USEFUL SERVICE AGAIN, I MUST FIRST GET YOU BACK ON YOUR FEET...
WELL, SOMEONE ELSE'S FEET, ACTUALLY.
FORTU-NATELY, I HAVE A VOLUNTEER...

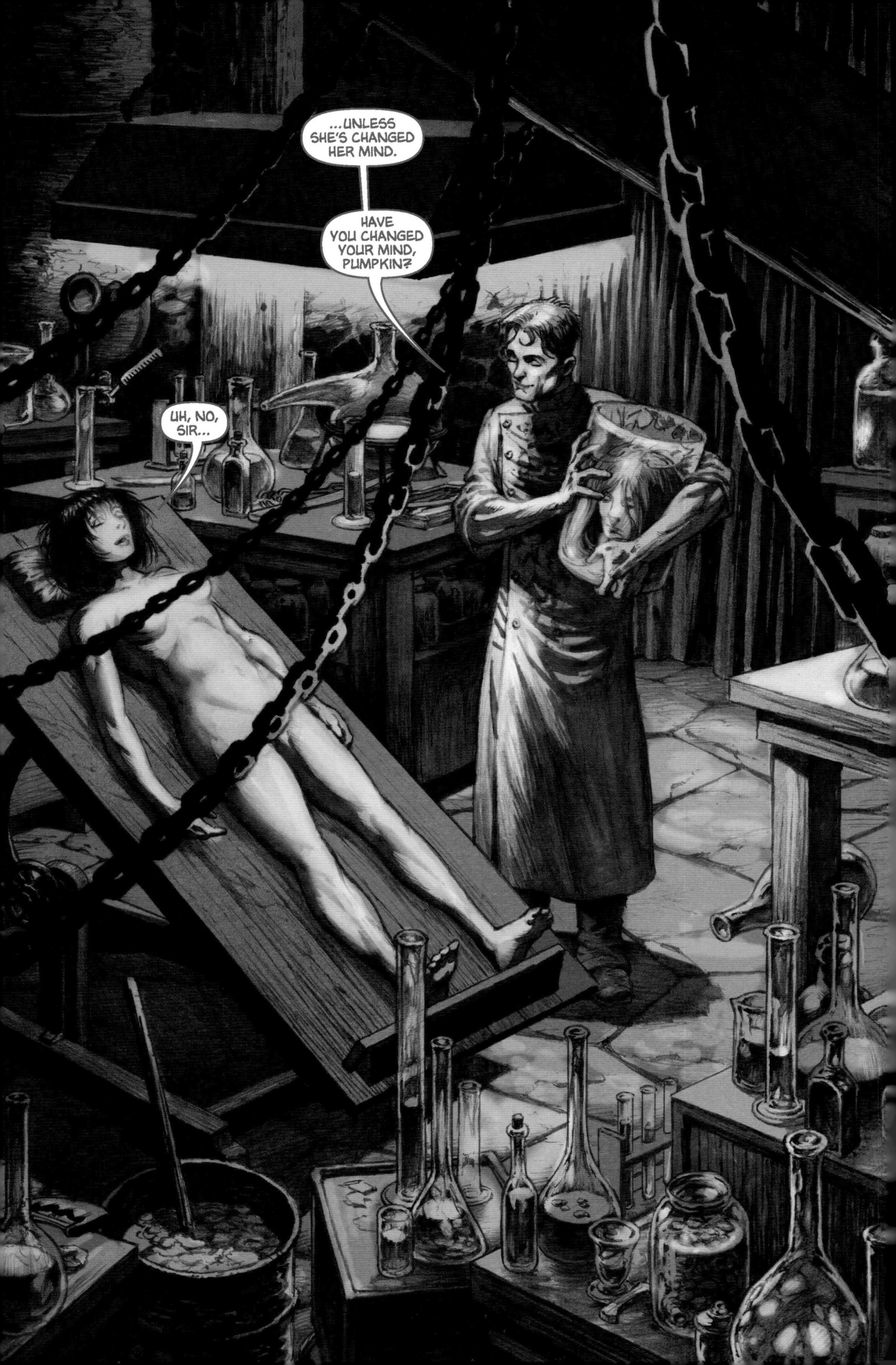
...UNLESS SHE'S CHANGED HER MIND.
HAVE YOU CHANGED YOUR MIND, PUMPKIN?
UH, NO, SIR...

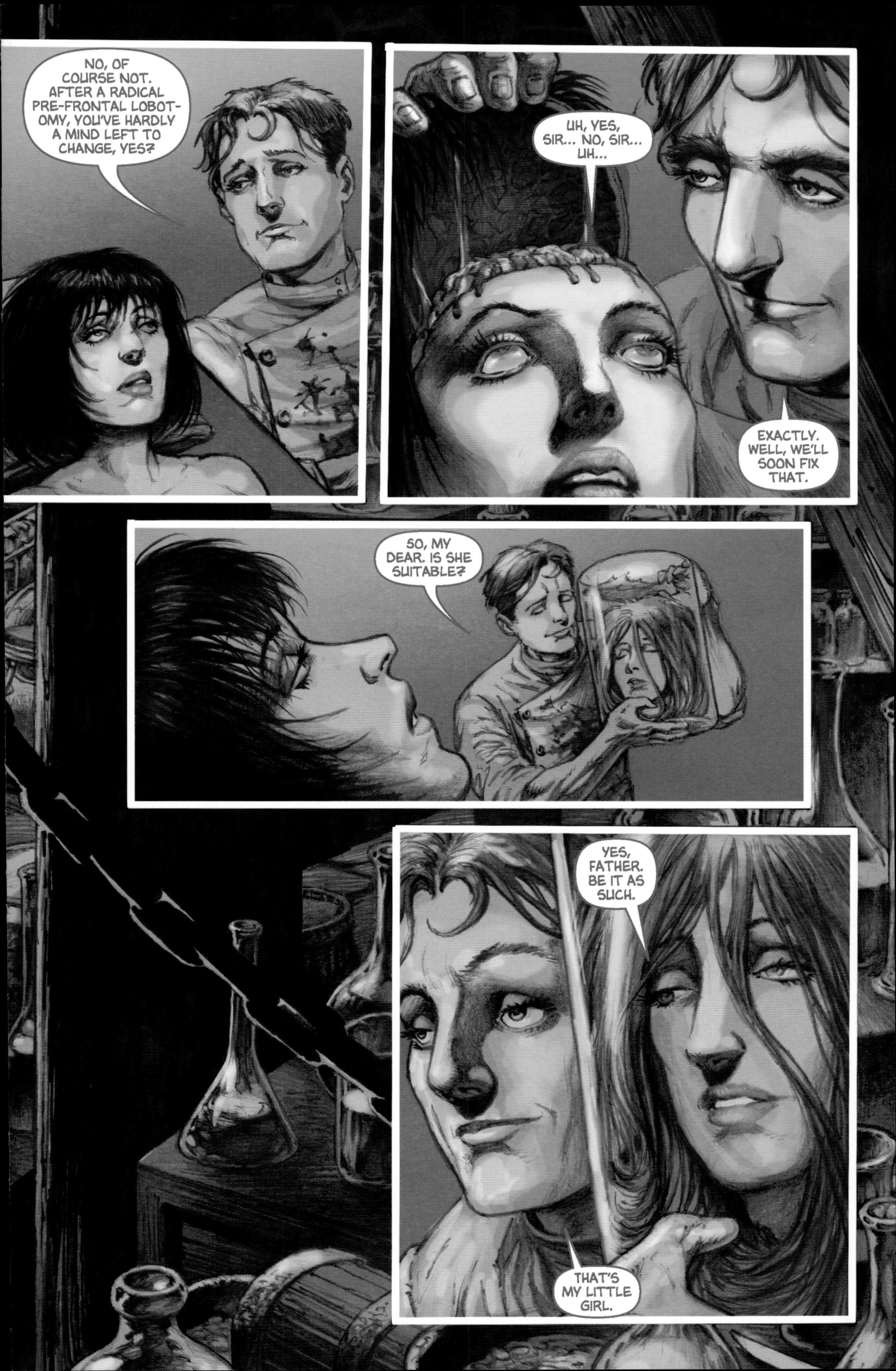
NO, OF COURSE NOT. AFTER A RADICAL PRE-FRONTAL LOBOTOMY, YOU'VE HARDLY A MIND LEFT TO CHANGE, YES?
UH, YES, SIR... NO, SIR... UH...
EXACTLY. WELL, WE'LL SOON FIX THAT.
SO, MY DEAR. IS SHE SUITABLE?
YES, FATHER. BE IT AS SUCH.
THAT'S MY LITTLE GIRL.

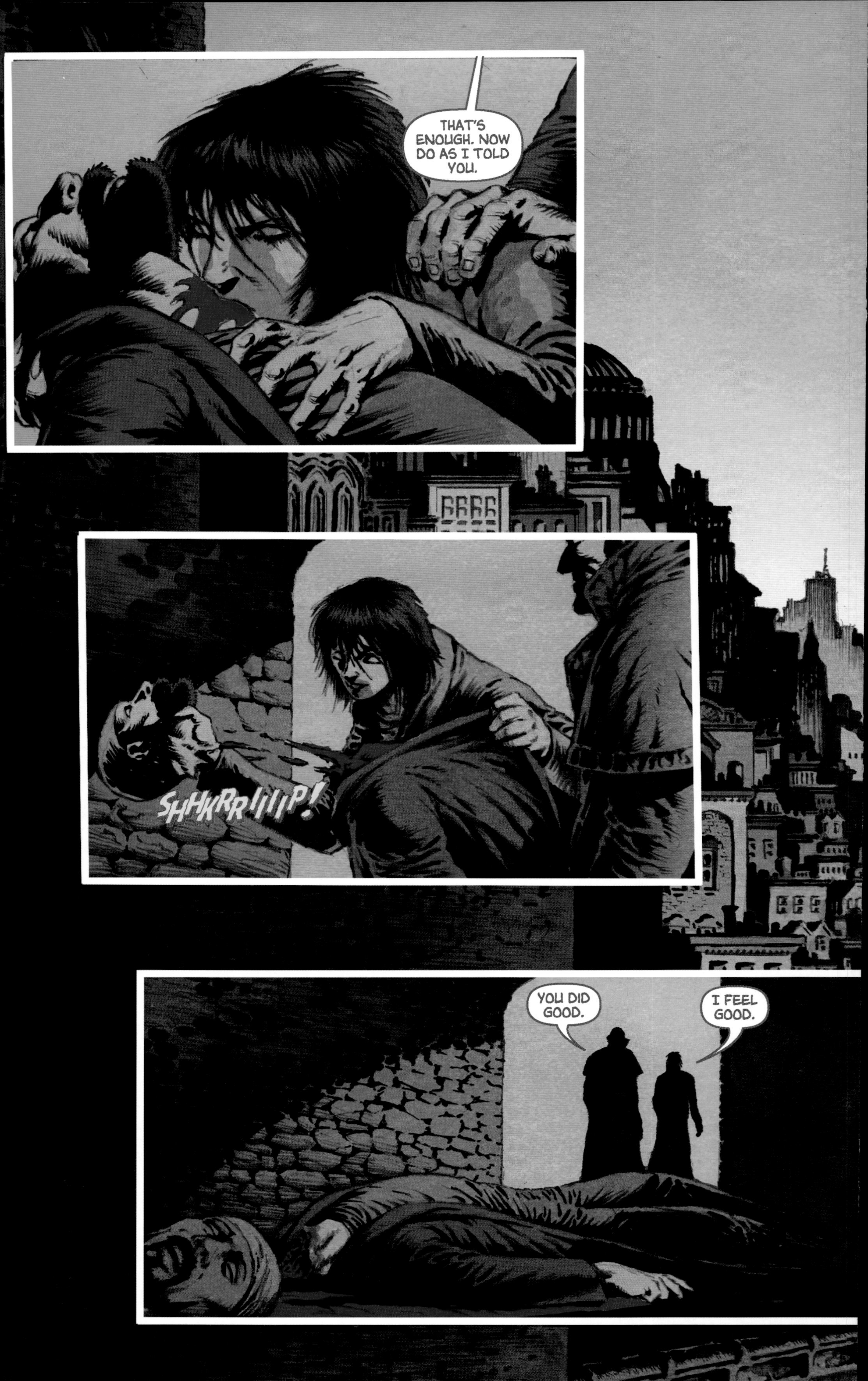
THAT'S ENOUGH. NOW DO AS I TOLD YOU.
SHHKRRIIIIP!
YOU DID GOOD.
I FEEL GOOD.

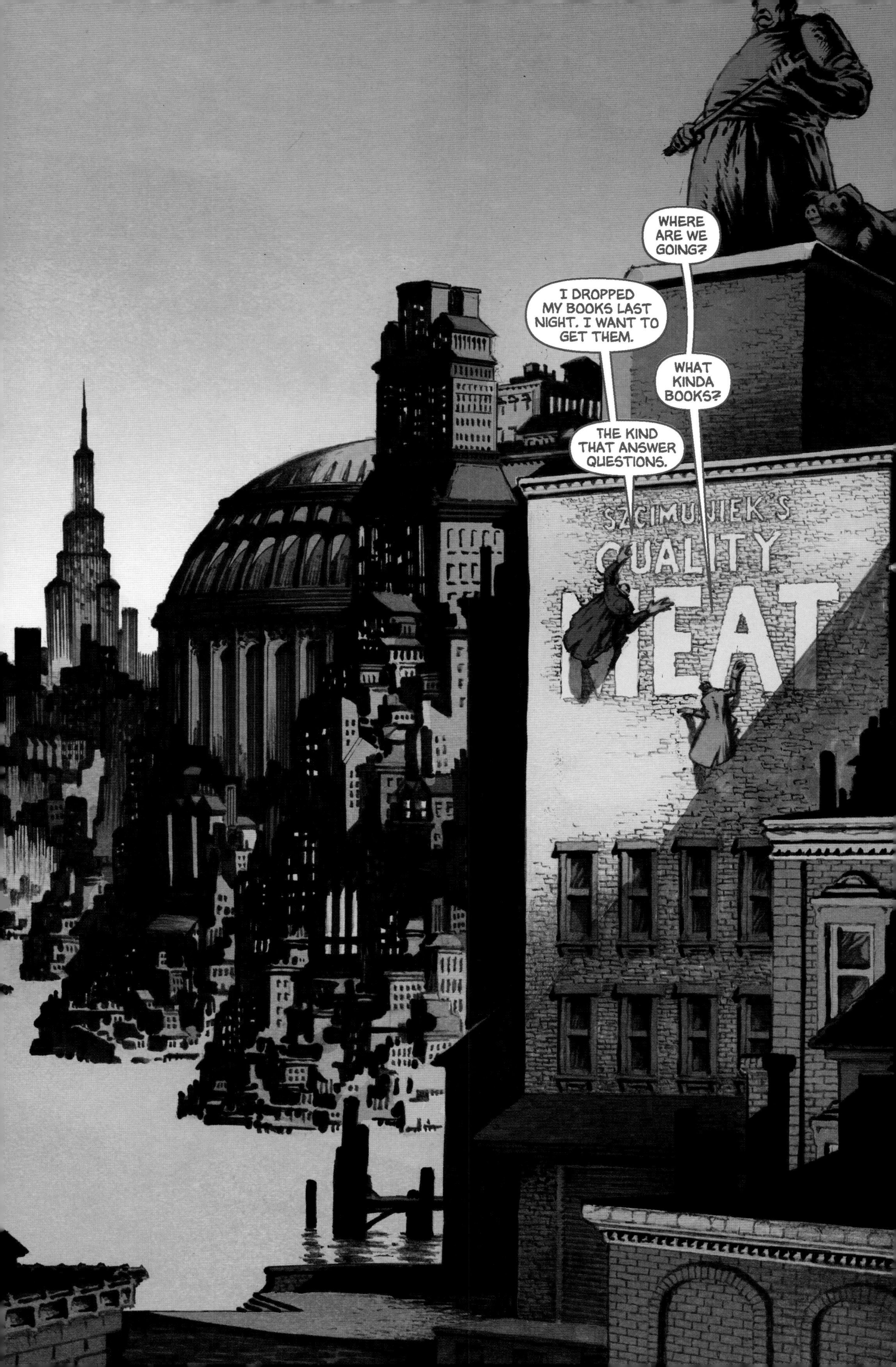
WHERE ARE WE GOING?
I DROPPED MY BOOKS LAST NIGHT. I WANT TO GET THEM.
WHAT KINDA BOOKS?
THE KIND THAT ANSWER QUESTIONS.
SZCIMUNIEK'S
QUALITY

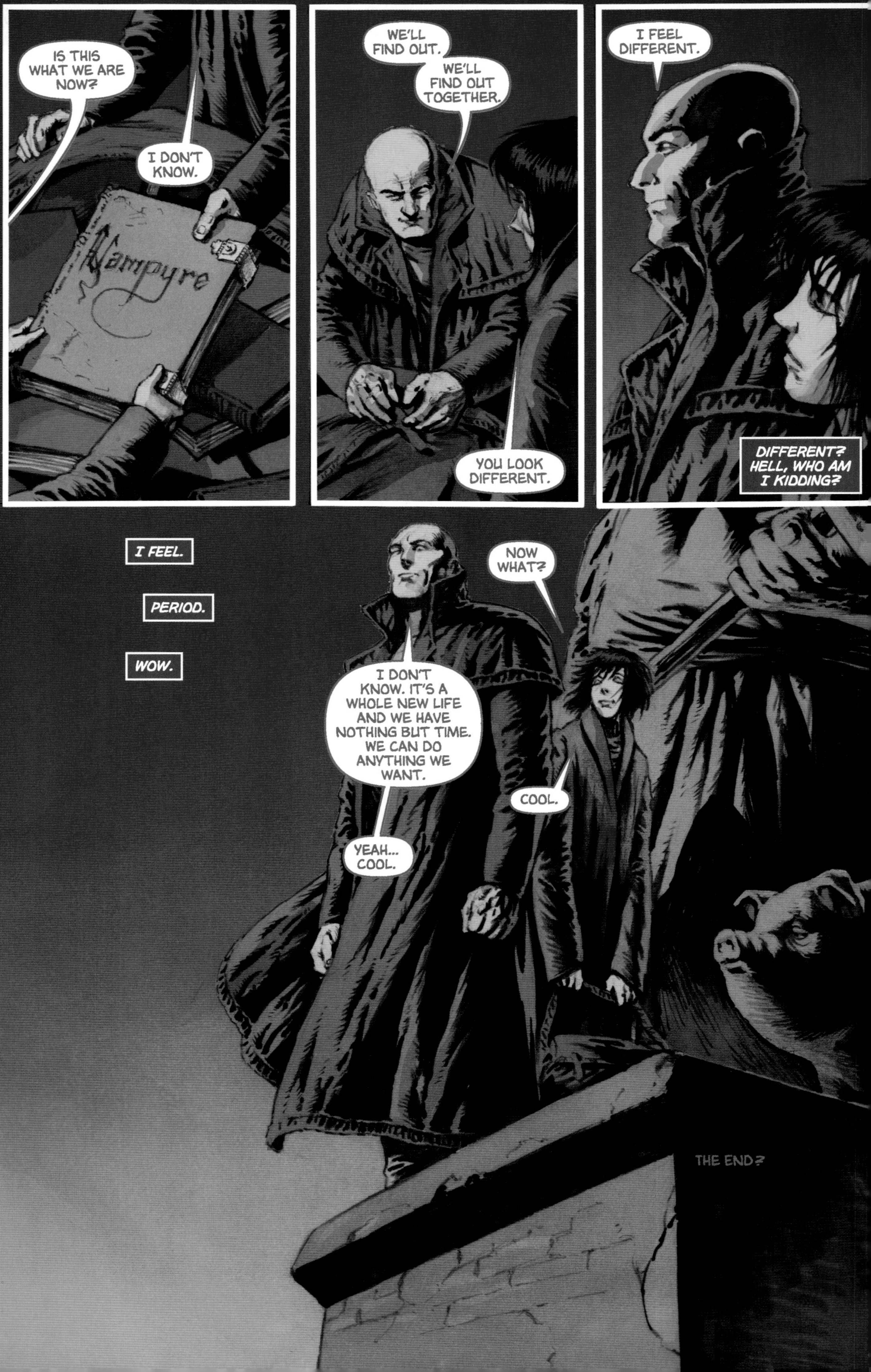
IS THIS WHAT WE ARE NOW?
I DON'T KNOW.
Vampyre
WE'LL FIND OUT.
WE'LL FIND OUT TOGETHER.
YOU LOOK DIFFERENT.
I FEEL DIFFERENT.
DIFFERENT? HELL, WHO AM I KIDDING?
I FEEL.
PERIOD.
WOW.
NOW WHAT?
I DON'T KNOW. IT'S A WHOLE NEW LIFE AND WE HAVE NOTHING BUT TIME. WE CAN DO ANYTHING WE WANT.
COOL.
YEAH... COOL.
THE END?

STEVE NILES creates monsters and releases them into our world with a fervor and flare that echoes throughout the horror genre. His hit series *30 Days of Night* jolted horror comics back to life. His other titles include such nightmare-inducing works as: *Criminal Macabre*, *Simon Dark*, *Mystery Society*, *Frankenstein Alive, Alive!*, *Freaks of the Heartland*, *Remains*, and *Batman: Gotham County Line*. He lives somewhere near Los Angeles with his wife, Monica, an unpredictable number of cats, several dogs, and Gil the tortoise. Hailing from the bowels of the Washington, D.C. suburbs, Steve has been writing comics since the Eighties and was once a member of D.C.'s legendary hardcore punk scene as a member of Gray Matter and Three.

BERNIE WRIGHTSON was a paragon of horror art in both comics and film, devoting most of his life and career to illustrating characters who were both monstrous, fun, and relatable. He co-created *Swamp Thing* with Len Wein and generated the definitive illustrations of Mary Shelley's *Frankenstein*. As a concept artist his fingerprints can be found all over some of Hollywood's biggest hits, including such titles as *Ghostbusters*, *Spider-man*, *Galaxy Quest*, Stephen King's *The Mist*, and George Romero's *Land of the Dead*. Bernie passed away in 2017 and is survived by his loving wife Liz, sons John, Jeffrey, and Thomas. His work has and will continue to inspire generation after generation of comics artists and writers.

Photographs by Tim Bradstreet

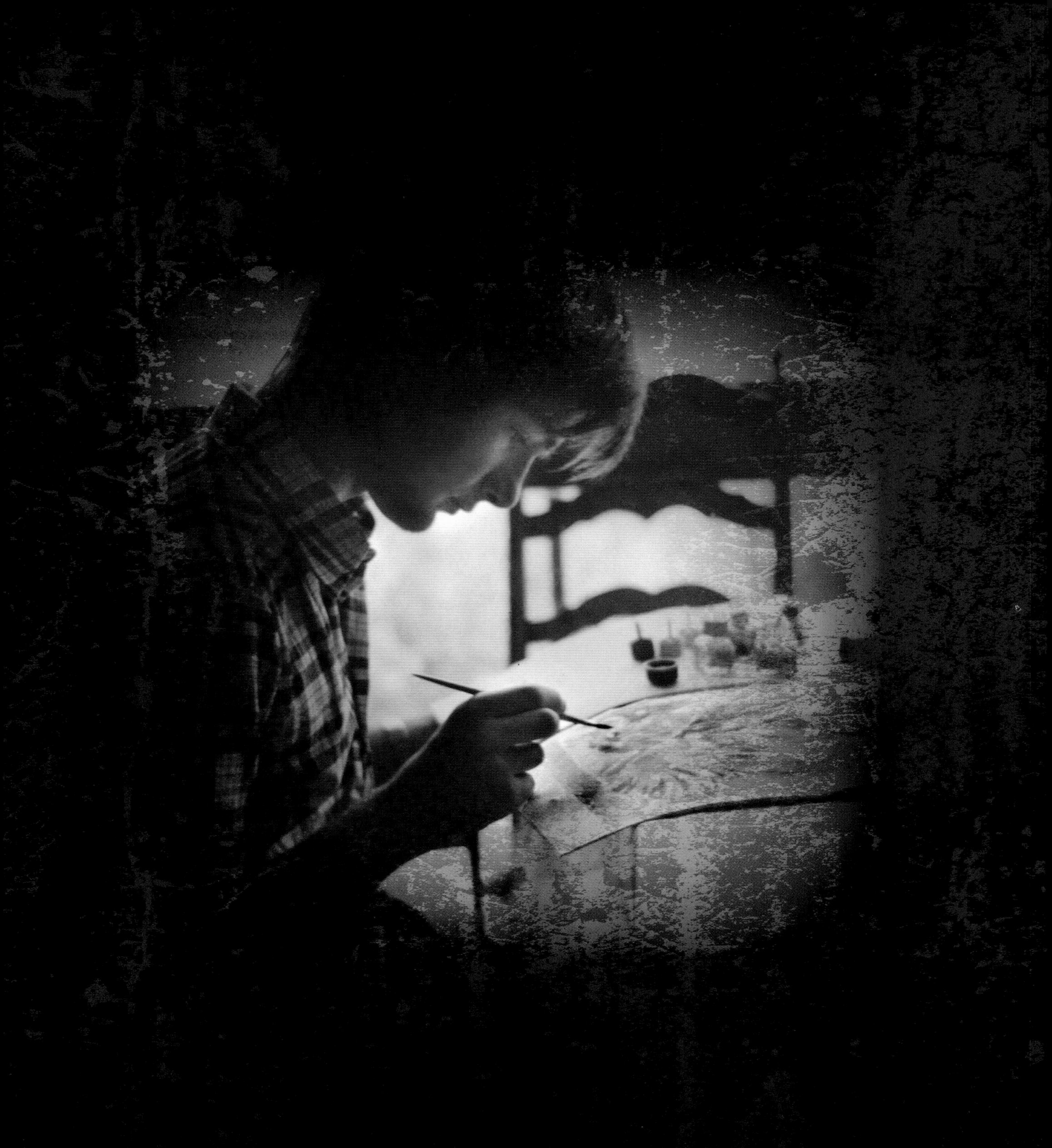

JOSÉ VILLARRUBIA is a Harvey Award-winning comic book colorist and college art professor with over twenty years of experience. He is the coordinator for the Sequential Art Concentration at the Maryland Institute College of Art and has worked as a freelance artist in fine art, photography, comics, and illustration. He is best known for his collaborations with Alan Moore, Richard Corben, Jae Lee, and Paul Pope. His most recent work includes *Anthony Bourdain's Hungry Ghosts*, *Sword Daughter*, and the critically acclaimed *Infidel*, which he both edited and colored. In 1975, he colored his personal copy of Bernie Wrightson's *The Monsters, Color the Creature Book*. Thirty-three years later he finally got to work with the master, fulfilling his dream.

Photograph by Luz J. Momediano

BERNIE WRIGHTSON'S
CITY OF OTHERS SKETCHBOOK

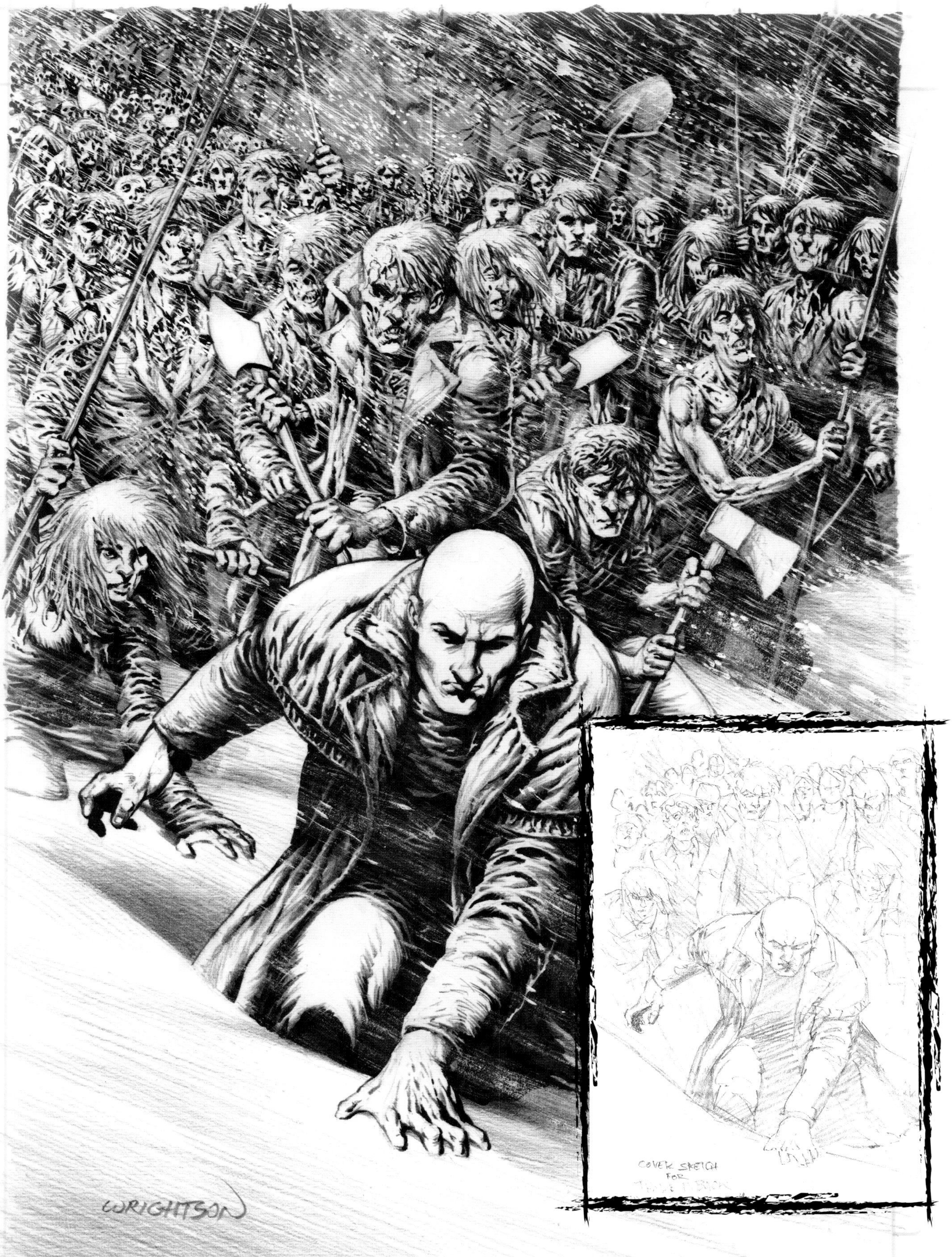
WRIGHTSON
COVER SKETCH
FOR

Above: The finished pencils for the cover of this book.

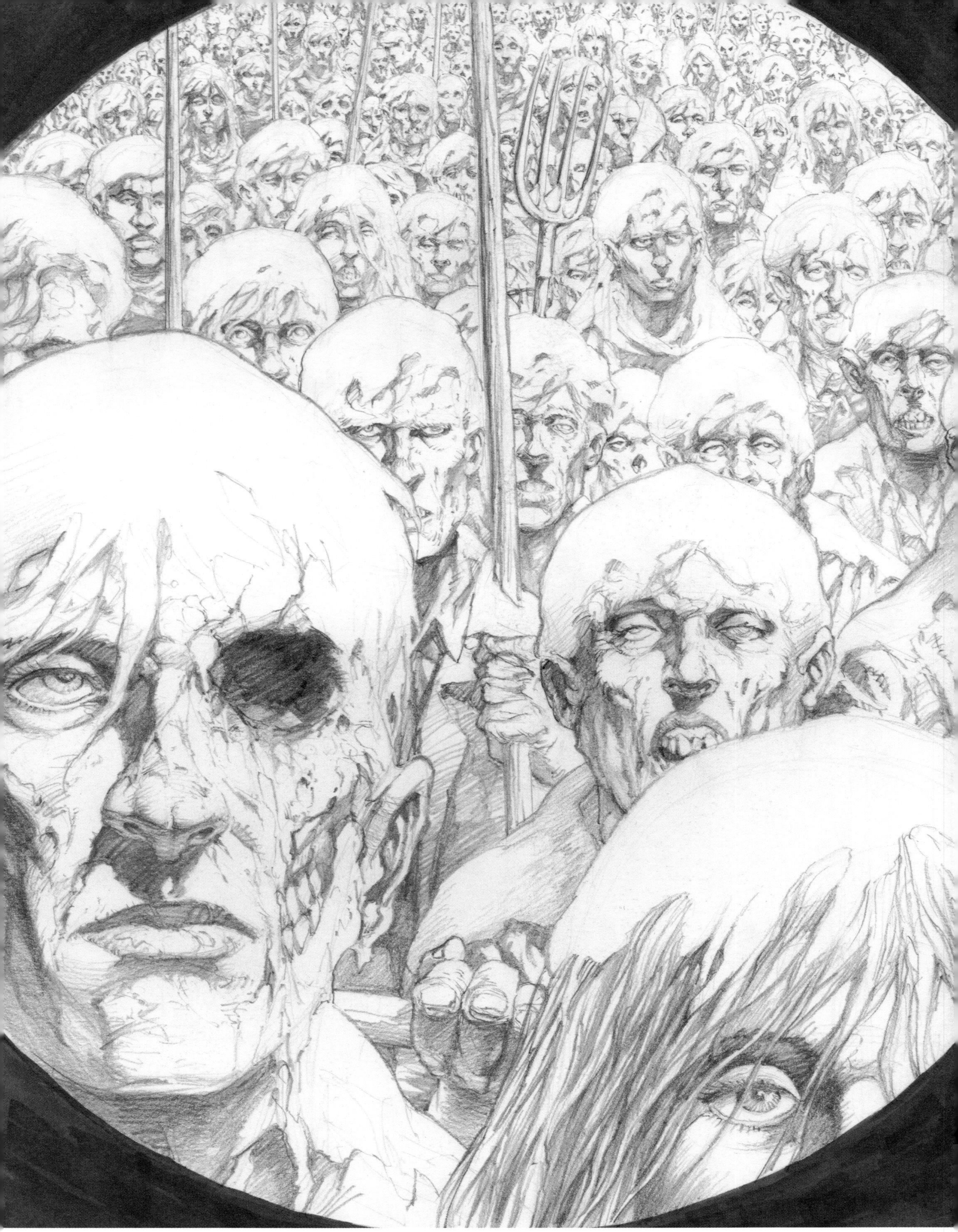

Above: Bernie's finished line art for the descending zombie horde from issue #2.

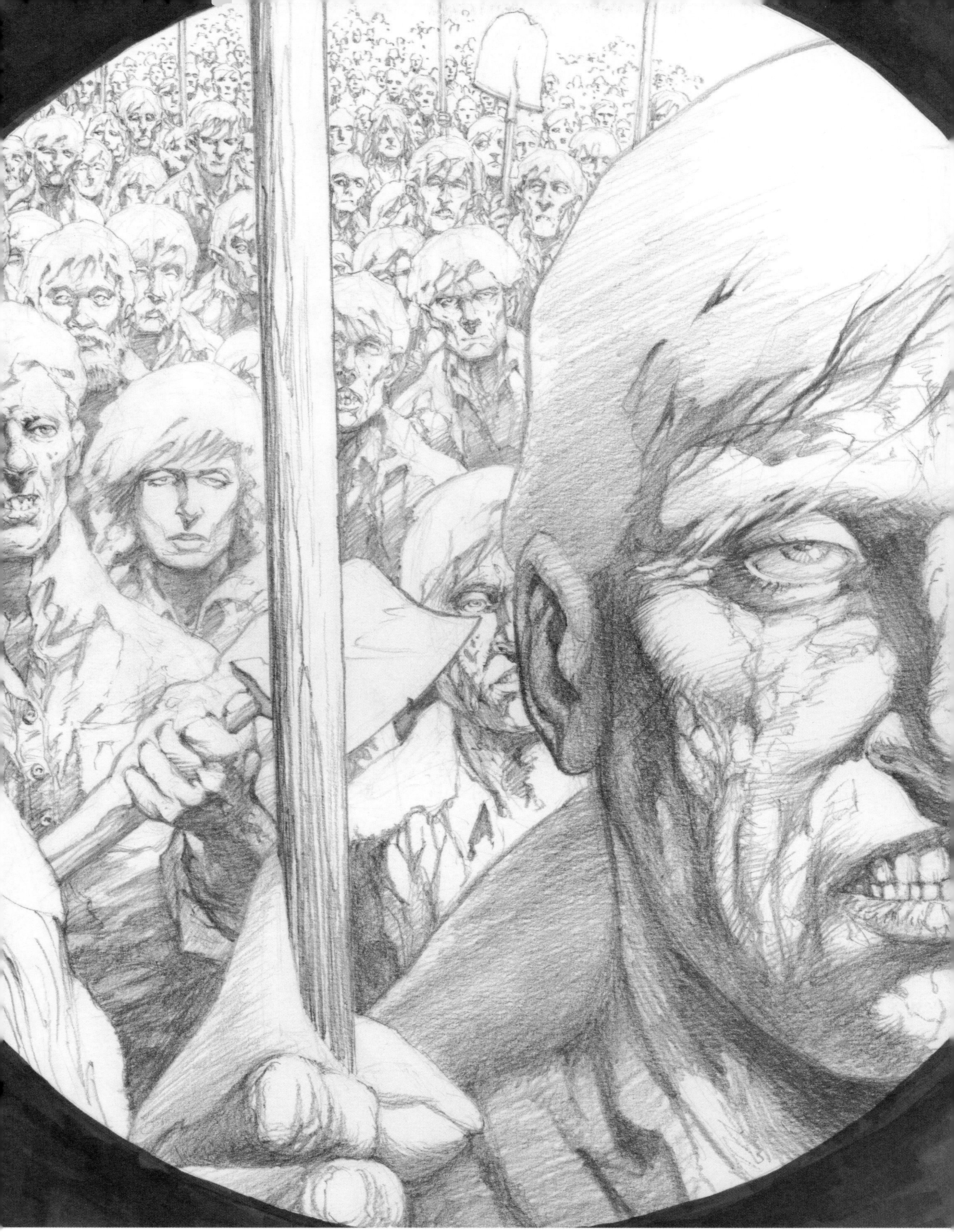

When we first began working on *City of Others*, it was remarkable to see Bernie's raw pencils as they came in. It's incredibly rare to see such fine detail work on a comic-book page anymore, and Bernie was pulling out all the stops. As the series progressed and the first issue hit the stands, we immediately began receiving requests to show just the pencilied line art as a bonus feature to the comic. We all liked that idea, but since there was limited space in the individual issues, we decided to save this feature for the series collection. I still think this is one of the most incredibly beautiful drawings I have ever seen, subject matter aside.

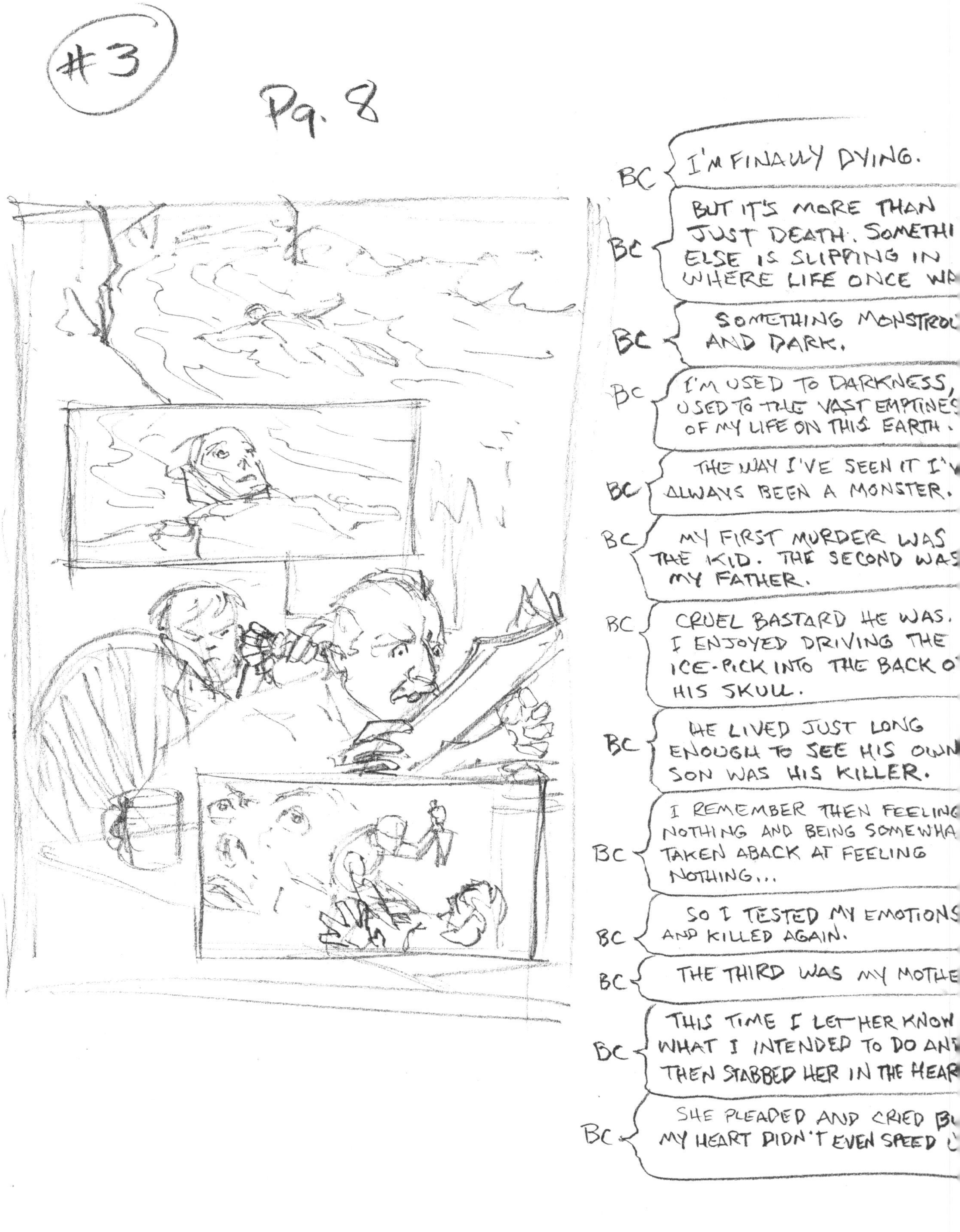
#3
Pg. 8
BC I'M FINALLY DYING.
BC BUT IT'S MORE THAN JUST DEATH. SOMETHI ELSE IS SLIPPING IN WHERE LIFE ONCE WA
BC SOMETHING MONSTROU AND DARK.
BC I'M USED TO DARKNESS, USED TO THE VAST EMPTINES OF MY LIFE ON THIS EARTH.
BC THE WAY I'VE SEEN IT I'V ALWAYS BEEN A MONSTER.
BC MY FIRST MURDER WAS THE KID. THE SECOND WAS MY FATHER.
BC CRUEL BASTARD HE WAS. I ENJOYED DRIVING THE ICE-PICK INTO THE BACK O HIS SKULL.
BC HE LIVED JUST LONG ENOUGH TO SEE HIS OWN SON WAS HIS KILLER.
BC I REMEMBER THEN FEELING NOTHING AND BEING SOMEWHA TAKEN ABACK AT FEELING NOTHING...
BC SO I TESTED MY EMOTIONS AND KILLED AGAIN.
BC THE THIRD WAS MY MOTHE
BC THIS TIME I LET HER KNOW WHAT I INTENDED TO DO AN THEN STABBED HER IN THE HEAR
BC SHE PLEADED AND CRIED BU MY HEART DIDN'T EVEN SPEED

Another great treat for this editor was learning Bernie's working process. Because Steve Niles and I both wanted to showcase Bernie's great visual storytelling, we came up with an interesting way to script the series. Bernie and Steve worked together on the general story outline for each series, then Steve would script it out to twenty-two story pages. Since the series allowed for twenty-six story pages per issue, this gave Bernie free rein to expand the scenes he was most compelled by and develop them with spreads or larger panels.

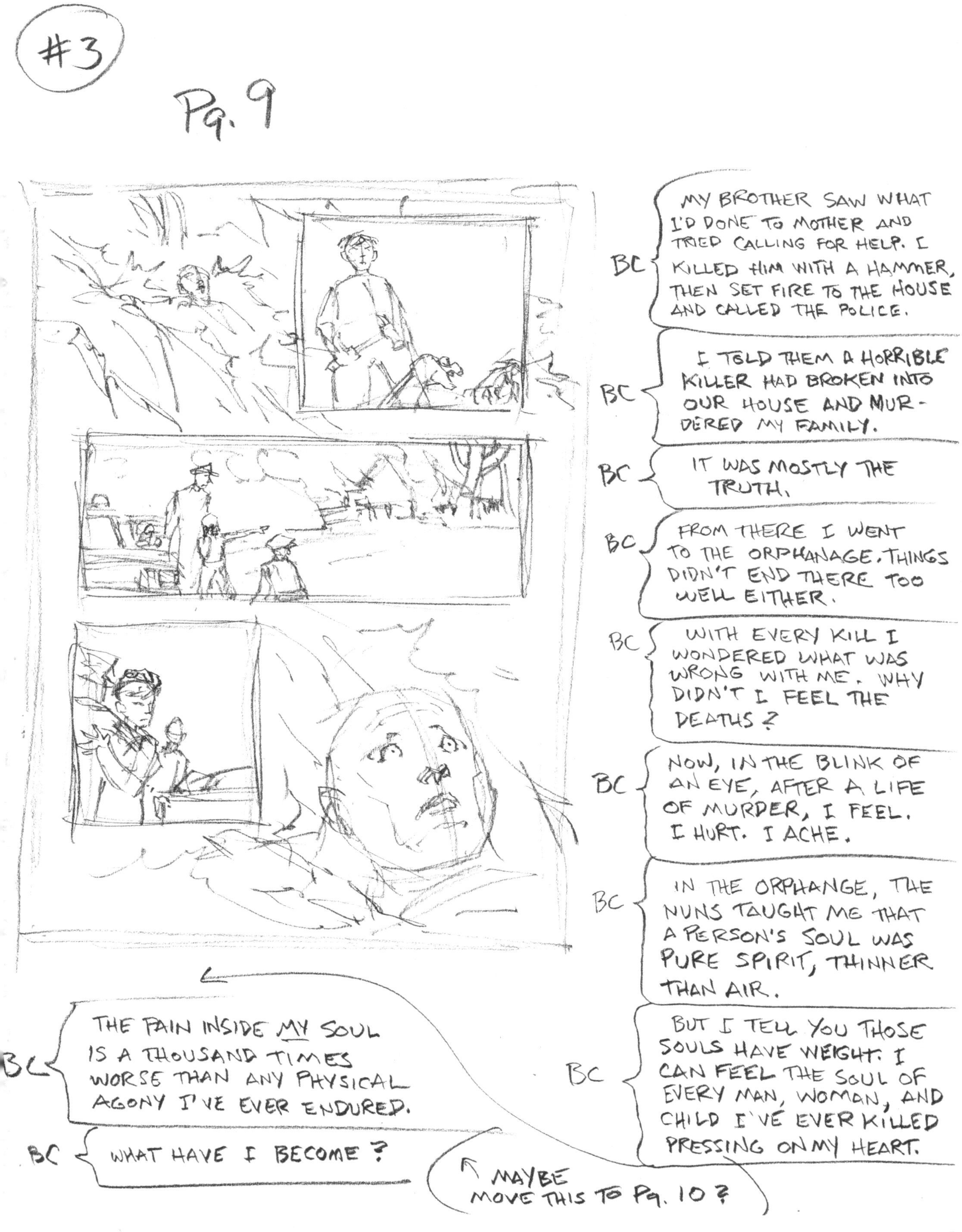
#3
Pg. 9
BC MY BROTHER SAW WHAT I'D DONE TO MOTHER AND TRIED CALLING FOR HELP. I KILLED HIM WITH A HAMMER, THEN SET FIRE TO THE HOUSE AND CALLED THE POLICE.
BC I TOLD THEM A HORRIBLE KILLER HAD BROKEN INTO OUR HOUSE AND MURDERED MY FAMILY.
BC IT WAS MOSTLY THE TRUTH.
BC FROM THERE I WENT TO THE ORPHANAGE. THINGS DIDN'T END THERE TOO WELL EITHER.
BC WITH EVERY KILL I WONDERED WHAT WAS WRONG WITH ME. WHY DIDN'T I FEEL THE DEATHS?
BC NOW, IN THE BLINK OF AN EYE, AFTER A LIFE OF MURDER, I FEEL. I HURT. I ACHE.
BC IN THE ORPHANGE, THE NUNS TAUGHT ME THAT A PERSON'S SOUL WAS PURE SPIRIT, THINNER THAN AIR.
BC BUT I TELL YOU THOSE SOULS HAVE WEIGHT. I CAN FEEL THE SOUL OF EVERY MAN, WOMAN, AND CHILD I'VE EVER KILLED PRESSING ON MY HEART.
BC THE PAIN INSIDE MY SOUL IS A THOUSAND TIMES WORSE THAN ANY PHYSICAL AGONY I'VE EVER ENDURED.
BC WHAT HAVE I BECOME?
MAYBE MOVE THIS TO Pg. 10?

Part of Bernie's process is adapting the script into layouts like the ones seen on this page from issue #3. Thumbnail sketches like this are commonly used by artists as they start work on a new script, but this also gave Bernie the chance to play with the placement for key scenes as he decided which plot points deserved more room on the page.

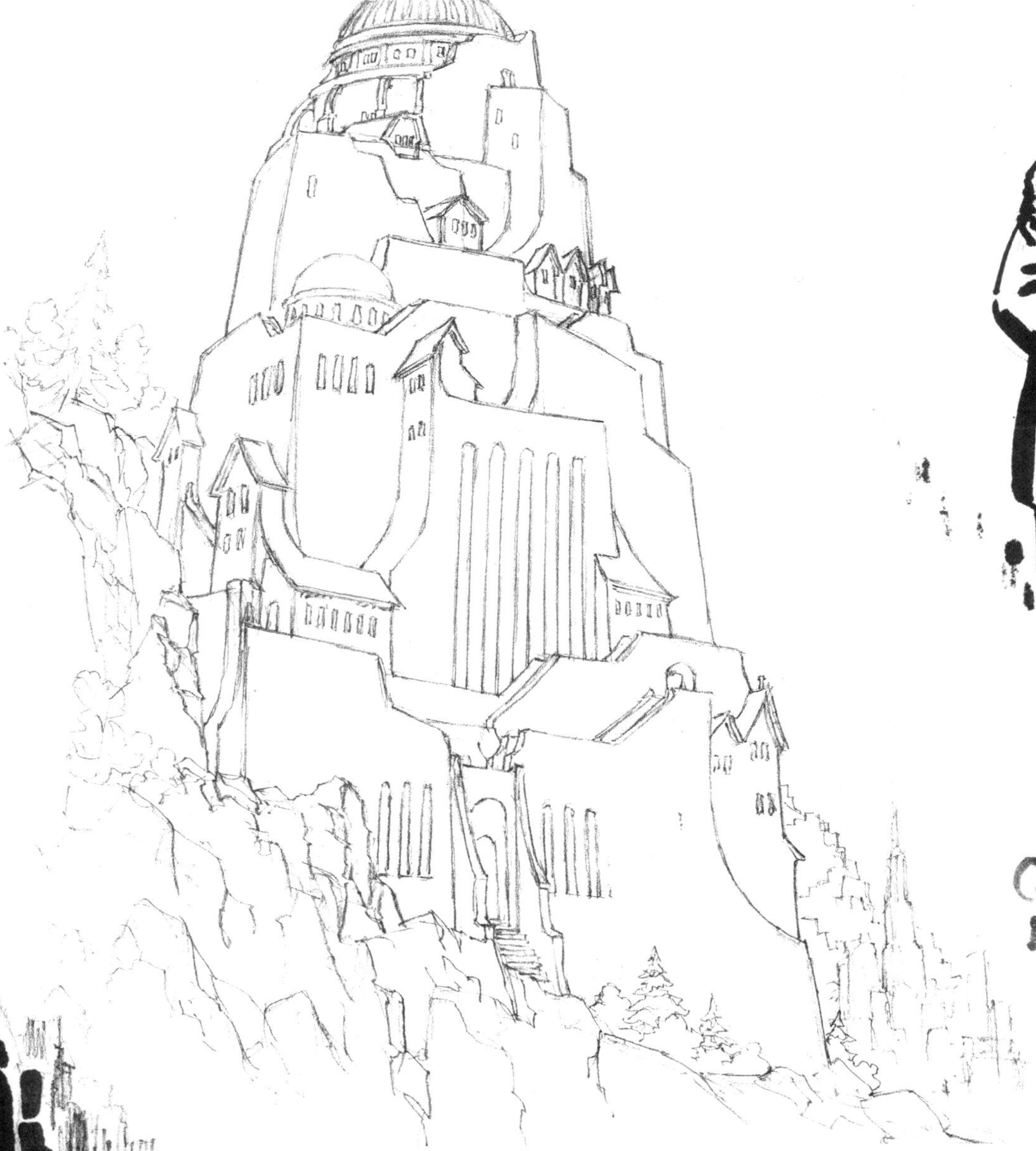

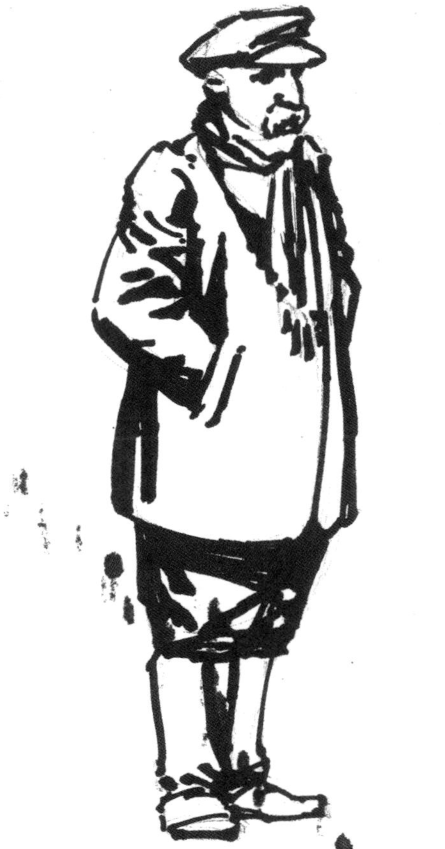

COASTAL EDDIE

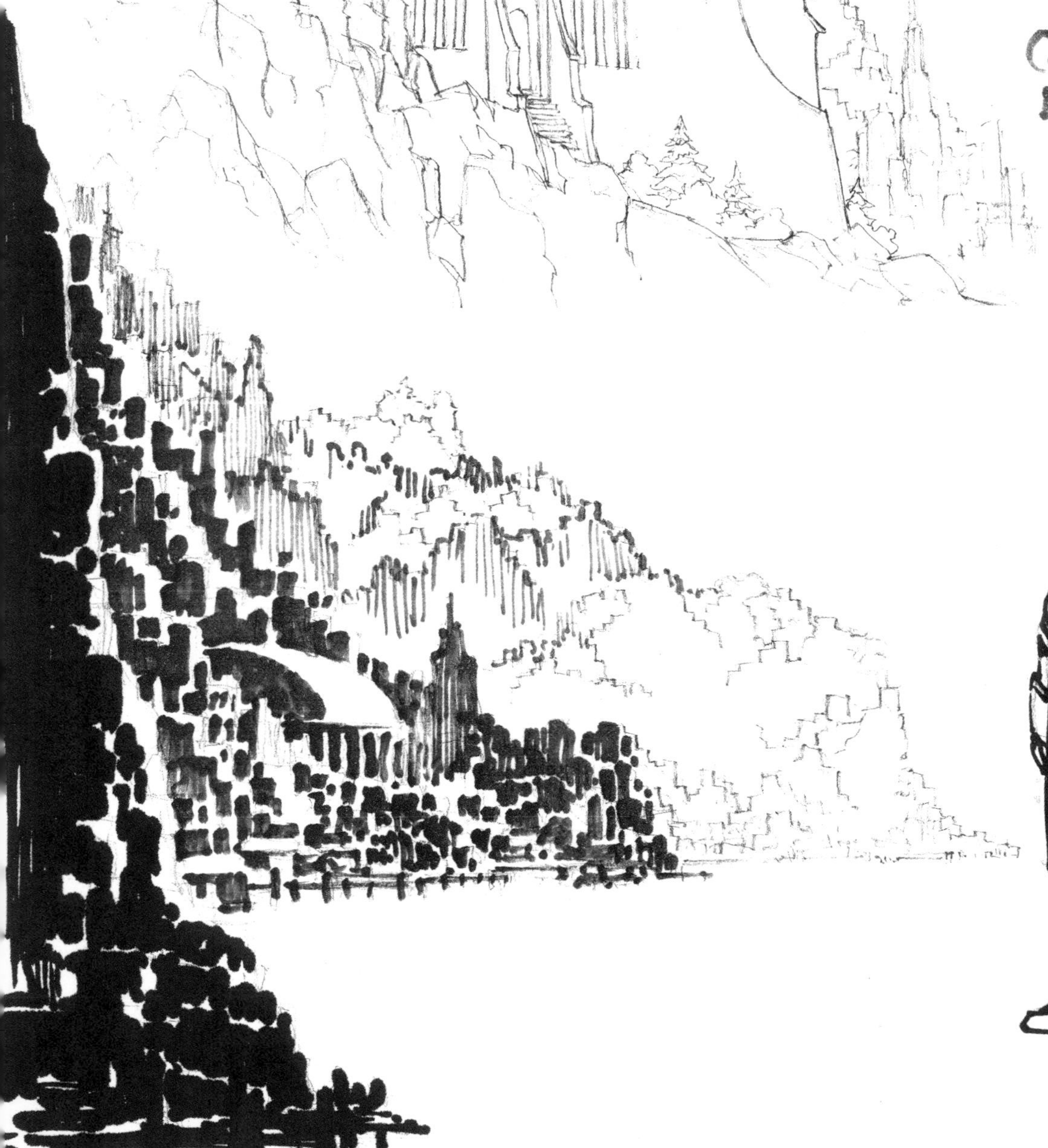

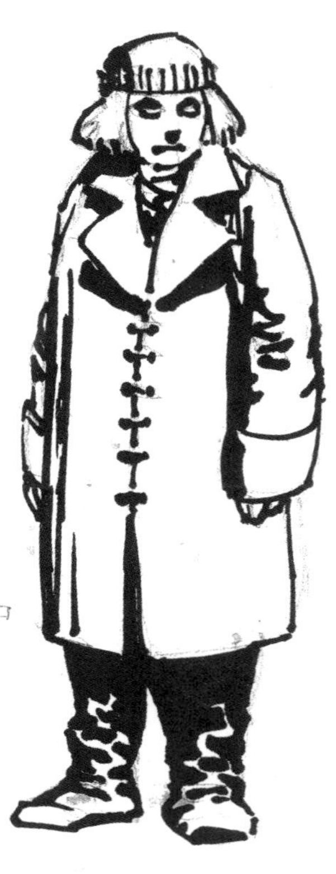

OFFSHORE FLO

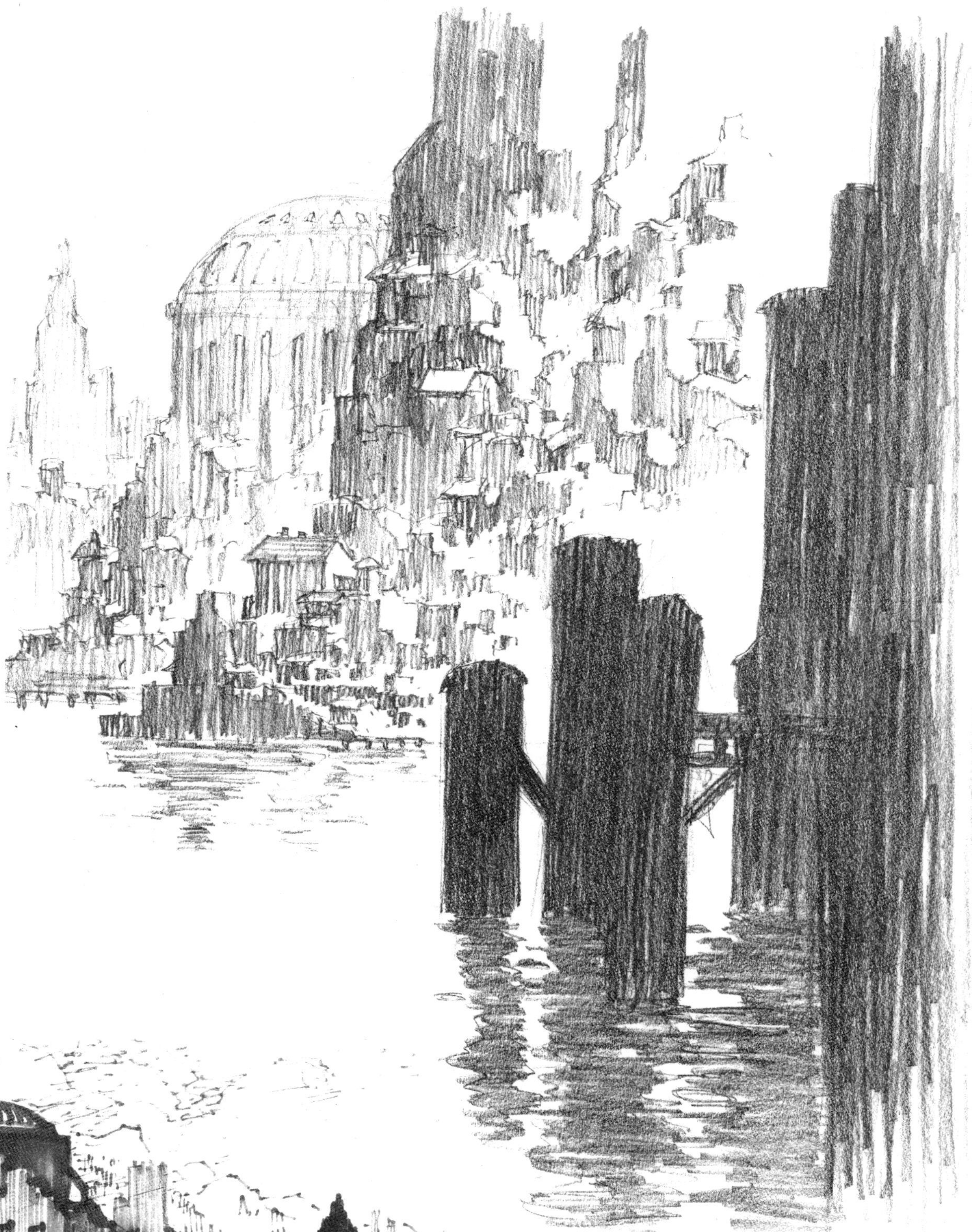

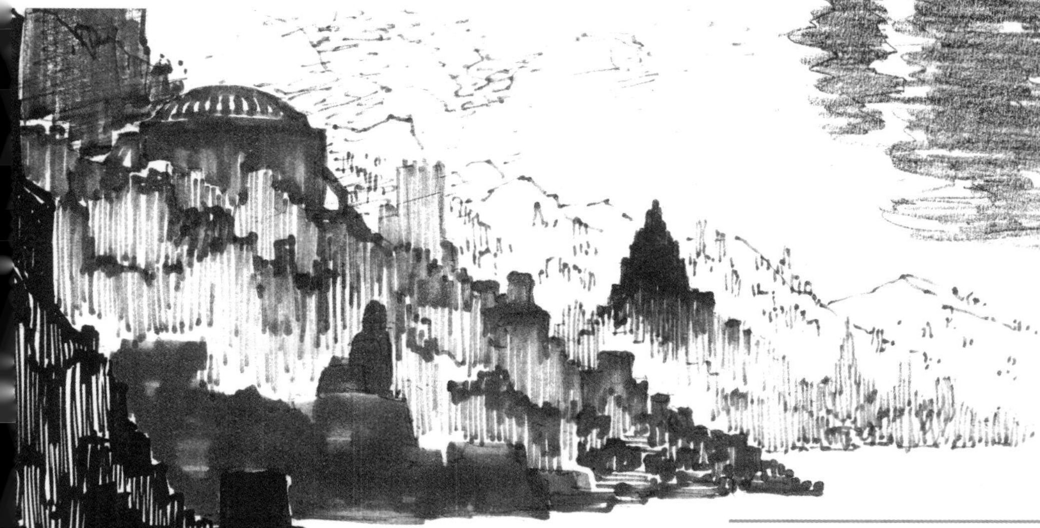

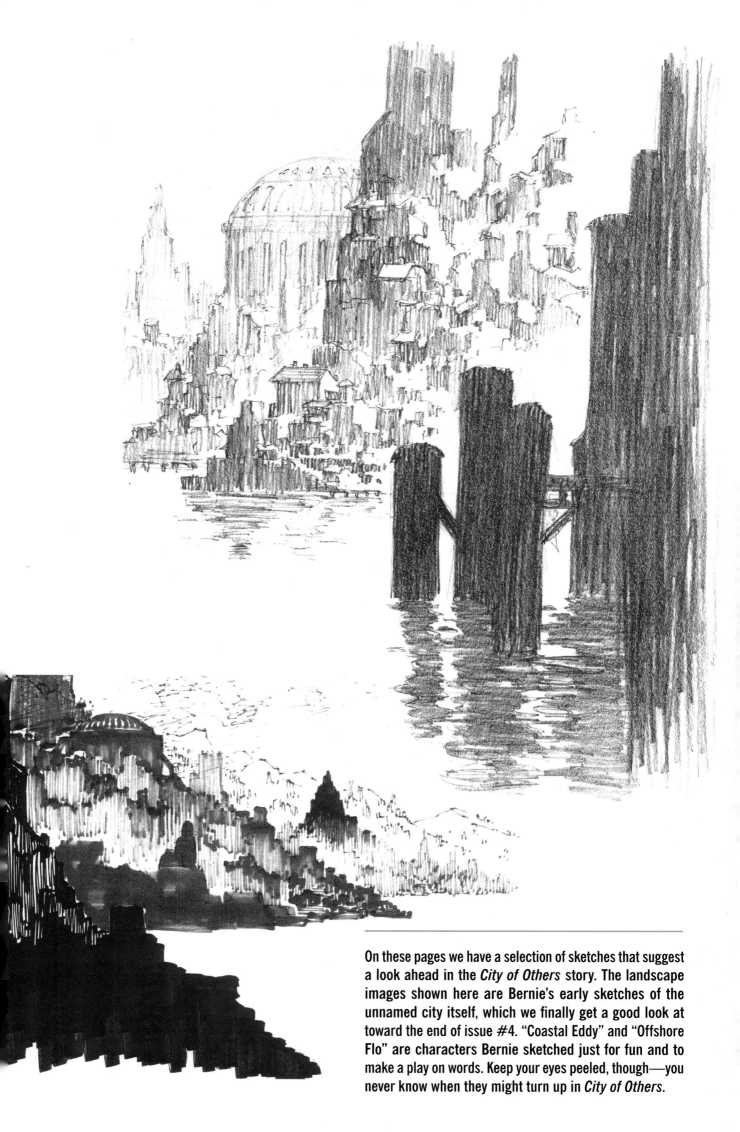

On these pages we have a selection of sketches that suggest a look ahead in the *City of Others* story. The landscape images shown here are Bernie's early sketches of the unnamed city itself, which we finally get a good look at toward the end of issue #4. "Coastal Eddy" and "Offshore Flo" are characters Bernie sketched just for fun and to make a play on words. Keep your eyes peeled, though—you never know when they might turn up in *City of Others*.

ALSO BY STEVE NILES

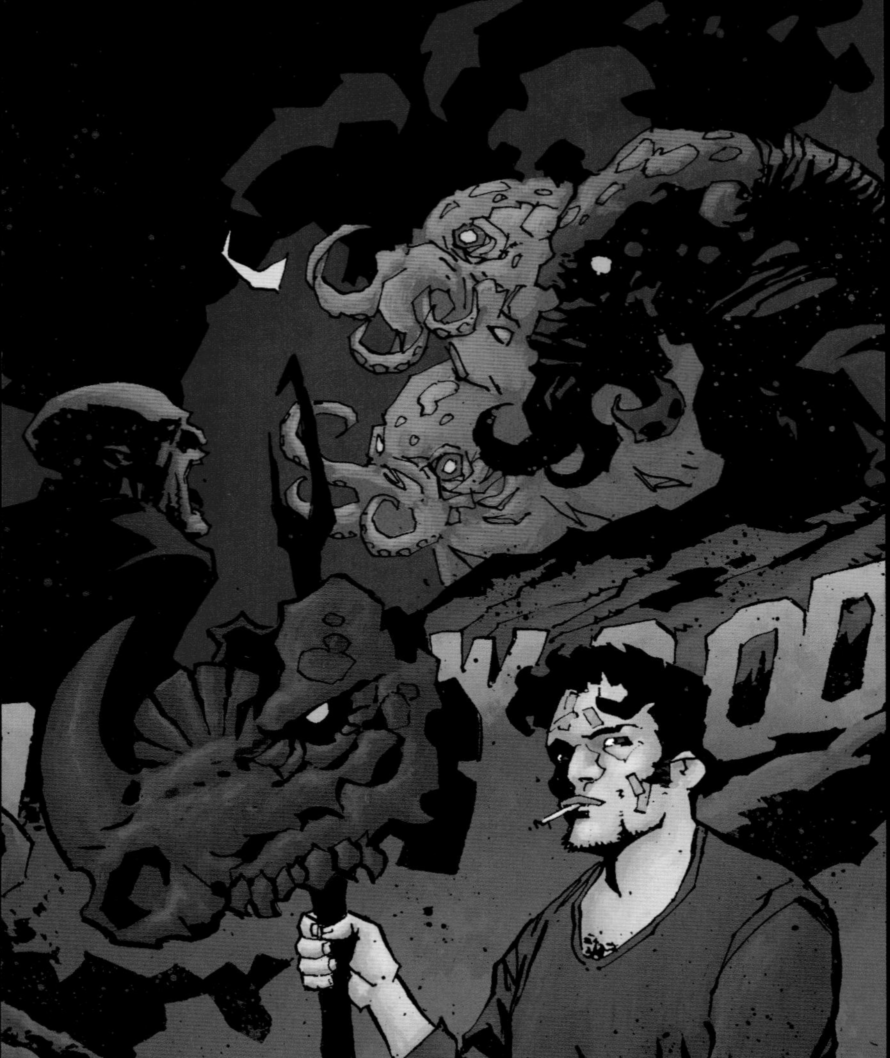

-Christoph

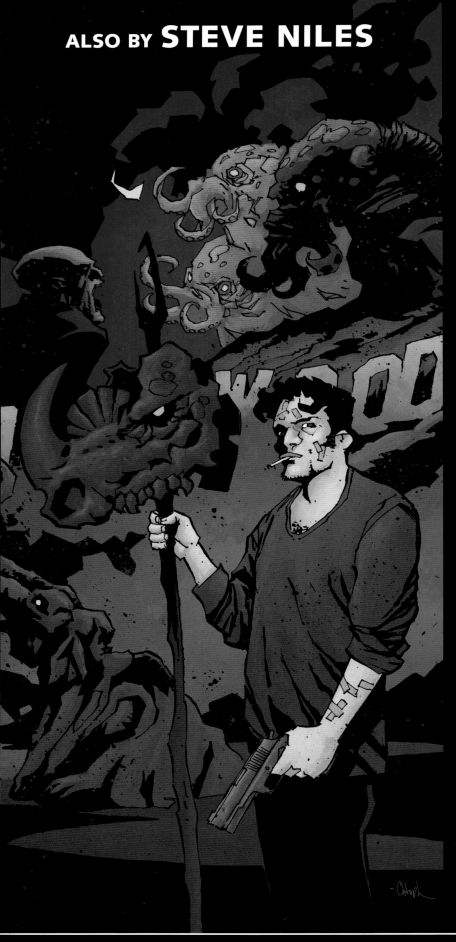

CRIMINAL MACABRE OMNIBUS

VOLUME 1
With Kelley Jones, and Ben Templesmith
ISBN 978-1-59582-746-3 | $24.99

VOLUME 2
With Kyle Hotz, Nick Stakal, and Casey Jones
ISBN 978-1-59582-747-0 | $24.99

VOLUME 3
With Christopher Mitten, Eric Powell, and Scott Morse
ISBN 978-1-61655-648-8 | $24.99

CRIMINAL MACABRE: THE IRON SPIRIT

With Scott Morse
ISBN 978-1-59582-975-7 | $19.99

CRIMINAL MACABRE: THE CAL McDONALD CASEBOOK

VOLUME 1
With Kelley Jones, Ben Templesmith, and Casey Jones
ISBN 978-1-61655-022-6 | $34.99

BREATH OF BONES: A TALE OF THE GOLEM

With Matt Santoro and Dave Wachter
ISBN 978-1-61655-344-9 | $14.99

FREAKS OF THE HEARTLAND

With Greg Ruth
TPB: ISBN 978-1-59307-029-8 | $17.95
HC: ISBN 978-1-59582-968-9 | $29.99

CITY OF OTHERS 10TH ANNIVERSARY EDITION

With Bernie Wrightson
ISBN 978-1-50671-202-4 | $29.99